Praise for *An Illusion of Equity*

"Written in an accessible and engaging style, this book asks us to face the atrocities humans have committed under the auspices of objectivity and righteousness. Refusing systematic racism disguised as scientific process and progress, Warren challenges us . . . to reject the testing premises and practices that destroy human lives and to work instead toward justice in education." —Alison Cook-Sather, author of *Co-Creating Equitable Teaching and Learning: Structuring Student Voice into Higher Education*

"Wendy Warren has written a compelling account highlighting the harm caused by our test-based educational policies, which . . . support a false linear hierarchy of intelligence, merit, ability and/or worth. Readers will better understand why the multibillion-dollar testing industry's house of cards is slowly beginning to, and should, collapse." —Jay Rosner, executive director of the Princeton Review Foundation

"As educators struggle with the disconnect between standardized test results and student learning and potential, *An Illusion of Equity* is the book we have been waiting for. Warren envisions a future where schools are relationship-centered ecosystems of mutual thriving. There is hope." —Jacqueline Battalora, author of *Birth of a White Nation: The Invention of White People and Its Relevance Today*

"Warren's book provides a weapon to confront the meritocracy myths, such as standardized tests, which continue to hinder improvement. Warren calls to action anyone who believes public schools are community institutions worth the investment." —Jacqueline G. Burnside, professor of sociology at Berea College

"Wendy Zagray Warren's carefully researched, enlightening book is an important contribution to this country's debate over systemic inequities. From decades of experience as a classroom teacher, Warren's love of students shines through and should motivate all of us to reimagine and strive for a system that values, respects, and nourishes each child." —Deborah Lauter, executive director of the Olga Lengyel Institute for Holocaust Studies and Human Rights

"Our nation's system of required standardized academic tests was built on a mountain of good intentions. . . . In *An Illusion of Equity: The Legacy of Eugenics in Today's Education*, Warren takes both the origins of these intentions and their real impact to task, exposing deeply systemic flaws in their logic and consequences. This work is deeply provocative, and the arguments and concepts it raises need to be brought to the table as we consider the future of standardized testing, and of public education itself."—Jason E. Glass, commissioner and chief learner of the Kentucky Department of Education

"Through the eyes of a teacher, Warren tackles the veneer of 'norm referencing' and 'cut scores' and shows how a historically rooted, racist, classist ideology has infused education with profoundly harmful, multigenerational consequences. This work makes visible an infrastructure of human worth and ability that has long been obscured, to our mutual detriment."—Ann Gibson Winfield, professor at Roger Williams University and author of *Eugenics and Education in America*

AN ILLUSION OF EQUITY

An Illusion
of Equity

THE LEGACY OF EUGENICS
IN TODAY'S EDUCATION

WENDY ZAGRAY WARREN

Foreword by
ERIC R. JACKSON

UNIVERSITY PRESS OF KENTUCKY

Scholarly publisher for the Commonwealth,
serving Bellarmine University, Berea College, Centre
College of Kentucky, Eastern Kentucky University,
The Filson Historical Society, Georgetown College,
Kentucky Historical Society, Kentucky State University,
Morehead State University, Murray State University,
Northern Kentucky University, Spalding University,
Transylvania University, University of Kentucky,
University of Louisville, University of Pikeville,
and Western Kentucky University.
All rights reserved.

Editorial and Sales Offices: The University Press of Kentucky
663 South Limestone Street, Lexington, Kentucky 40508-4008
www.kentuckypress.com

Because this page cannot legibly accommodate all the copyright and permission
statements for chapter epigraphs, these notices are printed in the notes section
(pages 223–38), which constitutes an extension of the copyright page.

The excerpt in the book epigraph is from john a. powell, *Racing to Justice: Transforming
Our Conceptions of Self and Other to Build an Inclusive Society,* Copyright © 2012, john a.
powell. Reprinted with permission of Indiana University Press.

Library of Congress Cataloging-in-Publication Data

Names: Warren, Wendy Zagray, author.
Title: An illusion of equity : the legacy of eugenics in today's education
    / Wendy Zagray Warren, Eric R. Jackson.
Description: Lexington : The University Press of Kentucky, 2023. | Includes
    bibliographical references and index.
Identifiers: LCCN 2023002349 | ISBN 9780813197661 (hardcover) | ISBN
    9780813197678 (pdf) | ISBN 9780813197685 (epub)
Subjects: LCSH: Educational tests and measurements—Evaluation—United
    States. | Educational equalization—United States. | Educational
    change—United States. | Discrimination in education—United States. |
    Education and state—United States.
Classification: LCC LB3051 .W37 2023 | DDC 371.2601/3—dc23/eng/20230215
LC record available at https://lccn.loc.gov/2023002349

This book is printed on acid-free paper meeting
the requirements of the American National Standard
for Permanence in Paper for Printed Library Materials.

Manufactured in the United States of America

Member of the Association
of University Presses

To the memory of Bob Warren who, as we lived and learned together for more than three decades, helped me to truly understand the power of love. And to Bobby Ann Starnes, a mentor and friend of a lifetime who, after Bob's death, became first reader and primary advocate for this work.

When we deny the fact that individual experience is necessarily filtered through the subjective lens of perception, the power to define "objective" truth resides with those whose perceptions are valued and validated. Thus, in our society, the subjectivity of white Europeans, shaped by their perceptions, culture, norms, and ideology, has been exalted as objective, and they have been empowered to determine what is normal and natural.

—john a. powell, *Racing to Justice: Transforming Our Conceptions of Self and Other to Build an Inclusive Society*

Contents

Foreword

I first read about the eugenics movement and scientific racism as a graduate student in the Department of History at the University of Cincinnati during my first few years in the doctorate program. Surprisingly for someone whose main focus had been on early American history, African American history/studies, and the history of race relations in the Americas, I was not aware until then of the highly violent and toxic eugenics movement, which has connections to concepts and historical time periods such as Social Darwinism and the doctrine of "separate but equal" as well as the passage of anti-interracial marriage laws during the 1920s and the regime and terror of Adolf Hitler during World War II.

The eugenics movement and scientific racism in the United States merged during the second half of the nineteenth century and lasted until the 1940s. Their tenets proclaimed that heredity and race were fundamental determinant factors of an individual's abilities to become successful in society, classifying individuals and groups as "fit" or "unfit." The "unfit" were defined with characteristics and concepts such as race, mental and physical disabilities, country of origin, and poverty. At the height of their influence, the eugenics movement and scientific racism were accepted by a good number of academics, politicians, intellectuals, local, regional, and federal government entities, and the US Supreme Court.

Once I discovered the impact of the eugenics movement on race relations in the Americas and US foreign policy during World War II, I was all in on studying the origins, development, and legacy of this and scientific racism. I began to read articles and books about these topics. At one point, I even pondered publishing an article on the impact of the eugenics movement on the plight of African Americans during the post-Reconstruction years. Thus Wendy Warren's meticulously researched and powerfully written book *An Illusion of Equity: The Legacy of Eugenics in Today's Education* continues my long interest in this highly important but often neglected topic.

In this well-crafted thematic volume, the author uncovers a potent connection between the eugenics movement and the public education system in the United States that is rooted in cultural-basis tests on all levels. More specifically, Warren contends that based on this linkage, "the use of large-scale testing . . . confirms that it has long served as one of [our nation's] caste's primary tools. And in a delicate operation at the turn of the twenty-first century, this dehumanizing practice replaced the beating heart of American public education." Also crucial are the author's central framework questions of this book: (1) "how tests are developed and how their scores are interpreted and used"; and (2) "the social conditions that have led America's leaders, and American society in general, to accept test-based policy."

An Illusion of Equity is divided both chronologically and thematically across twelve powerful chapters within three jargon-free sections that examine several intriguing topics, including the shifts in educational assessment and evaluation methods as a result of conclusions generated by warnings of our nation's failing public school systems noted in studies such as the 1983 report *A Nation at Risk*; the impact of test-based policies on individuals, racial groups, economic groups, and society at large; the changes to education polices during the last century; the idea that large-scale testing has been linked to the reinforcement of racism in public education; and the thesis that many current educational policies and ideas that primarily use standardized tests have their underpinning in the eugenics movement and scientific racism.

Warren's book is an eye-opening read for those interested in the link between the eugenics movement, scientific racism, and the recent history of America's public educational system. More important, this study is a must-read for anyone seeking a new perspective on the continued use of large-scale testing in our nation's public schools and its impact on students, parents, and society as a whole.

Eric R. Jackson
Northern Kentucky University

Introduction

Hartheim

What's most disturbing about the Nazi phenomenon is not that the Nazis were madmen or monsters. It's that they were ordinary human beings.
—David Livingstone Smith in Isabel Wilkerson, *Caste*

Our bus pulled up outside of Schloss Hartheim, a castle in the middle of a small town near Linz, Austria. My colleagues were American and Austrian teachers convened to study the Holocaust. We had traveled three hours from our meeting facility in Innsbruck to share this experience. A week of intensive learning and sharing had forged bonds of friendship. In this moment, however, the usual chatter was silenced by the thought of what the day would bring. During the Nazi regime, Hartheim had been a killing center created for those considered mentally or physically disabled. Entering this castle would require us to come face-to-face with the cruelest extremes of human behavior. Most disturbing of all, perhaps, was the thought that while the National Socialists held power, state-sanctioned murder had become normalized for much of the Aryan citizenry. Some ordinary citizens helped commit atrocities, and many stood by, convinced their government's dictates were righteous.

Difficult as it was, we felt a responsibility to bear witness to these events and to study the context that allowed them to occur. Our group had reached new understandings by hearing the testimony of survivors and witnesses and then processing the information together, adding new layers of meaning. While the Holocaust took place in a particular place and time, its lessons extend to all of humanity. Holocaust education takes us to the very edges of the human capacity for evil and for good. At some level, we understood that we traveled to Hartheim to learn more about ourselves.

National Socialist policy was based on Social Darwinist ideology, which had spread throughout the Western world. Social Darwinists believe that the human population is naturally evolving toward a superior being and that northern Europeans are the furthest along on an evolutionary chain. Eugenicists put this ideology into practice. They considered themselves social engineers who could speed up the evolutionary process. Eugenicists developed procedures that they claimed would determine which people carried traits worthy of being passed on. The government used these data to implement policy designed to support the reproduction of those *high-quality* people. Meanwhile, society's *useless eaters* would be forced to slowly die out by limiting their access to opportunity and resources, sterilizing them, and/or placing them in institutions removed from society.

Because the practices used to determine human quality involved measurement and statistical analysis, eugenics was considered a science. Eugenicists worked from charts based on a Social Darwinist conceptualization of race in which northern Europeans ranked at the top of a phylogenetic tree. The United States became a hub of eugenics research long before the German National Socialists came to power. In 1904, a Carnegie-funded lab at Cold Spring Harbor, New York was renamed the Station for Experimental Evolution. By the early part of the twentieth century, eugenics was taught at universities in the United States and across Western Europe.[1]

When Hitler became the German chancellor, social policy centered around eugenics. The data generated were presented as evidence to justify the regime's racist ideology. Laws were designed to benefit "superior" White people from northern European nations whom the Nazis dubbed Aryans. One of the regime's first acts was to pass forced sterilization laws to prevent those with "inferior" genes from passing them on. However, Nazi leaders could see that, with this approach, results would take at least a generation to play out. They grew impatient because they believed that in the meantime, valuable resources would be wasted on those they called *life unworthy of life*. Instead, they wanted to reserve the nation's assets for the *best and the brightest*, and they structured society around this goal.

Emboldened as Social Darwinist ideology gained favor among intellectuals across the Northern Hemisphere, Nazi leaders began to implement programs designed to permanently rid the world of those judged to be inferior. Eugenicists standardized an evaluative protocol to make these determinations. Hitler's Euthanasia Order declared that those who didn't meet a set standard of mental or physical functioning were to be eliminated. These murders were regarded as merciful. The government named the program T-4.

Schloss Hartheim was one of six facilities quickly converted into killing centers. Hartheim's so-called euthanasia program was directed by a psychiatrist and a physician. At this facility alone, at least thirty thousand people arrived by bus and walked down its stone hallways directly to their deaths. Of these, twelve thousand were inmates from work camps at Mauthausen, Dachau, and Gusen who had been declared too sick to contribute. The others were adults and children who had also been categorized as useless. The professionals who operated T-4 centers experimented with the use of gas chambers and crematoria, practice for the systematized mass murder to come. Each murder was government sanctioned, justified by evidence generated from evaluative tools designed for that purpose. Thus, society was framed according to an illusion that regarded some members of the population as inherently worthy and others as completely worthless. Government leaders claimed the evaluations were irrefutable because the evidence was based in science.[2]

As the bus door opened, a cold March wind whipped down the aisle. We pulled our coats tighter and stepped onto a cobbled walkway, passed through an arched doorway, and were led down a corridor lining an open courtyard. Our minds consumed by thoughts of those whose feet had worn these stones, we could barely take in the surroundings. But our bodies felt the cold.

Our guide invited us into a heated room just off the corridor. It was lined with books, some in German, others in English, but all focused on eugenics. Artifacts had been placed on the floor in the center of the room for us to examine: a rusted spoon, a plastic comb, a chipped ceramic cup, hair clips, a locket enclosing a small photo. We learned that these were a few of the over eight thousand artifacts that had been unearthed in the yard, the only visible remains of those whose bodies had been poisoned with carbon monoxide, then burned.

A few of the Austrian teachers had grown up only a few miles from Hartheim, yet they had never learned this part of its history. What took place there is not, after all, long past, and the instinct of parents and grandparents is to protect their young. The faces of these young educators registered their shock as they took in information that would forever cast a shadow over their memories. We circled close to the guide to see the only existing photo showing what happened here: smoke rising from crematoria chimneys right in the middle of this small town. Attempts were made to hide these artifacts. Governments, too, try to protect their reputations and shield their citizens. When evidence of evil is eventually revealed, some strive to justify their actions, even long after the fact. As I witnessed the tears welling in the eyes of Austrian teachers, however, I understood that denial merely delays pain. Healing can occur only by facing truth.

In condemning the Nazis' actions, it's tempting to think of theirs as a unique kind of cruelty, unrepeatable in any other time or place. This, however, is delusion. While every genocide is unique, the human capacity that drives it is not. We learn this as we study genocides in Armenia, Bosnia, Rwanda, Darfur, and Syria.

As I examined the collection of objects dug up from the yard, I considered what I'd only recently learned about the history of my own country, the United

States of America. The US government does not acknowledge genocide in its history. School textbooks taught me that America was a divine gift reserved for the European settlers who colonized it. Facts about the massacres of Native peoples, the murders of enslaved people who resisted, public lynching, and the slaughter of innocents in neighborhoods where people of color dared to show signs of success all are missing or downplayed in the national narrative.

Having never learned these historic truths, some American educators teach the Nazi Holocaust in isolation, as something that happened "back then" and "over there," atrocities perpetrated by the Germans, people we fought against. Simplifying a host of complexities, the story is broken down to portray good guys and bad guys. America is perceived as being on the right side of history, and for many American students, the message is left right there. If, that is, they study the Holocaust at all.

Holocaust education prompted me to view the history of my own country in a new light. Over the course of many summers, I've had the honor of traveling with educators onto the lands of Native nations. As we bear witness, many of us for the first time, to surviving descendants sharing stories of atrocities perpetrated by the US government, new layers are added to the image of the land we call home. Tears slide quietly down faces as we struggle with our own culpability. We remember that, all across the United States, plowed earth reveals artifacts of these victims, too. The soil retains these truths.

Strange as it may seem, this is the backdrop necessary for us to critically evaluate the impact of American education policy and practice on students and society. The silence around these parts of our history keeps us from remembering that American classrooms are filled with the descendants of survivors and of perpetrators. Violence comes in many forms: physical, cultural, spiritual, psychological and, I would add, intellectual. Imagine an Indigenous child or a descendant of enslaved people sitting in classroom after classroom, hearing stories of European conquest construed as if the land was a gift God awarded to those most deserving. Imagine contemplating the possibility of a god who would condone the murder or kidnapping of your ancestors in order to build a society for *better* people.

These are messages that impact identity. Many Black and Brown children also receive a postscript delivered in the form of a large-scale test score that they are told measures their success as students. Low scores are interpreted to mean that a child is not yet *ready* for, and therefore not offered, a challenging, engaging, high-quality education. Rank-ordered according to a number representing academic prowess or potential, students are organized into an educational hierarchy. This information is widely shared so that each child and their family can see exactly where they stand.

Imagine the cumulative impact of being told that historically your people were not good enough, and then receiving official confirmation that society has made the same declaration about you. From their first use, test scores created a hierarchy that aligns with eugenics ideology. Struggling to survive in a system that views them as failures, children are told that they must learn to be resilient to bear the onslaught.

There is, of course, an alternative. We can change the system of education so there will be no onslaught, creating instead places where every child will thrive. This is what justice requires of us. Reaching toward that goal is, ultimately, the aim of this book. We won't arrive at that point until the very end, however. First, we must take a hard look at where we are currently to clearly see how far we have veered from that path. Studying why and how we got here is a difficult but crucial journey. As I can personally attest, there is much to be learned along the way, knowledge that will inform our future.

Decades of propaganda have led us to accept an illusion: that test scores indicate something so valuable about human beings that they should be used to organize society. As we see in the example of Nazi Germany, those who draw the lines of success and failure, of worthiness and unworthiness, hold great power. A system of testing makes it seem that these decisions are not made by humans but are determined by the infallibility of science and statistics, as if test scores reveal a natural order.

At first glance, the topic of testing may seem like old news. Testing has been used in American education for more than a century. That is, in part, the point. Because testing has been normalized, the public has not vigorously questioned its use. While scholars have written about testing's history and critiqued social bias in test items, most of that information has not reached a wide audience. Moreover, few authors have followed the cumulative trajectory of ideas that supported the testing model's development and guides the interpretation of its scores. Interpretation, of course, assigns scores their meaning, an assumption critical to determining how test scores are used. In short, we must connect the dots from testing's conception to current practice. The model's procedures are, after all, not written in stone. They are malleable, each grounded in the ideology used to justify their application. When testing is placed into a framework of the evolution of racist ideas (as written by historian Ibram X. Kendi), which supports an American system of caste (as described by Isabel Wilkerson), we gain a better understanding of why—and how—large-scale tests were produced. From there, we can question the continued use of a tool to generate data that, in their application, perpetuate and appear to validate social inequity.[3]

While the book's focus may appear narrow, the knowledge gained by studying the specific example of large-scale testing reaches far beyond the realm of education. It is a study in how ideology impacts even those practices we mistakenly consider objective. It is a reminder to stay alert. The power of testing lies in the meaning people assign to test scores, because that meaning justifies their use. The example of large-scale testing reveals how the assumptions of a specific ideology can guide practice—even long after that ideology has been rejected.

The truth is that the American education reform movement of the twenty-first century fortifies a mirage created nearly a century ago. Then, test scores were used to justify a human hierarchy that those at the top believed to be naturally occurring. Large-scale testing, in fact, played a key role in maintaining this deception. Because contemporary education policy has exponentially increased the use of test scores, and because the testing model still relies upon its initial basic components, it is important to interrogate that hidden ideology. We need to know how that ideology might continue to impact the creation, interpretation, and use of test scores and therefore the outcomes of test-based policy.

Just as insights from Holocaust education reach beyond the specific, a close study of testing will strengthen our muscles of Criticality for use in other situations. Educator and scholar Gholdy Muhammad explained, "As long as oppression is present in the world, young people need pedagogy that nurtures criticality. And we have never had a world free from oppression. I differentiate between lowercase *c critical* and uppercase *C Critical* when defining criticality. While *critical* means to think deeply about something, *Critical* is connected to an understanding of power, entitlement, oppression, and equity." Capital C Criticality, then, invites us to explore how large-scale testing fits into an ongoing story of European colonization justified by an ideology that thrives in the shadows. Its key idea is that some people are inherently superior to others. This illusion, Wilkerson explained, supports caste systems throughout the world. Germany's National Socialists boldly promoted the notion of a naturally occurring human hierarchy. Although the supporting ideology may have changed, the idea of hierarchy continues to lurk beneath the surface in the United States. We can see its support in the endorsement of policy and practices that result in social stratification.[4]

The use of large-scale testing is one of those practices. Its history confirms that it has long served as one of caste's primary tools. And in a delicate operation at the turn of the twenty-first century, this dehumanizing practice replaced the beating heart of American public education.

I served on the front lines during this change. I am an educator who was limited by what I hadn't known about my own country. I was in my forties when I first learned there had been a eugenics movement in the United States, and that here, too, it led to policies of forced sterilization, institutionalization, and immigration restrictions. A decade later, I read that Nazi leaders came to the United States to study how Jim Crow laws were enacted to solidify a caste system. After twenty-five years of teaching and a doctorate in education, I had not known that eugenics ideology had prepared the soil in which large-scale testing took root. These omissions led me to feel I'd been duped into believing a national narrative that was simply false. I wondered how else I'd been misled.[5]

When regulators required my compliance in a system where critical educational decisions would be based on the scores from large-scale tests, I had questions. I knew these scores were not useful in my teaching. I had always felt that something about using large-scale test scores felt wrong, but I didn't know why. As I traced the history of testing, that feeling grew stronger. As a Holocaust educator, I understood how data and ideology can be misused. The questions raised by those uneasy feelings eventually led to this book.

In my classrooms, I facilitate an inquiry-based approach to learning. As a community of learners, my students and I raise complex questions that have no simple answers. I take a similar approach with this book, as I strive to create conditions conducive for learning. I envision us circled around a table, processing this information together, chapter by chapter, sharing our perspectives. Learning is, after all, change, and shared learning can be transformative. Shifting perspectives leads to new awareness, which carries new responsibility. This book is a response to my own transformation.

The text as a whole is organized as a spiral. The issues raised are so complex and interwoven that we return to them again and again, hoping to gain deeper understanding with each pass. We will consider how education policy, theory, and practice cycles and recycles, influencing and being influenced by national and international policy.

Our goal is to gain a broad view of how the twenty-first-century US educational system operates, its inputs and its outcomes, with a special focus on the assumptions and ideologies of the policies and practices of the last century. Public education plays a crucial role in crafting a nation's future. That role will become increasingly clear as we examine the transmission of norms and assumptions upon which our nation was built.

Experience is an important teacher, and decades of teaching experience allow me to understand things an outside researcher cannot. Throughout this book, I call upon what I've learned in the multitude of days I've spent with children. So while this book is grounded in research, my confidence in the statements I make about teaching and learning are unapologetically based on years of classroom experience.

The memory of my shock, as I read the many books and articles that form the basis of this study, is visceral. I highlighted, underlined, wrote arguments in the margins. Yet these annotations were too small to contain the horror I felt as I saw a larger picture coming together. Over the many years I've worked on this book, doubt crept in repeatedly. I thought that surely I must be misunderstanding. And back I would go to the sources, reconfirming my position before moving on. It was helpful that while I was writing, new sources were published that let me know I was on the right track.

Two main lines of inquiry frame this book. One involves how tests are developed and how their scores are interpreted and used. The second focuses on the social conditions that have led America's leaders, and American society in general, to accept test-based policy. Exploring the interplay of methods and ideology takes us beyond the moment large-scale tests were first constructed to interrogate the key philosophical assumptions that led to the development of the testing model.

Ideology is the reason this introduction begins at Hartheim. As the history of testing unfolds, we will be confronted by the fact that its tracks emerge from the same set of racist ideas that directed Nazi Germany's path to genocide. Due, in part, to public pressure, the United States chose to enact the ideology differently. We continue to see its ramifications, though, in the social inequities that exist at every turn, including in the educational system. Yet despite outcomes divided by race and class, the rhetoric used to justify test-based policy claims to be motivated by a desire for equity. This book is the story of the many interlocking factors that have led us to accept such large gaps between rhetoric and results.

Ibram X. Kendi argues that social inequity is caused by policy choices. Policies are created by people who can make different choices at any time. Yet policy change is motivated by ideological shifts prompted by evaluating the distance between where a nation stands and its promise to its people. Because public education charts the course of the future, we need to take a close look at where we are, how we got here, and where we'd like to be. Informed by patterns of the past, we can chart our course for the future.[6]

The book is therefore divided into three sections. The first, "The Illusion and the Spin," contains two chapters that invite us to take a close look at the changes made to American education policy around the turn of the twenty-first century. Although the seeds had been planted over twenty years earlier, these changes were codified in 2001 with the bipartisan passage of No Child Left Behind (NCLB) legislation. Chapter 1 explores the shifts in thinking about educational assessment and evaluation because of fears raised by warnings of failing schools based on evidence presented in the 1983 report *A Nation at*

Risk. Chapter 2 demonstrates the impact of the newly implemented test-based policy on individuals, racial and economic groups, and society as a whole.

Next, the five chapters in the book's second section, "Scaffolding Caste," take on a historical focus, inviting us to consider the evolution of education policy within a larger social framework. Chapter 3 interrogates America's social norms: why they were established, how they are taught, and how they were codified into policies built to advantage people who defined themselves as White and declared their superiority. Chapter 4 explores myths that arose during the nineteenth and twentieth centuries to feed and justify racist ideas and policies to uphold the social hierarchy, and the impact of the US eugenics movement on a newly consolidating national system of education. This leads to chapter 5, which demonstrates how large-scale testing was conceived as a tool to produce evidence to back the racist and classist ideas that justified the codification of eugenic ideology. Chapter 6 introduces some of testing's detractors, educational leaders who pushed back against the interpretation of test scores as truth, recognizing instead the role testing played in carrying out eugenic ideals. The section ends with chapter 7, which explores the notion of meritocracy, a term newly introduced in the 1950s.

"A Culture Framed by Illusions," the third section, has five chapters that involve a close study of psychometrics, a field created for the express purpose of developing large-scale tests. Chapters in this section explain how specific methods and procedures combine to produce a test score and how psychometric culture interprets the meaning of those scores. Chapter 8 provides an overview of the basics of test development, including the conceptual differences between norm- and criterion-referencing of scores. Chapter 9 examines processes involved in creating and selecting test items, and chapter 10 discusses the setting of cut scores used in criterion-referenced score interpretation. Chapter 11 takes a closer look at core assumptions built into the model's conceptual framework that are used to justify the interpretation of a score's meaning, including measurement error. The section concludes with chapter 12, which explains the cultural distance between how reliability and validity are defined in a psychometric context as compared to the world in which test scores are used to set policy and make educational decisions. This section ultimately invites readers to draw their own conclusions based on the accumulated evidence.

The extended epilogue focuses on hope, encouraging us to collectively imagine an educational system purposefully designed to nurture each child's growth and development.

My own hope is that the information and ideas presented here will serve as catalysts inspiring you to act. While it will become clear that I believe policy change is needed, and the sooner the better, I invite you to notice the questions the information raises for you as you read. I encourage you to resist the urge to rush to answers, but instead allow the questions to hover in your consciousness, serving as touchstones as you read. The conclusions you ultimately reach may disturb your spirit and your sense of justice, as they did mine. Despite that discomfort, I invite you to savor the feeling of a slowly shifting vantage point and to anticipate the possibility that, together, we will work toward a future that will ensure that no matter who we are, our children and grandchildren will be treated as equally worthy. I hope I have succeeded in creating an environment where you feel the courage to question what you think you know, replace old information with new, and allow your heart and mind to be transformed in ways that inspire action, for that is how this learning journey has affected me.

While each of us will place our shoulders in a different place on the wheel, together we can get it moving in the direction of justice. My greatest hope is that this humble offering adds a thread to a web of work being created by educators and writers who are, right now, reimagining American education. May our collective words spark a movement that will not rest until we have created new systems where every child will thrive.[7]

The Illusion and the Spin

1

A Façade of Assumptions
Myths, Beliefs, and Policy Mandates

The new caste system lurks invisibly within the maze of rationalizations we have developed for persistent racial inequality. It is possible—quite easy, in fact—never to see the embedded reality.

—Michelle Alexander, *The New Jim Crow*

Assessment and Evaluation

Teaching is my calling and my chosen career. I was one of those students who assessed each choice my teachers made and imagined how I would do things differently, honing my vision of the teacher I wanted to be. By the time I reached college, I was impatient to get started. So rather than taking college courses *about* teaching, I interned at a small, independent school. There I experienced the rich learning environment I had imagined. Under the guidance of the school's director, surrounded by students who inspired me, I learned to teach. This opportunity opened a path to the ideas that shape this book.

I graduated with a bachelor's degree in interdisciplinary studies in 1983 and stayed to teach full-time at the school I had come to love. Through teaching, I learned the importance of assessment. Carefully attuned to my students, I found many ways to gather the information I needed to plan the next steps in their learning. The approach was tailored to the child. The school's director, Bobby Ann Starnes, ensured that its teachers were well versed in child development, so we weren't surprised when our students grasped concepts and acquired skills at different times. This, we knew, was the way of the world.

Chelsea, for example, was reading fluently at age four. In contrast, Derrick struggled to connect words to make meaning despite daily practice until suddenly, at age eight, he began reading entire paragraphs and soon devoured every chapter book he could find. The school was structured around the understanding that children learn at different rates and in different ways. Instruction was therefore largely individualized, and group experiences were designed to be open-ended. Teachers gained valuable information by noting how each

13

child approached a task. No stigma was attached to learning differences, because there was never an expectation that there would be any other way. Students worked in flexible mixed-age groups. They had no concept that learning should look the same for everyone.

The school's approach required teachers to continually assess student learning. We were accountable to each other, to parents, and most of all to our students. At the end of each day when parents came to pick up their children, we informally reported the growth we had seen in their child that day. At a semester's end, teachers created more formal assessments. Rather than making comparisons to an artificial age-referenced norm, however, we wrote extensive narratives about each child we worked with. Each report documented the academic, social, and personal growth we had witnessed over the course of the semester. The information shared with parents was complex, nuanced, and individualized. This became my standard for assessment.

I understood that although Chelsea and Derrick learned to read in different ways and at different rates, it did not mean Chelsea was more capable than Derrick. Ultimately, they were both strong, confident readers. Yet had I been required to make a judgment about each child's overall academic ability or potential when they were six years old, I might have concluded that one was more capable or had greater potential than the other. If I had then used this information to place Chelsea in a class reserved for children perceived to be gifted, she, her family, and her future teachers would have assumed, from that point on, that she was academically advanced, a child of great promise. And based on a comparison made at that moment in time, Derrick and his family would have perceived that he was somehow deficient and in need of remediation. He may have been placed in a track for slow or remedial students. As a result of these comparisons, Chelsea would have been afforded educational opportunities that were withheld from Derrick based on an assumption that he was not "ready."

That would have been a grave mistake.

I say that with conviction because I know the ending of this particular story. At this school, students were never compared to each other or to an external norm. Derrick and his family therefore never received a message that he was in any way deficient. He was never placed into an educational track, and no labels constrained him. He had all the same learning opportunities as Chelsea, and, each in their own time, they both soared. Derrick is now a university professor who teaches, conducts research, writes, and publishes. He reports no memory of beginning to read later than his peers, and therefore carries none of the stigma that would be attached to that memory. Every child in America deserves this opportunity.

After a year teaching full-time at this school, love called me to Montana, which became my adopted home. The state has many small, local schools that I hoped would offer me the freedom to bring this kind of education to public school students. This meant I needed to become certified, so in 1987 I took the required courses, inspired by a vision of my future classroom.

I didn't view my teaching philosophy as a lofty ideal. Because of my first teaching experience, I knew what was possible. I used my evolving educational philosophy to enhance my coursework, vowing to glean something of value from each class. I soon learned, however, that in many ways my experience made things more difficult. Public schools are not organized around the fact that people learn in different ways and at different rates. The schools I visited seemed to be built around an entirely different set of norms and assumptions, yet I couldn't identify what they were.

The disconnect between my philosophy and lived experience and the course content was most evident in a class I took on educational assessment. The class was entirely focused on multiple-choice test design. Large-scale testing is rooted in an assumption that all students should be assessed at the same time and in the same ways and that their progress should be measured against a norm. The professor didn't name these assumptions; they were simply treated as a given. In fact, standardizing a test means making the test and testing conditions as uniform as possible. Standardization was presented as a goal, something we should strive for. The professor asked us to carefully study the structure of large-scale test items so we could emulate them in tests we created for classroom use. He extolled the virtues of statistical modeling and the sanctity of the bell curve.

I was bewildered. I had never even given a multiple-choice test. I'd had no reason to. I knew I didn't need a paper and pencil test to determine what a child can read and comprehend. I was there, beside my students as they read, witnessing and documenting their daily growth. Sometimes the growth was incremental, and sometimes, as with Derrick, pieces of learning fell into place with a burst of understanding. The rich assessment information I shared with parents could not have been reported as a number or even a letter grade. Yet this course ignored the many other ways to assess learning. The word *numbers* was treated as a synonym for the word *data,* and the only significant data, it seemed, came from multiple-choice tests.

Yet I struggled to even *find* meaning in these numbers. I couldn't understand how the complex information involved in learning could possibly be converted and condensed into a single simple representation. And I had no earthly idea how these numbers could help me teach. It all seemed a colossal waste of time and energy.

My experience had led me to conceptualize learning as a continuum of growth, where evidence of a new accomplishment would signify a child was ready for the next step. When students grasp letter/sound correspondence, for example, it often means they are ready to begin blending those sounds into words. This level of nuance can't be assessed on a paper and pencil test. Yet in this class, I was asked to create a test for that very purpose.

The models I had to follow were test items that directed a child to look at a simple line drawing of an object. Four words were listed underneath, each with a small circle next to it. The assumption is that if a child fills in the circle next to the word that names the object, it means the child has recognized and understood the word. Well, maybe it does and maybe it doesn't. Anyone who has taken a multiple-choice test knows the possibilities for misinterpretation. There is plenty of room for guesswork. In fact, people are often coached in the best way to make those guesses. Although such coaching actually invalidates test results, an entire test-prep industry banks on it. The system is, apparently, easily gamed, and it is important to learn the tricks.[1]

Many confounding variables simultaneously impact a test score. Even if a child *can* read the word she marked (which you could only confirm by asking her to read it), a teacher is still left with many questions. Did she distinguish only the first letter? How did she process the vowels? Could she read the other choices or is this the only word she recognized? In short, this information doesn't contain the richness needed for a teacher to plan the next step in that child's learning.

I realized then that even if I spent the time to give such a test, I would still need to rely on information from my daily classroom assessments in order to teach. So why go to the trouble of giving this test at all? It seemed an additional task that produced information with little meaning. At that point, I saw that testing twists learning into some unnatural form to fit the mold the model requires. It's like designing a ruler to try to measure the sky, and then adjusting the sky to fit the confines of the ruler. It's a pompously absurd notion. And because we are not able to adequately measure the sky, in the end, we adjust our sights to something that is measurable, perhaps a few particulates in the air, even if they do not directly relate to our original goal. We understand that these particulates are not the sky, yet we continue onward, extrapolating from those results and proceeding as if we have, in fact, measured the sky. While someone somewhere has intensely focused on the complexity of the statistical processes required, the integrity of the result's meaning has fallen quietly to the wayside, forgotten. Yet the outcomes are interpreted as if we now understand not only the sky but the entire universe.

As you might imagine, many convolutions are required to turn something nebulous like ability or achievement into a number. Each step in the process is like a funhouse mirror that distorts an image. As the image bounces from mirror to mirror, it becomes further removed from reality. In the end, I am still left with a number so abstracted that it is of little use. Yet teachers are put in the awkward position of trying to explain the presumed meaning of this number to parents and students.

The professor of my assessment course assured us that the testing model is actually far more complex than the brief overview he could present in a single-semester. He was certainly right about that. *Psychometrics* is the name of an entire field of study focused on test design and development. I began to wonder about the number of people who have built careers in this field and about the resources expended in the effort to produce large-scale tests. I could not understand what the payoff might be.

Here we were, trying to create a perfect measurement tool, but I couldn't see a reason to *measure* learning at all. Even if it were possible, how would it be helpful for a teacher to quantify a degree or amount of learning or to ascertain the speed with which it was acquired? Learning is not, after all, an object that can be held next to a ruler or weighed or timed.

My confusion deepened. I doubted my own thinking, but even more, I doubted my questions. No one else seemed to be asking them. The other students sat quietly in the lecture hall taking notes as the professor spoke. It was as if I had traveled to a foreign land and didn't understand the language or the culture. My classmates seemed simply to accept all this information without question, and I was expected to adapt. I felt increasingly alone, unable to express that something felt very wrong. The sounds of the joyful, busy classroom I envisioned were being muted by the sounds of pencils quietly filling in bubbles as students sat silently at their desks.

The assessment course tried to convince me that standardized testing data were superior to the information I had gathered about each student on a daily basis. For some reason, learning translated to numbers with assumed, generalized meanings was regarded as more trustworthy than the nuanced understandings I could gain by my direct classroom observations.

The rationale for placing such confidence in large-scale tests is that because teachers are human, we have biases that might influence our evaluation. True enough; I have no argument. Bias affects the judgment of every professional, including doctors, lawyers—and statisticians. In my education course, however, I was taught that because large-scale tests rely on standardized methods and statistical models, they are objective and therefore better than any potentially subjective information I can gather. We had learned nothing about the history and little about the design of large-scale testing models, so I had no context for a deeper understanding of how the scores are derived or the ideology used to justify their early use.

I finally recognized that the professor was operating from a set of norms and assumptions I hadn't learned and didn't share. It was, indeed, a culture foreign to me. If the purpose of the course was to ensure my assimilation, discomfort signaled my resistance.

Nothing put me at ease as the course continued. The professor explained that test development relies on a bell curve model with an established norm. The curve creates a spread that emphasizes the differences among scores. This makes it easy to compare scores and place them in rank order. These data are useful, the professor explained, to sort students into ability groups in a process known as *tracking*.

Tracking is often presented as helpful to educators who are put into the impossible situation of teaching large numbers of students. The industrial revolution left its mark on education by valuing economic efficiency above all. School consolidation replaced the small class sizes often found in local schools with the large class sizes housed in decentralized schools. Rather than fifteen or twenty students in a class, teachers are now commonly expected to teach thirty or forty.

The reason for standardization, then, had little to do with the quality of teaching and learning. Rather, it was introduced to meet the demands of efficiency. Tracking creates an educational hierarchy. Students perceived as having the most potential are separated from those presumed to have less. These judgments have always seemed arrogant to me. What could position any human to predict the potential of another? I have argued against tracking throughout my career without deeply understanding the reason for my objections. I was not yet able to think about it as a way to separate those considered worthy of a resource-rich, high-quality education from those determined to be unworthy. I had not yet visited Hartheim.[2]

While the professor didn't explain the reason for comparing students, the practice was treated as necessary. I came to recognize this as an unstated assumption that had been normalized. I was able to question it because it differed from my experience. Images of Derrick and Chelsea flashed in my mind. This was an early glimpse at testing's potential for harm.

Using large-scale test scores to track students is, in fact, based on a number of assumptions that were never identified in the class. The first is that these scores are capable of measuring nebulous traits like intelligence, ability, or potential. Test evidence is generalized such that the higher scores of some students are interpreted to mean they are more advanced or more capable than students with lower scores. This assumption is followed by another: that the most capable students deserve access to the best resources.

Based on this set of assumptions, students are separated into groups. Some students are labeled gifted, some average, and others learning disabled or simply slow. Each group is exposed to course content modified to meet their presumed needs. The material is often taught at different speeds and in different ways. The contemporary rationale for this differential treatment is that the students presumed to be less able may gain the skills they need to "catch up" to the others.

In reality, though, students tend to stay in the same tracks all the way through school. This stands to reason if, from the very start, the students considered advanced have access to better resources and richer opportunities. This select group of students is often invited to engage in project work that makes learning relevant and engaging, while students considered less capable are often asked to continually repeat the same rote learning that didn't work for them in the first place. These exercises are sometimes jokingly referred to as *drill and kill*—except it isn't a joke because the *kill* refers to what happens to a person's motivation and mental development as a result. Students placed in these categories typically remain in the lower tracts as they progress from grade to grade and often leave school before graduation, pushed out by unapologetic policy and practice.

The separation of students is about more than just efficiency. Treating a high-quality education as if it is a limited resource that should be reserved for the best and brightest is not a necessary conclusion. It is based on an ideology. The resulting model formats education as a competition that is, indeed, a race to the top. Any doubt about that is erased with evidence of wealthy parents doing anything and everything they can to try to secure their child a place in the best schools.

My experience in a learning environment that was instead purposefully structured around nurturing every child's growth helped me see that this competitive model is a choice. The creation of an educational system with a narrow path to the top of a hierarchy—with obstacles purposefully placed along the way to bar some from advancement—is based on a worldview that best serves the "exclusive few who have the power to create policy."[3]

This outcome of educational testing troubled me enough to seek a different perspective. I found it in Stephen J. Gould's *The Mismeasure of Man*, which had been published a few years earlier. To my relief, Gould raised questions similar to my own. His book probed and rejected "the argument that intelligence can be meaningfully abstracted as a single number capable of ranking all people on a linear scale of intrinsic and unalterable mental worth." Gould's research provided thought-provoking conclusions that, I now realize, planted the seeds of ideas that disturbed my thinking. Buried deep within me, these seeds have lain dormant for many years.[4]

Gould, an evolutionary biologist, approached the topic of intelligence testing from that vantage point. He recognized that in order to understand the testing model, he needed to study the context of its development. This allowed him to identify the key assumptions that led to the statistical models and influenced the interpretation of scores. His book was my first encounter with the term *scientific racism*: the use of seemingly scientific methods to justify policy and practice that produce racist outcomes.

In fact, Gould's close study of the origins of mental testing shifted his thinking about science in general. Studying the specific example of large-scale testing helped him clearly see that the effect of culture overrides claims of objectivity. "Culture," Gould recognized, "influences what we see and how we see it." Even for scientists.[5]

My own responses to the educational assessment class helped me understand that life experience, too, influences the questions people are able (or unable) to ask. Gould's grandparents, for example, were Jewish immigrants from eastern Europe, the very people, he explains, that early proponents of large-scale testing were trying to keep out of the country. This life-connection may have sparked his initial interest or motivated him to dig deeper into the topic. His findings compelled him to write.[6]

Gould truly believed that science has the potential to reveal truth. What he learned about the development of large-scale testing, however, helped him recognize that this can't happen unless or until scientists recognize the cultural norms that influence their thinking. Only then can they identify the assumptions on which those norms are based. Once a norm is identified, the next—critical—step, Gould explained, is to ask "how questions might be formulated under different assertions." In other words, scientific thinking has to free itself from the confines of culture so a theory can be interrogated from multiple perspectives in order to consider alternatives. If its findings hold in many different contexts, the theory is strengthened. Science, in fact, relies on such continual probing of the ideas it postulates.[7]

Gould identified two things that weaken scientific theory: "the twin myths of objectivity and inexorable march toward truth." The notion of objectivity that surrounds large-scale testing, for example, fails to consider the fact that the tests and their statistical models were created by humans enacting their cultural norms and assumptions. Based on the evidence Gould gathered, he concluded that the context in which tests were developed clearly impacted the results. Early psychometricians were, in fact, influenced by the ideology of

Social Darwinism, and large-scale testing was used as a tool to generate evidence proponents used to claim eugenics as a science.[8]

The eugenic movement's clear influence on the assumptions that supported the testing model's development led Gould to challenge nearly everything about it. His critique encompassed "the abstraction of intelligence as a single entity, its location within the brain, its quantification as one number for each individual, and the use of these numbers to rank people in a single series of worthiness, invariably to find that oppressed and disadvantaged groups—races, classes, or sexes—are innately inferior and deserve their status."[9]

Mental testing, Gould explained, was based on the theory of biological determinism, which "holds that shared behavioral norms, and the social and economic differences between human groups—primarily races, classes, and sexes—arise from inherited, inborn distinctions." Based on this belief, the social hierarchy suggested by test scores is perceived as "an accurate reflection of biology." Gould focused on exposing "two deep fallacies" of biological determinism. One is the representation of a "complex and multifaceted set of human capabilities" as a single measurable entity. The second fallacy is based on the idea that a human hierarchy is part of the natural order. Gould invited his readers to deeply question the reasons for the continued use of an instrument built upon these two fallacies. Gould calls the result the "mismeasure" of man, which became the title of his book.[10]

Gould's research gave me language to frame some of my own questions about large-scale testing, and it helped me feel not quite so alone in raising them. Perhaps the rhetoric around testing was not meshing with my experience because of my own assumption that assessment's purpose is to support teaching and learning. Gould's book led me to consider that perhaps tests were created for a different purpose entirely. At the time, however, I was woefully unprepared to delve into questions of scientific racism, because, well . . . because I was raised White in America. The seeds of these ideas could not take root in soil that had been depleted by racist ideas.

While *The Mismeasure of Man* had gotten a lot of attention in the press, this challenge to large-scale testing had not been mentioned in class. I wondered what my professor thought of Gould's claims. So one afternoon, I navigated my way through the auditorium-style seating as the professor stuffed papers into his satchel near the podium. There were so many students in the class he didn't know me, so I introduced myself. My hand trembled a bit as I held out Gould's book and asked if he had read it.

"No," the professor snapped, eager to be on his way. "I have read reviews, though, and it sounds like a bunch of hogwash." And with that, he clicked his bag shut and walked away.

At first I was surprised. A cutting-edge book about educational assessment is, after all, a rare occurrence. What should I make of the fact that a professor teaching a course on assessment dismissed it without even reading it? But then I realized that Gould's book challenged the very assumptions on which the course was based, and therefore perhaps even the professor's core beliefs. But Gould's thinking helped me understand that if testing is to be considered scientific, its basic tenets must hold up under scrutiny from multiple perspectives.

As much as I wanted to pursue this conversation with my professor, the reality was that I wanted to be a teacher, and I had to pass this course. So despite this evidence to support my views, I tamped down my skepticism and tried to accept the explanation that large-scale tests are objective and efficient, and they maintain their validity when used as one measure among many.

For the first fifteen years of my teaching, test scores *were* used as one of multiple measures. The consequences attached to their use were, in most cases, fairly low. I was expected to administer only the occasional large-scale test, and the results had little influence on the daily life of the school. While I would rather not have used precious class time for something I felt was unproductive, it was only a few hours every other year or so, and I thought some parents might value the information. As long as I was able to reassure my students that this was just one form of evidence, I didn't feel too bad about being asked to administer a test. In this context, it seemed little more than an inconvenience.

A Policy Shift

My resigned acceptance of large-scale testing changed, however, in 2002. I was teaching in a Montana middle school when No Child Left Behind became the law of the land. New mandates dramatically changed the way test scores were to be used. NCLB and subsequent policies require that test scores serve as the basis for judgment in decisions made throughout the US educational system, although, as will soon become clear, the exclusive use of test scores counters the recommendations of psychometricians and even the testing manuals. Nevertheless, these school reform policies directed educators to treat test scores as proxies for academic achievement and to make decisions based on that flawed assumption. Many of these decisions carry such high stakes they can determine the course of a student's future.

Newly removed from the assessment loop, educators are expected to act as if we believe that test scores reveal a greater truth than we can possibly ascertain from our ongoing work with students. Nonbelievers like me are left with two choices: follow guidelines that challenge your integrity or leave the profession. Many teachers continued their careers, hoping the nightmare would be short-lived. Yet, as I write nearly twenty years later, test-based policy continues its reign, and teacher shortages loom in many states.[11]

Proselytizing at the time of NCLB was intense. Policy makers claimed that testing data were needed to hold teachers accountable for closing the demographic divides in scores they had newly defined as achievement gaps. Although tests have produced scores divided by race and class throughout the history of large-scale testing, policy makers feigned shock and outrage at the existence of these gaps. They called it a civil rights crisis and placed blame squarely on the shoulders of teachers, claiming the scores as proof that they were leaving children of color and poor children behind. Selling this idea to the public advantaged policy makers in two ways: by relieving mounting public pressure to equalize the wide discrepancies in school funding cited as a reason for educational inequities, and by allowing NCLB legislation to claim equity as its intent.

Based on this version of reality, policy makers created a system that rewarded or punished teachers according to their students' test scores. This move was based on the assumptions that teacher negligence had cause the scores gaps in the first place, and that we needed greater incentives to motivate us to help students learn. For the nation's many devoted teachers, nothing could have been more insulting.

Without supporting evidence, educators were expected to simply accept that social divides in test scores represented gaps in student achievement. No mention was made that these score patterns had existed since the tests were invented during the time of eugenics. Stephen J. Gould's book had apparently been excluded from the assessment and evaluation courses of other educators as well. Now Gould's cautions came flooding back.

Adding insult to injury, mathematician Cathy O'Neil explained that the rationale for this policy shift was based on a novice-level error in statistical analysis. A 1983 study showed SAT scores in decline across the nation. The government report announcing these findings was ominously titled *A Nation at Risk*. The report blamed failing schools, and teachers in particular, for declining test scores.

As it turned out, the reason for the overall decline in scores was the score gaps themselves. Over the course of the study, from 1963 to 1980, test takers had become increasingly diverse. More people of color and more people from economically disadvantaged families were taking the SAT. Because the scores of these groups have historically been lower than those of White or wealthy students, the increased numbers of test takers from these groups created a downward trend in SAT scores overall. When the scores are broken down and analyzed by subgroups, however, as Cathy O'Neil explained they should have been, SAT scores had actually *risen* within each and every group. For those prone to accept SAT scores as indicators of truth, the evidence actually showed that teachers were successfully teaching the increasingly diverse students in their classrooms. Rather than sounding a dire warning, the report should have celebrated—and encouraged schools to build upon—this success.[12]

If you are a teacher, the false rhetoric generated by this report is enough to make your blood boil. This mistaken interpretation of data has been used to justify the most dangerous *misuse* of testing data since the time of eugenics.[13]

It was never widely publicized that the justification for test-based reforms was based on error, however, and well into the twenty-first century, teachers continue to be held responsible for raising test scores and closing score gaps. Teacher negligence is still assumed to cause these demographic discrepancies. The public was told that more testing was needed to monitor what were now called "achievement gaps" and hold teachers accountable for closing them. We were told new tests were being designed to measure academic achievement, the meaning newly attributed to test results. In the meantime, educators were instructed to simply rely on scores from existing tests, as if any test-based data would serve the policy's purposes.

Based on the new guidelines, test scores are now used to decide, for example, who is retained in third grade, who is allowed to take AP classes, who is qualified to graduate from high school—and who is not. Schools and teachers are rated *exemplary* or *failing* on the basis of student test scores. These changes were not recommended by researchers or educators or psychometricians. They were conceived and delivered by policy makers desperate to appear as if they were holding teachers accountable for school improvement according to a paradigm the policy makers themselves had created.

Since 2002, these new policies have reframed the entire system from kindergarten through high school graduation, and they are now influencing university accreditation standards as well. The entire system of education is focused on data collection and interpretation. The required data are quantitative, much of it produced by large-scale standardized tests. As test scores are increasingly conflated with reality, the highest priority is now placed on passing a test rather than on demonstrating what skills have actually been mastered. Whether a student can actually read and comprehend, for example, has become a moot point. If the test score is high, it is assumed that means a child can read and understand. Yet educators and anyone who has taken a large-scale test knows that the two are not the same. The interpretation of test scores' meanings and the corresponding use of testing data have been left to the dictates of policy makers, however, and test-based policy requires us to treat scores as if they have revealed truth.

On the surface, all may seem well with this system . . . unless, that is, you are aware that this policy also locks the existing social hierarchy into place, just as large-scale tests were initially developed to do. After all, who would disagree with policies called No Child Left Behind or Every Student Succeeds? At face value, the titles make it seem that equity is the central goal of these policies. It is, therefore, natural to assume that the resulting practices must bring about greater equity. Yet nothing could be further from the truth.[14]

As Michelle Alexander demonstrated in *The New Jim Crow*, if we turn our attention to a policy's impact rather than its intent, we get an entirely different view. In the case of test-based policy, the gap between intent and outcome makes the policy look like a bait and switch. Over one hundred years of test score evidence shows that large-scale tests have always produced scores divided by race and class. If a system of rewards and punishments is attached to these scores, then the consequences are easy to predict. The highest scorers, those who are White and wealthy, will be rewarded. Those who receive the lowest scores, people of color and those who live in poverty, will be sanctioned. The impact of test-based policy on poor communities and communities of color should have been quite clear. With such significant demographic discrepancies, whenever scores are used as gatekeepers, policy makers have always known who would be allowed through the gate and who would not. For well over a century, far higher percentages of students of color and economically disadvantaged students have been left behind by test-based policies.[15]

The increased use of test scores demanded by twenty-first-century policy has, predictably, amplified the intensity and scope of this impact. The injustice now plays out at every grade level in every public school in America. At each juncture where test scores are used to make critical decisions, higher percentages of White students and wealthy students are awarded opportunities denied many students of color and students from backgrounds of poverty. Given these results, NCLB would have been more accurately named NWWCLB: No White or Wealthy Child Left Behind. Twenty-first-century education policy therefore quietly maintains America's caste system.

If we believe what we are told test scores mean, these outcomes make it appear that White and wealthier students deserve their place at the top of a hierarchy where they are awarded positions of power. Yet historian Ibram X. Kendi cautioned, "Racist ideas love believers, not thinkers."[16]

As the number of required tests began to increase at the school where I taught, I felt powerless. When I discussed my sense of foreboding with administrators and fellow educators, reactions ranged from quiet resignation to arguments that the tests were both useful and necessary. The policy left no recourse for educators and parents who disagreed because legislators tied federal funding to these test-based mandates. No one had a choice. My initial trepidation about testing returned as it became detrimental to my goals as a teacher. Increasingly, we were expected to use test scores to guide our work with each class and each child. In many schools, the curriculum changed to match the content and format of the tests.

The arm of this new policy stretched to educational research as it, too, had been reframed. Decades of qualitative research were suddenly ignored as quantitative studies were proclaimed to be the *gold standard*. The research arm of the Department of Education became the Institute of Education Sciences. Decisions about what "counted" as research were made by politicians and policy makers rather than researchers or scholars.[17]

Policy guides action, and actions have consequences. Policy is, of course, based on the worldviews of the people who create it. It rests on the foundation of societal norms and assumptions that serve as backdrops for daily life, as difficult to see as air.

Once an assumption like *Standardized tests are the best tools for measuring aptitude, intelligence, or achievement* becomes normalized, and when people accept the idea that society should be organized around these traits, it becomes very hard to remember that alternatives even exist.

Policy makers asked us to believe that the goal of twenty-first-century education policy reform was to achieve equity. Yet it seems like a shell game. While our attention was focused on the right hand of intent, perhaps we were not supposed to notice the outcomes created by the left hand. While one set of regulations demanded the use of tests to track the score gaps teachers were responsible for closing, other protocols doled out rewards and consequences based on those demographically divided test scores. Educators and parents, researchers and scholars were expected to simply trust, believe, and follow.

Yet I didn't believe, so I couldn't follow. After nearly two decades of close study and attention, the knowledge I had gained about teaching and learning whispered in my ear constantly, reminding me that testing, comparing, and ranking students has nothing to do with nurturing children's growth and development. Although I vaguely wondered what purpose these practices *do* serve, at that point, my mind was not yet ready for the seed of that question to take root.

2

A Nation at Risk

The Damage Done

The question . . . is whether we've eliminated human bias or simply camou-
flaged it with technology.

—Cathy O'Neil, *Weapons of Math Destruction*

A Cycle of Inequality: The Power of Policy

Being asked to enact No Child Left Behind policy challenged my integrity. All
that inspired me as a teacher was quickly being destroyed by policy mandates.
The damage to our educational system made me fear for our country's future.
As a disempowered teacher in a solitary classroom, I felt helpless to do anything about it. So when the opportunity arose, I accepted a three-year position
as a visiting professor in education studies at Berea College, a small private
school in Kentucky. This tuition-free college serves students primarily from
the Appalachian region who show great promise and have limited financial
means. Since its founding in 1855, Berea has intentionally served students of
color. The college's "Eight Great Commitments" light the path of its mission. I
hoped this new role might increase my ability to push back against these
policies.[1]

As NCLB proceeded, however, its power enveloped everything in its wake.
Waves of policy changes washed over us, fast and furiously. By the time I joined
Berea's faculty in 2012, the nation was ten years into NCLB. Little did I know
its waters already lapped at the shores of teacher education.

Kentucky was an early adopter of NCLB, so the impact on schools and
classrooms was more visible than it had been in Montana. I was disturbed by
what I saw. Still, I clung to the belief that in my new role as a teacher educator,
I, along with my colleagues, might be able to help our students retain a collective memory of learning environments free from the bondage of test scores. At
Berea College, I hoped, we would become keepers of a flame, ready to reclaim
education once the testing madness ended. The strong conceptual framework
of Berea's education studies program and the commitments of the college gave

me hope that if an ember of this flame could be kept alive anywhere, Berea College was the place.

When I first began supervising student teachers, Kentucky policy required them to pass the Praxis II exam to earn certification. Praxis II is a large-scale standardized test designed by the Educational Testing Service (ETS), creators of the SAT, the GRE, and many other tests. I hadn't been at Berea long when Kentucky added an additional testing mandate that created another barrier. The regulation decreed that students must pass a Praxis I exam before they were permitted to even *enroll* in a teacher education course. While Praxis I and II have somewhat different formats, "a primary difference . . . is how states use the exams." Praxis I is described as a test of "basic abilities in reading, math, and writing," and Praxis II "is designed to evaluate candidates' specific content knowledge and skills in teaching this knowledge in the classroom."[2]

Kentucky's requirement that students must pass Praxis I before they could begin teacher education coursework shifted the locus of decision making. Colleges and universities normally set their own standards regarding what students they admit into programs. When it came to teacher education, however, this regulation left that decision in the hands of the state, even for private colleges. I was astonished that institutions of higher learning would accept such a bold reach, especially given that the decision was based on the use of test scores with long-standing demographic score divides. Anyone who studied test data would be aware of the ramifications. The brunt of the regulation's impact would land squarely on the very students Berea College serves, restricting their opportunity to take a series of courses the college offered. Yet despite the protests of teacher educators, it seems the mandate garnered little attention from college and university administrators. As a result, the dreams of some Berea College students were deferred at the outset. Paradoxically, while test-based policy removed higher percentages of low-income students and people of color from the pool of teacher candidates, accreditation standards simultaneously required teacher education programs to demonstrate their attempts to diversify that pool.

Clearly, policy can create opportunity gaps for some students. In fact, exclusionary mandates have been used for this purpose throughout American history. Kentucky, for example, had overtly interfered with Berea's interracial mission once before. In 1904, during the Jim Crow era, legislators passed the Day Law, which prohibited White students from attending school with people of color. The law was targeted specifically at Berea College, which had been integrated since its founding before the Civil War. The Day Law was prompted by legislators worried about the fact that President Theodore Roosevelt had recently invited Booker T. Washington to lunch at the White House. Some feared this might open a floodgate, releasing waters that threatened to destroy a carefully constructed caste system built to advantage White people. During the Day Law's hearing, the state superintendent of education warned, "If the Berea ideas were carried out to logical conclusion, there would be social equality of the races in Kentucky"—as if that should be avoided at all costs. The very idea threatened the illusion of White supremacy. Legislators agreed, and the Day Law passed. Berea College appealed this decision all the way to the US Supreme Court, but its justices must also have feared White supremacy's downfall. The law was upheld.[3]

However, no lawsuits were filed when additional testing mandates were implemented in Kentucky's teacher education programs, despite an impact that would fall especially hard on Berea's students. College administrators instead decided they would do their best to serve the teacher education candidates who managed to pass Praxis I. Perhaps they agreed with politicians who justified this change by claiming that the Commonwealth desperately needed to raise teacher quality, and testing pre-service teachers was a way to do that. For policy makers, it was a simple solution. All the complexities of defining and testing teacher quality were removed from their hands and instead turned over to testing companies.

Carefully chosen words made test-based policy's demographic discrepancies more palatable. The term *unworthy*, for example, is not used in contemporary settings to refer to low-scoring students. Instead, educators are coached to explain that some students are not yet *ready* for an educational opportunity. While this may change the way we perceive the practice, the impact is the same: far higher percentages of White and economically privileged students continue to be granted access to the best the educational system has to offer.[4]

Assimilation

The mantra of failing schools and failing teachers began with the 1983 report *A Nation at Risk*. Although the report's conclusions were drawn from a flawed statistical analysis, as chapter 1 explains, that fact was never widely publicized. Instead, propaganda about bad teachers and failing schools fanned the flames of public fear. The need for testing was justified by calls for greater accountability throughout the system, which led to public acceptance. After all, parents who believe that teachers are failing to educate their cherished children are desperate for a remedy.[5]

New language framed the redesigned paradigm. In teacher education, for example, the term *classroom-ready* became a proxy to reference the intricate weave of skills and dispositions needed for effective teaching. At the same time, new evaluations required young children to demonstrate they had met standards of kindergarten-readiness before they were granted entry to public schools. Children who did not meet this standard, along with their families, felt the sting of exclusion before their school experience even began. The concept of kindergarten-readiness flips educational practice on its head. Rather than expecting that schools should be ready to meet the learning needs of every child who walks through the door, policy now decrees that children will be admitted to school only once they meet certain qualifications.[6]

The term *ready* is not new to educational circles. It has long been used to refer to a sequence of human development. Teachers watched for signs that a student is ready to read, for example, and instruction was tied to the developmental needs of each child. Used in this way, the word *ready* allows children the grace of developing, each in their own time.

A developmental model, however, does not mesh with a standardized, test-based culture. In a world divided into winners and losers, the word *ready* is part of a vocabulary of exclusion. Readiness, after all, is a nebulous concept. When a test evaluates a child's readiness, the standard, like the test, has been defined by people who then decide how the resulting numbers will be interpreted and used. Historically, large-scale test scores have been used to justify the exclusion of some from opportunities awarded to others. Unlike the term *worthy*, readiness implies that the exclusion is only temporary. The resulting segregation and its message of deficit, however, are often not.

The justification for the exclusion of those who are not *ready*—for kindergarten, third grade, high school graduation, or teacher preparation—is that a delay might increase their chances of later success, giving them time to *catch up*. It makes it sound like the exclusion is for the good of the student. This might be an effective approach if systems were in place to offer students learning opportunities tailored to meet their individual needs. Instead, as discussed in chapter 1, if the excluded students receive any additional support, the materials used for remediation are often standardized, and teachers are expected to follow their directives with fidelity. One look at school retention statistics for a child held back a year demonstrates the ineffectiveness of these programs.[7]

In reality, a standardized approach is about economic efficiency. After all, industrial models show standardization to be cost-effective. The system operates most efficiently, to this way of thinking, if students can be taught the same things in the same way. Since NCLB became law, standards regulate the entire educational system. Attempts are made to assimilate students to grade-level norms and preordained teaching methods so they can be uniformly taught.

The problem with this expectation, of course, is that humans are not standard. Further, a system's efficiency can be defined and measured in many ways. While the ability to assimilate might be valuable in a test-based paradigm, conformity may be detrimental in other circumstances. Test-based policy, however, decrees that resources that could be directed toward meeting students' individual needs must instead be used to purchase standardized instructional materials that mimic the tests. Learning standards are assigned and scores representing minimum standards, called cut scores, are established. Students who, for any number of reasons, don't make the cut are labeled and separated, as they were during the time of eugenics. Schools with large numbers of so-called failing students are required to pour even more resources into remedial programs designed to tailor their students to fit the requirements of a system where success is defined as a passing score.

When passing a test is the only goal, however, students can lose opportunities to actually apply knowledge and skills in meaningful ways. Politicians seem to ignore the fact that test scores are not actual proxies for learning, so teachers are asked to use scores to guide their teaching. I, for one, found them to be of little value for classroom use. Nonetheless, testing has changed the entire discourse about teaching and learning. Rather than inquiring about a child's passion for reading the word and the world, the standard question has become "What is Sarah's reading score?" However, few have a clear understanding of what that score really means.[8]

This lack of understanding about the implications of the greater system seems to include policy makers, educators, and the public. The fact that some professions require certification is a case in point. In any profession, certification is explained as the way the state can protect the public from harm. The purpose of teacher certification standards, in that case, is to ensure safe educational practice. In the language of testing culture, this translates to protecting children from teachers who are not classroom-ready. But the gap between a score and its meaning is exposed by the fact that a passing score varies from state to state. If we are to believe that cut scores represent the lowest acceptable standard of classroom-readiness, are we then to presume that the danger posed by an ill-prepared teacher varies from state to state? Of course not.[9]

The fact is, teaching is a complex, relational process that involves all the intricacies of human interactions. The dimensions of good teaching are difficult to even define, let alone evaluate. Yet when certification decisions rely on Praxis scores, the power to define the standards for solid entry-level teaching is handed over to the Educational Testing Service, which then also determines how those standards should be evaluated. In reality, of course, there is a multitude of ways to define and evaluate good teaching. All meaning is lost, though, when we pretend that a cut score actually represents a standard of classroom-readiness, or that a multiple-choice exam magically reveals teaching ability. The absurdity is easy to recognize, but for some reason, we continue to play the game.

The Human Cost

I felt the impact of test-based policy with all of my heart. After my first year mentoring student teachers at Berea College, I stood by helplessly as students who excelled in classroom practice were barred from certification because of a single test score. Despite four and a half years of evaluations that consistently demonstrated that these students had the potential to become outstanding teachers, policy had designated the Praxis score as the final point of decision. The loss is irretrievable, not only for each of these devoted pre-service teachers but also for the generations of learners who would have benefited from their teaching.

Because the impact of such outcomes is often obscured in a haze of statistics, allow me to humanize it by briefly introducing three of my former students.

After Ronald's college career, filled with stellar reviews from the professors and cooperating teachers who mentored him, tears of frustration shone in his eyes as we discussed his newly limited possibilities. Ronald is a gifted teacher of elementary children. Yet even after repeated retakes, Ronald did not pass the Praxis exam and therefore did not gain Kentucky certification. The direct evidence obtained by all the educators who had worked with him over a number of years was trumped by the verdict of a test score. Despite years of successful classroom practice, because Ronald's number fell below the cut score, he was suddenly deemed to not be *classroom-ready*. Anyone who saw Ronald teach knew that verdict to be ridiculous. Yet it brought a quick end to Ronald's plan to become a Kentucky-certified teacher.

I'm happy to say, however, that Ronald *is* a gifted teacher, because like many resilient people, Ronald found an alternate path to his dream. He moved to a different state to work in a KIPP school. KIPP is a network of public charter schools, and the school's program did not require Ronald to be certified. Ronald completed a master's degree and he is now an award-winning teacher and team leader at his school. While we celebrate Ronald's success, we must also examine the flaws in the system that rejected him.[10]

Jocelyn was Ronald's colleague in that cohort of student teachers. Jocelyn's cooperating teacher had mentored pre-service teachers over many years, and he made a point of letting me know that Jocelyn was among the best. The entire education studies faculty agreed, as had each of Jocelyn's prior cooperating teachers. In fact, the elementary school where Jocelyn completed her student teaching wanted to hire her immediately. Like Ronald, however, Jocelyn did not pass the Praxis exam. The last I heard, she was working as a paraprofessional in a local school. The classroom Jocelyn serves is no doubt enriched by her presence, as she resolutely follows her calling despite the immense frustration of not being certified. State policy completely ignored the solid evidence that showed Jocelyn is, in fact, highly qualified. Her impact, to say nothing of her salary, has been limited by a test score.

Last, I'll introduce Roxanne, who completed her student teaching in high school English at a model lab school affiliated with a state university's teacher education program. Roxanne was placed with a group of high school juniors described as extremely challenging, yet her abilities set her apart from the other pre-service teachers at the school. Roxanne designed projects that clearly engaged these students. Her experienced cooperating teacher was impressed and awarded Roxanne the highest ratings. Yet Roxanne, whose first language is Spanish, never passed the Praxis exam, even after retaking a version with language adaptations. Like Ronald and Jocelyn, Roxanne also found her way to teaching, but only for a few years. After college, she joined Teach for America (TFA), a program that accepts candidates with no prior teacher preparation and places them in some of the nation's most challenging schools. Given her talents and her teaching degree, I'm sure TFA was thrilled to have Roxanne join their ranks. Like many TFA teachers, however, Roxanne ultimately decided to pursue a different career path.

The social identities of each of these students is significant when we consider how testing impacted their careers. Ronald is African American, Jocelyn is White Appalachian, and Roxanne is Latina. Each comes from a background of economic disadvantage.

The damage wrought by testing's demographic score gaps is even more extreme for underprivileged candidates who are also Black or Brown. Unlike the overt exclusion of Kentucky's Day Law, which forced out all students of color, testing outcomes vary for individual students. Therefore, despite the odds stacked against them, many Berea College students do manage to pass required large-scale tests. Viewed as a whole, this makes the detrimental impact of the high-stakes use of test scores more subtle, but no less damaging.

Students in low-scoring demographic groups who pass large-scale tests are held up as models for what is possible, as if their success means that students who don't pass the tests just didn't work hard enough or were simply less able. At Berea College, I find little evidence to back that conclusion.

Witnessing the impact of test-score based policy on the lives of students like Ronald, Jocelyn, and Roxanne watered the seeds of my discontent that had been planted years earlier. A policy's impact is measured in human lives. The injustice exemplified by my students' experiences was the driving force for the research that informs this book.

The Damage Done

To comprehend the impact of using scores with demographic gaps to make high-stakes decisions, we need to know the size and consistency of those gaps. Harvard professor and psychometrician Daniel Koretz wrote, "The mean difference [in scores] between whites and African Americans . . . in every credible study of representative groups of school-age students [is] in the range of 0.8 to 1.1 standard deviation." To simplify, Koretz explained that the *smallest* of those mean differences, 0.8, "would place the *median African American* student . . . the student who would outscore half of all black students . . . *in only the twenty-first percentile among whites.*" This means the placement of the cut score that determines passing or failing impacts groups of White and African American test takers quite differently. A cut score set in the lowest quartile of the White group's scores would mean that well over half the African American groups would fail the test and a far higher percentage of White test takers would pass. This result can be predicted before the test is even given. And Koretz makes it clear that most often the gap in median scores between groups of Black and White test-takers is even larger than that.[11]

It may surprise you that Koretz can generalize about the size of the divide between Black and White test takers. That's because the score gaps across the broad array of large-scale tests are so consistent that test takers' scores from one test can be used to predict their scores on others. We'll look at the reasons for these score consistencies in a close study of the testing model and the ideas that gave rise to it, but for now, let's consider the implications of the twenty-first-century policy decision to rely on a testing model with outcomes known to be divided by both race and class.[12]

African American students or students from economically disadvantaged families study in the very same teacher education programs as White students or wealthy students. Yet testing outcomes are used to tell the story of a world in which a far higher percentage of White students are, in the end, classroom-ready. This brings us to a moment of historic reckoning. Are we willing to believe, without question, that these test results truly mean that, as a group, higher percentages of White people and wealthy people are and always have been—fill in the blank—more intelligent, more able, and/or higher achieving than all other groups of people? Because that's how score-based evidence is being interpreted by testing advocates who, apparently, agree.

The impact of this practice is clear. The testing gauntlet for students I worked with began with Praxis I. Its scores, remember, determined who would be allowed to take state-specified teacher education classes. The passing rates published in a national study of first-time test takers show that on the reading portion of the test, 81.5 percent of White students met or exceeded their state's cut score compared to 40.7 percent of African American students. On the same test, 79.5 percent of White students and 44.2 percent of African American students passed the writing exam. And 78.2 percent of White students passed the math section compared to 36.8 percent of African American students. In every subject area, then, African American students passed at about half the rate of White students.[13]

When Praxis I is used as an entry requirement, then, the data described above mean that for first-time test takers, we can predict that roughly 60 percent of African American students who wanted to become teachers will be barred from even *beginning* the teacher education program that leads to certification. The same would be true for approximately 20 percent of White students. In Kentucky, policy makers presumably accepted these outcomes, claiming this raised the bar used to determine who would be admitted to teacher education. As testing advocates, they would have interpreted the score to mean that over half of African American students who took Praxis I lacked the basic skills needed to become teachers.[14]

Those who were admitted to teacher education programs completed their coursework, fieldwork, and student teaching, and then, as in many states, they faced the Praxis II exam. If they didn't pass that, they didn't become certified. Nationwide, the standardized differences between Whites and African Americans who take the Praxis II exam range from between 0.74 to 1.41. Score gaps over 0.8 standard deviation are considered statistically large. In all but a single example cited in the study by Nettles et al., the gap was greater than 0.8. So when a large-scale test is used to determine certification, as compared to their White colleagues, we can predict that a far lower percentage of the African American teacher candidates who managed to pass Praxis I and successfully complete their courses and fieldwork will, in the end, be allowed to become teachers.

The study of Praxis passing scores cited here was conducted for the Educational Testing Service, the company that produces the Praxis Series. It is important to note, however, that this example is not an anomaly. These researchers did their best to tease out the effects of other social factors, and still they found that "race/ethnicity explained the most variance in the scale scores." In fact, the study revealed statistically "very large" score gaps between African American and White teacher candidates on every Praxis I and Praxis II test they studied. Koretz clarifies that large score gaps have also been found "in every credible study of representative groups of school-age students."[15]

There are strong correlations between test scores and socioeconomic status (SES) as well. SES is an amalgam of the income, educational level, and occupational status of a student or their parents. Studies find that students from wealthy families receive significantly higher scores than children from economically deprived families. The social factors of race and SES correlate with test scores so strongly that they can be used to predict a test taker's score. White test takers who are also wealthy, for example, predictably receive the highest scores.[16]

For generations, the meaning of these scores has been interpreted in ways that justify granting greater access to White and wealthy students pursuing higher education and professional careers. The assumption is that students earn these privileges because their scores have shown them to be more intelligent or higher achieving. Yet despite decades of research, no one has provided conclusive evidence to explain why these score gaps exist. Test results are influenced by many factors. Some are related to education, and some are not. As Koretz writes, "Everyone who studies educational achievement knows that differences in scores arise in substantial part from noneducational factors. A huge body of research collected in the United States over half a century documents this." Educational testing scholar Wayne Au cites a study that claims that about 20 percent of test score variance has to do with schooling, while about 60 percent is related to other, noneducational factors, including, for example, food insecurity, medical and dental care, the number of times a student has moved, and a host of other complicating factors.[17]

While it is impossible to eliminate the influence of these confounding variables, the statistical model tries to account for at least a few of them. For this and many other reasons, psychometricians recommend that a test score *never* be used as the sole piece of evidence in making any decision.[18]

Yet in twenty-first-century education policy, test scores—and their gaps—have been assigned new meaning and greater significance. Rightly or wrongly, test score gaps are assumed to represent gaps in student achievement. Policy also requires that test scores be reported and used *as if* they are accurate measures of student learning. As you will see in chapters to come, establishing a test score relies on a great deal of inference. Inference and accuracy, of course, do not go together. Yet the entire twenty-first-century test-based reform movement is built upon these assumptions.[19]

For many of us, the inner workings of the testing model are a mystery. Yet the consistency of demographic gaps throughout testing's history makes the winners and losers of any test-based policy quite clear. The verdicts are justified by a belief that test scores are worthy indicators of some valued trait, even when few are sure what that trait is or how the scores are attained.

In the twenty-first century, education policy exponentially increased reliance on large-scale tests, exacerbating the impact of demographic divisions. Daniel Koretz, for one, is worried. Students now experience the consequences of a test score's verdict year after year. To those who consistently receive low scores, it must feel like repeated blows. Koretz wrote, "Clearly, these are very large differences, large enough to have very serious implications for the students' later success." Indeed, we see the results as they influence all areas of society.[20]

Koretz's concern is particularly significant because he understands the ins and outs of the testing model. This leads us to a crucial question: can we really trust the meaning of test scores enough to use them to determine the course of students' lives? Should they be allowed to shape the social structure of our nation? Because that is exactly what's happening. When test scores limit opportunities for individuals, they also limit possibilities for the nation's future.

Weapons of Math Destruction

Perhaps the public's willingness to accept the meaning attributed to test scores is complicated by the fact that the scores are produced using complex statistical models. We have been conditioned to believe that test results are objective and scientific, but it is difficult to work out how a score is derived. We now live in a data-driven society where racist ideas have reigned for many generations. We've therefore been socialized to expect racially divided outcomes, and somehow we've been convinced to consider the entire system just.

Much as Stephen J. Gould's research into the origins of large-scale testing led him to understand that racist assumptions and outcomes can hide beneath claims of scientific objectivity, Cathy O'Neil's study of the 2008 market crash gave her an unexpected "front-row seat during the financial crisis and a terrifying tutorial on how insidious and destructive math could be." O'Neil is a Harvard-educated mathematician who has taught at Barnard College and worked at both a hedge fund and at an e-commerce start-up company. These experiences gave her unique vantage points to evaluate what she calls the Big Data economy. The disillusionment that grew from her conclusions led her to write *Weapons of Math Destruction: How Big Data Increases Inequality and Threatens Democracy*. The book explains that a Big Data economy is defined by the many decisions that are made through the use of algorithms. These are decisions that affect our lives, and some, she found, perpetuate cycles of inequality. Her explanation helped me place test-based education policy into a broader framework of contemporary American society.[21]

O'Neil's expertise and experience helped her see how advancing technological capabilities allowed the use of algorithms to ramp up in scale. She noted that predictive models once used in banking and business are now being applied to people's lives, calculating and ranking our potential societal value as contributors and consumers. In the shift to a Big Data economy, O'Neil wrote,

> mathematicians and statisticians were studying our desires, movements, and spending power. They were predicting our trustworthiness and calculating our potential as students, workers, lovers, criminals. This was the Big Data economy, and it promised spectacular gains. A computer program could speed through thousands of resumes or loan applications in a second or two and sort them into neat lists, with the most promising candidates on top. This not only saved time but also was marketed as fair and objective. After all, it didn't involve prejudiced humans digging through reams of paper, just machines processing cold numbers. By 2010 or so, mathematics was asserting itself as never before in human affairs, and the public largely welcomed it.[22]

If this sounds strangely familiar, it's because these are the arguments employed to justify using data produced by large-scale tests. Yet rather than eliminating human bias as supporters claimed, O'Neil found that "many of these models encoded human prejudice, misunderstanding, and bias into the software systems that increasingly managed our lives." In the Big Data economy, algorithms determine outcomes at crucial turning points in our lives. In addition to whether we will be admitted to college, algorithms often regulate whether we will be granted a loan, sentenced to prison, or hired and retained as an employee. O'Neil explains that these statistical models operate on a grand scale and in an alternate universe, far removed from the lives of those impacted by the consequences.[23]

After the market crash, O'Neil came face-to-face with the human impact of faulty algorithms and their applications. She could clearly see who lost, who gained, and why. This shift in perspective led her to examine outcomes in many other areas where statistical models are applied. What she saw moved her to speak out. Despite her love of mathematics, O'Neil concluded that many of the modern world's problems were based in growing inequality "aided and abetted by mathematicians wielding magic formulas."[24]

O'Neil despaired that when the world of finance was confronted with the human suffering caused by the market crash, it did not seek redemption. There was no recalibration. Instead, it callously returned to business as usual. As O'Neil's career shifted from finance to tech-driven data science, the move allowed her to understand the pervasiveness of Big Data mentality. She explained that the shift to "data-driven" practice has ushered in a new cultural mindset and a new way to define success. Hired out of top universities, tech and data science employees have "focused on external metrics—like SAT scores and college admissions—their entire lives. . . . In both cultures," O'Neil wrote, "wealth is no longer a means to get by. It becomes directly tied to personal worth." Those who operate in this world view their high salaries as confirmation that they have earned their elite positions in the social hierarchy. It seems that in the Big Data culture, big money sits alongside intelligence or achievement as a measure of worth.[25]

Based on what she learned, O'Neil coined the term "weapons of math destruction" (WMDs), using it to describe some statistical models that were built to serve the Big Data economy. Reviewer Evelyn Lamb summarized that WMDs "are mathematical models or algorithms that claim to quantify important traits: teacher quality, recidivism risk, creditworthiness but have harmful outcomes and often reinforce inequality." Lamb explained that in her book, O'Neil "shares stories of people who have been deemed unworthy in some way by an algorithm."[26]

O'Neil provides a broad range of examples to show how data is increasingly being collected, interpreted, and used in ways that advantage those with great wealth and disadvantage all others. In every case, O'Neil wrote, the model's "verdicts, even when wrong or harmful, were beyond dispute or appeal. And they tended to punish the poor and the oppressed in our society, while making the rich richer." In short, the algorithms are used within a system constructed to convince people their findings are just.[27]

The cases described in O'Neil's book are all contemporary, beginning with a scathing assessment of the value-added model of teacher evaluation she calls a "statistical farce." Yet as I read, I could not stop thinking about large-scale testing. The century-old model perfectly fits O'Neil's definition of a WMD. What I've learned leads me to wonder if it might be the granddaddy of them all.[28]

O'Neil reiterated Gould's claim that statistical models are influenced by the worldview of the people who create them. She stated simply, "Models are opinions embedded in mathematics." Further, "WMDs are only primitive tools which hammer complexity into simplicity." The examples she shares show how often Americans are caught in a bait and switch. Based on a false belief that any data-based system is inherently objective and fair, statistical models serve as smokescreens, hiding the inequities their algorithms produce. If people mistakenly assume the models are somehow capable of revealing unbiased truth, O'Neil explains, their results are considered beyond reproach. The results can then be used as evidence to justify racist and elitist outcomes.[29]

O'Neil's findings also directly counter a narrative of infallibility. She explained that "the math-powered applications powering the data economy were based on choices made by fallible human beings. . . . Many of these models encoded human prejudice, misunderstanding, and bias into the software systems that increasingly managed our lives. Like gods, these mathematical models were opaque, their workings invisible to all but the highest priests in their domain: mathematicians and computer scientists. Their verdicts, even when wrong or harmful, were beyond dispute or appeal. And they tended to punish the poor and the oppressed in our society, while making the rich richer."[30]

Use of these algorithms leads to dire social consequences, O'Neil explained, because while some are advantaged, many others suffer. She wrote, "These models, powered by algorithms, slam doors in the face of millions of people, often for the flimsiest of reasons, and offer no appeal. They're unfair." In his criticism of the algorithms eugenicists created, Gould cautioned us to beware of scientific racism. O'Neil agreed, explaining that we need to "start putting the 'science' into data science." She continued, "We must equip ourselves with sufficient skepticism [so] that we can see, understand, and defend the data that goes into our algorithms and the results they produce."[31]

It takes some effort to view these models with a critical eye. Few choose to wander into the haze of statistics to find out how they actually operate, let alone examine the assumptions that drive their use. That is, however, the only way to gauge the distance that exists between a model and reality. We need to understand how the model operates in the context of its use. Although the use of large-scale test scores has advantaged White and wealthy test takers for over a century, society's devotion to Big Data allowed education policy to exponentially *increase* the social damage wrought by this particular weapon. Yet test-based education reform policy has been spun as if equity is its goal.

Based on O'Neil's taxonomy, it seems testing easily meets the qualifications of a WMD, which O'Neil explains are "opaque, unquestioned, and unaccountable, and they operate at a scale designed to sort, target, or 'optimize' millions of people." In addition, "Ill-conceived mathematical models now micro-manage the economy, from advertising to prisons. . . . By confusing their findings with on-the-ground reality, most of them create pernicious WMD feedback loops." While the chapters to come will take a close look at how testing data is produced, for now, let's set the contemporary test-based educational model within O'Neil's WMD framework to get a broad view of how the system as a whole operates.[32]

WMDs Are Opaque

Opaque is the opposite of transparent. If an object is opaque, you can't see through it. When a system is described as opaque, it means its steps or procedures are hidden or unclear. While testing manuals are available to all, most educators and parents don't have the time or the will to cut through their convoluted use of language or untangle the web of statistical procedures that produce a score. O'Neil wrote, "WMDs are, by design, inscrutable black boxes" whose inner workings are hidden from the people most affected by them.[33]

Few outside the testing industry really understand how these tests are created or how their scores are produced. In fact, Nicholas Lemann, author of *The Big Test: The Secret History of the American Meritocracy*, claimed that even many of the presidents/CEOs of the Educational Testing Service didn't understand the psychometrics involved. In my experience, neither do school administrators, educators, parents, or those who design test-score based policy. Without this understanding, though, we are prone to accept the meaning of test scores as they are marketed, without knowing why or if they are worthy of our trust.[34]

If we can't place our complete trust in the meaning of the scores, we certainly shouldn't trust the conclusions drawn from them. Trust is gained through information and evidence. The latter part of this book is devoted to shining a light into some of testing's dark corners, exploring how test content is selected, how cut scores are set, the degree of estimation and measurement error involved, and the many assumptions that underlie the model's conceptual framework. The system of testing is particularly opaque, in fact, due to the limits placed on outside research. As we will learn, large-scale testing organizations control their own data. Without access to this data, it is especially difficult for outside researchers to answer, or even raise, critical questions. These multiple layers of opacity hide outcomes that reveal test-based education policy as a WMD.

WMDs' Results Go Unquestioned

Because of the model's complexity, we tend to rely on policy makers' interpretation of what test scores mean and their appraisal of how scores should be used. Educators and parents are expected to trust their judgment and follow their mandates. The expectation of obedience without question is another marker of a system that functions as a WMD.

When twenty-first-century policy makers decided that test scores represent student achievement and redefined long-standing test score divides as achievement gaps, all arenas of educational practice shifted to accommodate this new presumed to be accurate reality. Educational researchers and education reporters, for example, regularly cite test scores as evidence of academic achievement.

The use of large-scale testing has become so normalized in education that although we may complain about these tests, we treat them as if they are an inevitable part of schooling. Although critics have questioned the educational use of large-scale testing since its inception, the public at large has not yet recognized or protested the social damage caused by falsely equating test scores with truth. Meanwhile, the testing industry thrives.

As an educator, I assumed that someone somewhere must surely have proven that test scores are accurate measures of student achievement. But I couldn't find evidence that convinced me. In fact, quite the contrary. Yet when we don't hold leaders accountable for policy outcomes they have free rein. This lack of accountability is, in fact, another marker of a WMD.

WMDs Are Unaccountable

Given the consequences of test-based policy, it is hard to believe that there is no external oversight, public or private, of the testing industry. The only vetting takes place internally. ETS, for example, conducts and publishes its own research and maintains complete control over its data. This closed system makes it easy to avoid critique from unsanctioned research, freeing the organization to focus on marketing its products and services. Clearly, this lack of oversight works in favor of the testing industry and against the public interest. It sets up a scenario where the government claims to protect the public from harm by certifying teachers, yet it not only allows but *requires* the use of data from an unregulated industry to make those certification decisions.[35]

The public, however, certainly has reason to question the veracity of data used to justify a century-long pattern of racial and economic injustice. In the twenty-first century, politicians promoting the need for greater educational accountability created policy mandates requiring states to accumulate and track huge amounts of testing data. Yet where is the accountability for the testing organizations that produce the data? And who holds policy makers accountable for the impact of its use?

By calling score gaps *achievement gaps* and successfully deflecting the blame to teachers, schools, and communities, policy makers have seemingly absolved themselves of responsibility for the outcomes of policies they created. Explicit statements of good intent, like naming a policy No Child Left Behind, offer a layer of protection. In the United States, legal precedent decrees that for a racial discrimination charge to hold, plaintiffs must prove racist *intent*. Intent is, of course, internal, and therefore almost impossible to prove. This was quite clear to policy makers. So while the impact of test-based policy would be divided by race and class, they knew courts would consider that information irrelevant if equity was the policy's stated goal. The proof of intent requirement leaves the public with little recourse, as it prevents most claims of discrimination from ever reaching the courts. The law, in other words, allows for discriminatory outcomes as long as a court has determined they aren't intentional. This framework spins discrimination to look like justice and enacts the illusion of human hierarchy as if it is reality.[36]

WMDs Operate on a Large Scale to Sort or Target People

Test-based policies target and sort millions of people, as O'Neil explains is also typical of a WMD. That was the initial purpose of large-scale testing, and testing data is still used to that end. Before the development of large-scale tests, educators created their own tests to assess the learning of the students they worked with. No statistical modeling was needed because there was no reason to extrapolate a larger meaning from the score.[37]

In the chapters to come, however, we will see that eugenicists, deciding it would be beneficial to categorize large numbers of people, developed testing's statistical models for that reason. Social Darwinists had drawn maps of human hierarchies formed by the racial divides they imagined. The demographically divided scores of large-scale tests were cited as evidence to back these beliefs. Testing data was created to support social engineering. Large-scale tests were not created for a teacher's use; their purpose was to justify an educational hierarchy and ensure "efficiency." Scores granted some students access to the finest educations in the country while others were declared only worthy of training in rudimentary skills.

Ibram X. Kendi, Isabel Wilkerson, and Michelle Alexander each demonstrate ways an American caste system is upheld by policies that result in the oppression of some and the elevation of others. From the time large-scale tests were first marketed for use in US education, scores have been used to categorize, label, and track students, determining the course of their futures. In short, testing is the blunt instrument that divides those considered worthy of the best of society's resources from those who are not.

WMDs Create Toxic Cycles and Harmful Feedback Loops

When a system operates as a WMD, the social and economic consequences of its use are hidden behind a smokescreen of complex algorithms backed by rhetoric created to justify the results. Large-scale testing is no exception. Contemplating the impact of test score–based policy soon has us thinking in circles because the requirement mandating the high-stakes use of test scores exacerbates the very problem policy makers say they are trying to solve. The fact is that the high-stakes use of test scores creates and maintains demographic gaps in schools and in society, even as policy makers claim exactly the opposite intent.

Every student of research learns the importance of triangulating the data used to make any claim. In order to be trustworthy, we are told, information used to confirm or deny a claim must come from at least three sources, different in form. Yet without corroborating evidence outside the realm of testing, educators are told to use test scores as the sole indicators of student achievement or "readiness." Based on a single data point, the assumption is that students of color and students with lower SES are actually achieving at lower levels than White students and wealthy students. Rather than question what Kendi defined as a racist idea, we are asked simply to believe.

Belief sets the toxic cycle of a WMD in motion. We are told that test scores are needed to determine whether score gaps are closing. Student opportunity is awarded or restricted and teacher success or failure is measured on the basis of test scores. Resources are withheld from districts with large numbers of "failing" students, while districts with high-scoring students are rewarded. Given the long-standing demographic divides in test scores, anyone drafting this policy could have predicted the impact. Schools in poor areas or with large numbers of students of color would be sanctioned. Schools in wealthy areas or where the student body is mostly White would be rewarded. This is an age-old story.

The cycle is powered, in part, by confusion between statements of equitable intent and conflicting outcomes, a common feature of systems that operate as WMDs. O'Neil explained that "the model itself contributes to a toxic cycle and helps to sustain it." The system relies on public trust that policy outcomes will match statements of purpose . . . even when they don't.[38]

The problem is, as O'Neil described, we are confusing the policy's conclusions with reality. When we allow student achievement to be defined solely by test scores, advantaging those with high scores and denying access to opportunities for others year after year, the scores become self-fulfilling prophesies. Once people are convinced that scores truly represent some form of merit, those at the top of the test score hierarchy gain confidence, while all below them feel less worthy. Equally harmful is that students who receive higher scores also learn to see low-scoring students as less deserving. Self-perception affects human behavior. When students' low scores cause them to feel inept as learners or as test takers, they internalize that message and feel less confident as they take the next test—or they stop trying to learn completely. This establishes a cycle. At the same time, students who receive higher scores grow more confident with each test they take. With the increased testing demands of twenty-first-century policy, students receive test–score based messages from the very start of their educational experience, and they are repeated year after year. Sorting students on the basis of presumed merit results in an educational hierarchy that both reflects and perpetuates the social structure of the nation.

Another harmful feedback loop involves how test-based mandates impact teacher expectations, which in turn affect student learning. As test scores are increasingly treated as truth and teachers are held accountable for the scores of their students, deficit thinking takes hold. Score-based accountability focuses attention on fixing presumed educational deficits of lower-scoring students rather than on building upon their assets. In other words, instead of focusing on student strengths, teachers are responsible for "fixing" areas of perceived weakness so students can "catch up" to an arbitrary standard set for a child of a given age.

The entire process is dehumanizing. As testing data have become the sole measure of student and teacher success, students are sometimes referenced by their test scores rather than their names. Teachers are told that their goal should be to raise those scores. I've seen test scores charted on *data walls* in places actually called *war rooms*. I've witnessed well-meaning teachers referring to certain students as *gap kids*. The fact that children internalize such labels brings us to the final characteristic of a WMD.

WMDs Create Systems with Winners and Losers

In a paradigm that treats life as a competition, weapons of math destruction create systems in which there are winners and losers. This score-based game leads the White and the wealthier segments of society to believe in the truth of test scores because they designate them as winners. Once the public is convinced that test score evidence is an actual measure of a person's merit, testing data are used to justify denying opportunity to the losers—those who have not made the cut. This is how WMDs operate. Because they create self-perpetuating systems, O'Neil wrote, "the algorithms would make sure that those deemed losers would remain that way. A lucky minority would gain ever more control over the data economy, raking in outrageous fortunes and convincing themselves all the while that they deserved it." These words describe the position we now find ourselves in.[39]

There is no doubt that industries are also winners in an age that gives rise to test-based entrepreneurship. Beyond the expansion of the testing industry itself, test-based policy also expands the market share of test-prep companies. The punitive measures attached to low test scores have created a boon for other businesses as well. Publishers promote "research-based" curricula as remedies for "failing" schools. Required remediation ranges from hiring on-the-ground consultants, mandating standardized, scripted curricula, or school takeovers by the state or by private, for-profit companies. Consulting companies train teachers to teach their students test-taking skills. In a system built around a single indicator of student success or failure, raising scores and boosting the economy have become the end goals that matter.

Given the inequitable school funding formulas and the economic and racial segregation in US schools, the results of policy have played out exactly as would be expected. Because of low test scores, the poorest schools are forced to pay the costs of these additional mandated services. If test scores remain low, schools in these neighborhoods lose local control, while those in Whiter or wealthier neighborhoods continue to offer high-quality service. From the Blackfeet Nation to Chicago's South Side to the heart of Appalachia, the schools that can least afford it are paying the highest costs—economically, educationally, and emotionally.[40]

Thanks to Cathy O'Neil's work, we can see how each part of a system that operates as a WMD acts in concert, and we can identify the role large-scale testing plays. In a model where data are not triangulated, test scores have replaced the demonstration and application of skills as evidence of learning. Teacher education programs are forced to teach students how to disaggregate test score data, yet few pre-service teachers learn how those scores are obtained. This ensures the system remains opaque as the cycle continues.

For educators forced to enact policy mandates, it soon becomes difficult to remember what once was obvious: a child is not a test score; skills like reading and writing are best assessed in a meaningful context; learning is difficult, and often impossible, to quantify.

As American society has shifted to a Big Data economy where decisions are based on extrapolating results from mountains of data, there is a strong tendency to be drawn into the language and mindset of models that refer to humans in terms of numbers. Accepting inequitable impact is "easy to do, and to justify," O'Neil writes, "when success comes back as an anonymous score and when the people affected remain every bit as abstract as the numbers dancing across the screen." In other words, if we are removed from the beauty of Ronald, Jocelyn, and Roxanne, if we don't witness their tears, it is easier to define them as *losers*.[41]

Studying the characteristics of WMDs allows us to question a system that allows a test-based education model to operate even as it produces racist and elitist outcomes. We are told that test-based policy will resolve societal inequity when in fact it exacerbates it. Once I recognized the size of the test-score divides and began to understand the devastating impact of mandates that increased their high-stakes use, I was puzzled by how I, a life-long educator, could have been so blinded. Conversations with fellow educators and parents let me know I was not alone. Colleagues could see the harmful effects of classrooms focused solely on test content but, like me, few seemed aware of how the system fit into a pattern of a national policy that advantages some and oppresses others.

It's as if educators could see only a few threads in one square of a national quilt. The pattern had been quickly rewoven by NCLB policy. Educators and parents were so busy trying to keep up with the speed of the changes that we couldn't attend to the outcomes of the new test-based policy. It has been difficult to gain a vantage point that allows us to see how this change fits into a larger pattern of a society configured to serve a Big Data economy. Yet because public education impacts nearly every person who lives on American soil, the threads extend to reach all parts of the quilt. Inequities resulting from education policy are therefore woven into the social structure in ways that will reverberate for generations.

The goal of my research was not only to reveal the impact of twenty-first-century education policy on society as a whole but to understand the conditions that led to its acceptance. By interrogating that context, we find more threads of racist and elitist policies to disentangle. For me, this involved a journey inward as well as outward, as I struggled to learn how this illusion of equity had been so carefully constructed.[42]

SECTION 2

Scaffolding Caste

3

Constructing an Illusion

Assigning Human Worth

Once you've experienced one other way of seeing, you begin to realize there are many different ways to describe the universe, many different ways to transmit knowledge.

—Sandra Lopez in Jessica Singer Early, *Stirring Up Justice*

Cuts in a Prism

Berea, Kentucky, the town where I live, was founded by abolitionist John G. Fee, who established Berea College there in 1855. Before the Civil War, African Americans and women taught at Berea College. The early town of Berea was platted to ensure that Black and White people lived side by side. Fee's goal was to create the college and the town as inclusive communities.

People who supported slavery and believed in White supremacy tried to disrupt Fee's dream of inclusivity by driving his family and college faculty away. They returned, however, and quietly continued their work. In 1904, the state government intervened by mandating educational segregation across Kentucky, justified by the idea that White students would be "contaminated" by attending schools with African American students. The law was aimed at Berea College, the state's only integrated institution.[1]

Berea's public schools, like those in the rest of the Commonwealth, were segregated. In 1927, Middletown School opened to serve the African American children in the Berea area. It was one of thousands of schools funded by Julius Rosenwald who, in partnership with Booker T. Washington, designed schools specifically to serve Black children. Collectively, they became known as Rosenwald Schools. Middletown School operated until Berea's K-12 schools were integrated in 1963. In the summer of 2016, Middletown School had its first reunion, and Berea's mayor, a White lawyer, was invited to speak. He explained that although he had spent his childhood in Berea and graduated from its high school during that time, he was embarrassed to say he had never realized Middletown School existed. This, of course, implies he had also never wondered about the absence of African American students in the schools he attended.[2]

51

As he spoke, a hush fell over the crowd of Middletown School's alumni. The mayor confessed that although he had studied civil rights law, he was just beginning to examine his own life experience through the lens of race. People in the audience began to nod. The mayor continued, saying that he understood this meant he had not had a clear picture of the life experiences of some of the people he represented or about the shared heritage of our nation. He admitted shame at his ignorance. He vowed to do better.

Although the circumstances are different, in many ways the mayor's story is my own. Like over 80% percent of American teachers, I am White. I was raised in a middle-class, Christian family. I am a cisgender woman. These parts of my identity fit the norms we've been socialized to in American society. Like the mayor, I don't know what I don't know. I grew up in a family who made sure their young daughter was aware of their support for the civil rights movement, and yet this same family chose to live in a nearly all-White city because it was a "good place to raise children."

Codified into law and policy since colonial times, racist ideas have shaped American institutions and invaded the lives of every individual. It took me a long time to become aware and then to acknowledge that as a result, generations of my family have benefited from racist policy. Because of social positioning awarded by my Whiteness, I have not directly experienced racism's impact. Ongoing segregation ensured that I had rarely witnessed individual acts of racism. My lack of awareness, of course, didn't mean that racism has disappeared, as some claim. As I learn to recognize its ongoing impact, I also see the many ways I've been encouraged to look away.

One example is the fact that, although I teach in a country shaped by racism, nowhere in my education was I asked to even examine, let alone question, a social hierarchy that author Isabel Wilkerson identifies as a caste system. James Loewen's many studies show how rarely the words *race* and *class* appear in American textbooks. Not one of my teacher certification courses asked me to consider the impact of the ideas I'd absorbed about what is *normal* or taught me the history of racism and classism upon which this country, and its system of public education, was built. I'd lived forty years before I finally found myself in a situation where someone asked me to consider the history of the land on which I walked and pointed out that someone's gain is often someone else's loss. I was unable to identify the interlocking systems that perpetuate ongoing cycles of racism and elitism because until I actively chose otherwise, I was rarely around people negatively impacted by these systems. In short, I was blind to things that were happening right before my eyes, largely because they weren't happening to me.[3]

I failed to recognize that I operated in a world structured around White, Christian, middle-class norms because those norms matched my cultural identities. I have been socialized to accept them without a thought, taking them for granted like the air I breathe. I didn't know there were other ways of interacting with others and with the world because I saw few alternatives. Segregation narrowed my view. In my neighborhoods and throughout my education, I heard the stories of people whose backgrounds and life experiences were much like mine.

Now I see how carefully American society and its institutions are constructed to create a mirage for White people, especially focused on those of us in the middle and lower classes. Little in my world disrupted the idea that the United States is an inclusive society where all are welcomed. I hadn't yet recognized that when a school textbook uses the word *American*, it most often refers to someone who operates within White, Christian, middle-class cultural norms. I was socialized to believe that all Americans should strive to live by these norms and, by implication, that anyone who chooses not to assimilate is not truly American. This narrative maintains the social order of a country whose policies were built to advantage those who are White and those who are wealthy.[4]

As one of the privileged, I was raised to assume that the values maintained by these norms were, well, "right." I was socialized to assume policy was built to achieve goals espoused in a national narrative claiming to uphold equality, liberty, and justice for all. My segregation from people who are negatively affected by racist policies and practices ensured I would rarely see their impact. At the same time, my schooling prompted me to accept, rather than question, the social order the policies upheld. In fact, I was led to believe that these are the norms and values that constitute civilization itself, something people around the world should strive for. From my vantage point, I believed that American policy aimed to ensure that everyone shared in the American Dream.

Like many educators, I had learned these lessons well. For too many years, I passed this false narrative on to my students.

I was shocked into reality by the No Child Left Behind mandates and by Indian Education for All, an educational requirement that all people on the lands now called Montana learn about the history and perspectives of the tribal nations there. While I immediately knew that something was wrong, I couldn't put my finger on exactly what it was. Around the time NCLB practices took hold in Montana, I was spending a few weeks each summer co-directing National Writing Project Summer Institutes in Browning, Montana, on the Blackfeet Nation. The impact of NCLB on children and teachers in Browning Public Schools was profound. Based on low test scores, schools that served as the heart of the community were quickly declared to be failing. Curricula infused with local cultural knowledge was replaced by nationalized scripted curricula, prescribed as a cure. One teacher told me, for example, that she received standardized lesson plans the day before she was to teach them. The rest of the year's lessons were locked away in a cabinet until they were to be taught, forcing all teachers to follow the same script. The districts hired support staff to rotate among classrooms to record interactions so that any teacher who strayed could be quickly brought back in line.

Teaching in a school just over the mountains from Browning, where my students were mostly White, there were no such mandates. I had no scripted curriculum; I was free to teach according to my professional knowledge and experience. This was the moment my eyes began to open.

The opportunity to learn from Blackfeet colleagues slowly helped me recognize that I had only ever seen one small piece of the large mosaic that comprises America. When I was finally ready, some kind and patient teachers graciously guided me until I learned to perceive reality as a prism with many different cuts in the glass. Looking through the prism from any other vantage point allows me to understand the world differently. This new awareness set the course for a learning journey that will last a lifetime.

I came to realize that equity, in schools and elsewhere, will never be achieved if we are blind to the policies and practices that perpetuate inequity. People can't oppose what they can't see. Yet identifying the many policies that uphold social norms takes conscious, active effort, especially for people like me, whose interests the policies are designed to protect.

Despite the national narratives, the fact is that American society was not created on a model of equity. It was, instead, deliberately constructed as a social hierarchy. Those in power create policies that maintain that structure. We might be aware of it, but this truth is rarely spoken in White society. Yet, if asked, even children can identify the demographics of people at the top of the social pyramid: White, male, wealthy, Christian. These were, in fact, the people whose positions of power the law was created to uphold. Regulations allowed them to own land, and in many jurisdictions, land ownership determined the right to vote.[5]

Yet from its inception, the United States has called itself a democracy. As American students study the construction of caste systems in other places, their textbooks imply that they are fortunate to live in a society where everyone has a say in their government, and all have the opportunity to rise to the top. Even as they experience its effects, students are rarely encouraged to name the social hierarchy in the United States, let alone examine why and how it operates. Despite their own observations and statistics that demonstrate ongoing inequities, many Americans defer to a narrative that tells us our country values equality above all. This is the nature of hegemony.

Contemporary Hegemony

Encyclopedia Britannica defines hegemony as "the dominance of one group over another, often supported by legitimating norms and ideas." In other words, the dominant group crafts the rhetoric used to justify its right to govern. That rhetoric is based in ideology. Hegemony reigns as these ideas become normalized to the point that they seem "commonsensical and intuitive, thereby inhibiting the dissemination or even the articulation of alternative ideas." The rhetoric of American hegemony certainly influenced my thinking well into adulthood.[6]

There are several ways people explain the demographic similarities of those who maintain their positions at the top of the American hierarchy. One is based on the belief that White, wealthy men have proven themselves to be more worthy than all others and have therefore earned their right to occupy their positions of power. This position was once argued as biological superiority. We now hear other reasons: that their test scores were higher or they worked harder or they knew best how to take advantage of opportunities available to all. The concept of race, however, has been politically assigned and enacted. A different view, therefore, is that the segment of the population at the peak of the social pyramid has been and continues to be advantaged by American law and policy.

Historian Ibram X. Kendi contends that policy, not personal failure, creates the racial divisions in our country. Any view that ignores the role of policy is based on racist ideas that have become normalized. Kendi explains, "A racist idea is any notion that suggests one racial group is inferior or superior to another racial group in any way. Racist ideas argue that the inferiorities and superiorities of racial groups explain racial inequities in society." In other words, pinning the reason for social inequity onto members of marginalized groups by saying "they" are not as intelligent or ambitious or hardworking is a racist idea.[7]

Individuals within racial groups are, of course, different from one another. Yet politicians, data analysts, and journalists frequently reference Black or Indigenous or communities of color as if they are internally homogeneous. This is why the *Essential Understandings regarding Montana Indians* states: "There is great diversity among individual American Indians as identity is developed, defined and redefined by entities, organizations and people. A continuum of Indian identity, unique to each individual, ranges from assimilated to traditional. There is no generic American Indian." The fact that tribal leaders needed to include this reminder shows how deeply racist ideas are embedded in American society.[8]

Public acceptance of racist ideas allows racist policies to continue. Kendi describes a racist policy as "any measure that produces or sustains racial inequity between racial groups." Kendi's books cite many examples of such policies throughout history, educational testing among them. When education policy is built upon "standardized tests that produce racial inequities," Kendi wrote, it stands to reason that its outcomes are also racially divided. Yet in spite of this racialized impact, pundits continue to claim test-based policy is "race neutral." This is how hegemony operates. It fools us into thinking there is only one way to perceive the world.[9]

Anti-racism, then, is a system of policies created from anti-racist ideas that results in equity across every demographic: race, class, gender, religion, and beyond. Equitable intent is irrelevant; a policy's impact is evaluated by its outcomes. Throughout this book, my use of the terms *racist* and *anti-racist* rely upon Kendi's demographically inclusive definitions. Equity, after all, requires inclusivity.[10]

In her book *Caste: The Origins of Our Discontents,* Isabel Wilkerson adds a new layer to the conversation about America's social hierarchy. Wilkerson suggests that because of the cultural blindness that often surrounds racism, a change in language provides new vantage points. In researching her book, Wilkerson read the works of writers publishing during the time of racial terror known as the Jim Crow era. To her surprise, she discovered these authors frequently used the term *caste* to describe the social order. Wherever they operate, Wilkerson explained, caste systems are created to rank and to separate groups of people. Jim Crow laws codified a class of citizens separated from White Americans. Caste was enforced by the legal system, aided by public lynchings and other acts of terror.[11]

In the United States, caste and racism are so interwoven it is difficult to separate the two. Both ideas are politically constructed. Wilkerson argued that because the term *race* is used to describe acts that are personal as well as institutional, racism is too easy to deny. Caste, however, is purely organizational. It's the framework that grants racism its power. Wilkerson defined caste as "any action or structure that seeks to limit, hold back, or put someone in a defined ranking, seeks to keep someone in their place by elevating or denigrating that person on the basis of their perceived category." The organizing principles of caste are clear. Wilkerson explained, "Casteism is the investment in keeping the hierarchy as it is in order to maintain your own ranking, advantage, privilege, or to elevate yourself above others or keep others beneath you." Her book demonstrates how in the United States policies are enacted to uphold the social rankings defined by the ideology of race.[12]

What we call "race," on the other hand, is defined by a set of traits, some observable, others imagined, assigned for the purpose of differentiating among human groups. These perceived differences are prevalent in the cultural narrative and therefore in people's minds. Race is illogical, Wilkerson explained, yet "it is a fiction told by modern humans for so long that it has come to be seen as a sacred truth." The concept of race supports a hegemony that maintains White dominance.[13]

Public acceptance of the illusion and ideology of race renders the caste system's structure invisible, giving it power and longevity. Left unseen, it is easily ignored. Once we begin to identify systems that uphold caste, however, we can finally name it, as Wilkerson has done. At this point, we have a responsibility. For the sake of our own integrity, the United States must either change the policies that keep the caste system in place or redefine its rhetoric to match the reality of a racially divided social structure. Integrity, in other words, demands that the impact of a nation's policies square with its statements of intent.

As things now stand, Americans have been socialized to a racist system. The role policy plays in its maintenance is rarely acknowledged. While both India and the United States have abolished many of the laws that overtly lead to inequity, Wilkerson wrote, "both caste systems live on in hearts and habits, institutions and infrastructures."[14]

In democratic systems, leaders hold power through public consent. Maintaining hegemony is therefore a bit tricky. The public must somehow be convinced that an oppressive system works in their favor, even when, and maybe especially when, the data demonstrate just the opposite. Policies that uphold hierarchy must either be concealed or justified in a way that the public will accept. Otherwise, "when people believe they've been disadvantaged by a rigged system," Nathan Palmer explained, "they get angry and they start to use words like injustice, occupy, and revolution."[15]

Because "hegemony is the act of convincing another that it is in their best interest to do what you want them to do," its function is to counter the possibility that a hierarchical system will be overthrown. An alternative is simply to encourage public complacency. People who feel powerless or overwhelmed by responsibility may disregard unjust policy or downplay its effects. Silence, however, amounts to acceptance. In short, hierarchical social structures remain in place until dissatisfaction reaches a tipping point. Change relies on a large number of people deciding they will no longer accept policy that creates social divisions.[16]

Hegemony is also difficult to maintain when there is a mismatch between rhetoric and outcomes, as there is in the United States. As inequities grow, it takes a clever use of propaganda to maintain people's faith in systems that oppress them. Nazi Germany, for example, never tried to convince Jews that anti-Jewish laws worked in their favor. In fact, James Whitman reports that Nazi leaders who came to the United States to study its racist laws were puzzled and bemused by the degree of deception required to maintain such a clear disconnect between policy and rhetoric.[17]

Even today, there are large gaps between a narrative of equality and the lived experience of many Americans. The rhetoric required to maintain hegemony must therefore continually convince us that the system is not rigged, that everyone has equal access to positions at the top of the social hierarchy (and soon, it might be you!), and that a person's social position is one they somehow deserve. In short, the continuation of caste relies on us believing that some people are more deserving than others. While this position was overtly declared in Nazi Germany, eugenics fell out of favor after the Nuremberg trials, and it has not been a position the United States would claim. The fact that a caste system persists, however, begs a deeper dive.

Framing a National Narrative

Just as O'Neil helped me place test-based education policy within a contemporary context of a data-based economy and Wilkerson enabled a careful look at social structure, Ibram X. Kendi provided a critical historical framework for this interplay of intent, policy, ideology, and outcomes. Kendi's book *Stamped from the Beginning: The Definitive History of Racist Ideas in America* highlights a long-standing pattern in which racist ideas emerge to justify policies that allow the upper caste to maintain its authority. In other words, Kendi argues that racist ideology is repeatedly invented to support the structures that maintain the caste system. Racist ideas are woven into an illogical and complex narrative that frames inequality as just. Test-based evidence, it turns out, plays a major role in supporting this narrative and therefore sustaining the illusion of hierarchy.[18]

Self-serving policy intertwined with racist ideas as the warp threads in the fabric of a fledgling American nation designed to serve its landowning elite. For some, the emerging patterns woven onto its surface tend to draw attention away from this underlying structure. For others, however, the ongoing impact of these policies is so obvious it is impossible to imagine how anyone could overlook them.

Racial and class divisions are visible in every aspect of American life, yet few understand that they were deliberately created or how they have been maintained. In fact, those advantaged by these demographic divides seem to perceive them as somehow natural, as just the way things are. The deliberate invention of "race" is missing from our national narrative. It exemplifies what author and educator Lee Anne Bell called a concealed story. Concealed stories, when told, disrupt America's carefully crafted self-image as an egalitarian nation. They thwart the false perceptions of equality that are promoted through norming narratives "passed on through historical and literary documents, and celebrated through public rituals, law, the arts, education and media." Bell named these stock stories. As they are told and retold, stock stories reinforce the norms and values of those who hold power. Bell explains that stock stories portray reality for the benefit of the dominant group. Eventually, stock stories come to define a culture, serving as powerful tools to hold a caste system in place.[19]

As dominant group values are woven into the fabric of a nation, all others fall to the wayside. When stock stories become normalized, they are viewed as the neutral stance, an unbiased truth, despite all evidence to the contrary. Any view outside these norms is considered exotic and strange. An example of this perceived neutrality is highlighted by the addition of courses in African American and Native American history. This reveals that courses *called* US history are taught from a European perspective, which is represented as the history of the whole. Of course, the nation's history is not merely the story of its European colonizers. Yet that stance has traditionally been perceived as neutral, referred to as, simply, history. And some still argue for its exclusive place in the curriculum of our nation's schools.[20]

Language, too, is a vehicle of culture. Analyzing its use reveals the American power structure. The term *minority*, for example, is often used to refer to those who are not White. It implies a White majority, even when that is not the case. The term therefore creates and reinforces the idea that Whiteness is normal and anything else is not. This leads many White Americans to see themselves as raceless and cultureless and to view their norms and values as somehow neutral and objective. Asked to name their identity, White people often describe themselves as simply "American." The metaphor of America as a melting pot implies the necessity of assimilating to these "American" norms and values.[21]

The language of assimilation often marginalizes historic and cultural narratives of all but White Christians living in the United States. When educators or textbooks introduce traditional stories from non-European cultures, for example, they are often called myths or legends, implying they are not only imaginary but "primitive." They are often described as the stories of *diverse* groups, adding another layer of remove. While *diverse* is a synonym for *various,* here it is code for people who are not White. Misuse of the word *diverse* has become quite common, used to separate Whiteness from everything else, further reinforcing Whiteness as a norm. *Ethnic* is another term used in reference to non-European cultural groups as if it is a synonym for *exotic.* This implies, oddly, that European ancestry is not an ethnicity, reinforcing the falsehood that *Americans* are Christians of European heritage.

Concealed stories become buried beneath the weight of this dominant narrative, often hidden from the view of those who fit the norm. Members of the dominant group therefore tend to perceive their life experience as everyone's reality. This is evident in conversations about racism, for example, when White people declare that because they don't see racism, it doesn't exist.

Concealed stories, Bell explains, invite us to think critically about all we've been taught. They disrupt the false notion that America is a post-racial society. Bell wrote, "Concealed stories reveal both the hidden (from the mainstream) stories told from the perspective of racially dominated groups, as well as stories uncovered through critical analysis of historical and social science data that illustrate how race shapes experience in our society."[22]

Because of their potential to disrupt hegemony, those in power consider concealed stories dangerous, even though they are true. Stock stories, on the other hand, uphold hegemony. That's why they have been used as the foundation of the public school curriculum. Movements to include ethnic studies continue to be met with resistance across the nation. The fear of hegemony's disruption appears in the form of a president who opposed *diversity* workshops, for example, which might reveal perspectives carefully concealed from the majority of society's middle and upper castes. A president trying to uphold hegemony might, instead, promote a "patriotic education," comprised of stock stories alone.[23]

Try to discover, for example, what your local school teaches about the history and contemporary lives of the Indigenous peoples who have long cared for the land on which you walk. Unless you live in Montana or a handful of other states where this is an educational mandate, you will likely find that this information is absent. The same is true for local histories of slavery, Jim Crow, or eugenics. Missing, too, is any connection to their legacies. The history of those who were colonized or enslaved appears as a few sentences or a sidebar in America's history books, if it appears at all. Just as the Austrian teachers who grew up near Hartheim had never heard of the killing center that operated in their town, local histories of oppressed peoples are concealed as state history courses reflect the perspectives of colonizers, who are hailed as heroes. This amounts to an attempt to silence the voices and worldviews of what will soon be a majority of Americans. Standardized curricula, created for a national audience and often forced into schools categorized as failing, exacerbates the impact of this erasure.

Concealing all other lived realities from the view of society's most privileged lulls us into complacency. Stock stories, though, can be powerful teaching tools for anti-racist leaders. Used alongside concealed stories, they provide a window to understanding how hegemony operates.

In America, stock stories uphold a rhetoric of equity by attempting to hide or justify racial and class divides. Disrupting the systems that maintain these divides requires complicating the narratives used to uphold the power dynamics of our nation. Unless or until American schools take this as their charge, we are left to learn on our own.

Fortunately, as Kendi wrote, "Antiracists of all races" have been writing disruptive narratives for decades. They recognize this as critical work because "preserving racial hierarchy simultaneously preserves ethnic, gender, class, sexual, age, and religious hierarchies." The subjugation of one group reverberates throughout the entire nation, resulting in a social pyramid where the greatest benefits are reserved for the very small group at the top. I hope Wilkerson's use of the term *caste* will shock us out of complacency and inspire us to identify and disrupt its scaffolding. In a hierarchical system, Wilkerson explained, the top priority is for the lowest caste "to remain low in every way at all times, at any cost." If equity is our goal, we have no choice but to destroy the tools used to keep the lowest caste in place. As Kendi wrote, "Human hierarchies of any kind . . . do little more than oppress all of humanity." Breaking those chains will therefore liberate us all.[24]

Hierarchical Thinking

A step on the path to liberation is to understand how we got to our present position so we can avoid circling back to the same mistakes. In the twenty-first century, we continue the practice of categorizing people into what we call racial groups. Census forms, job and college applications, tests and surveys all ask people to identify their race, even as defining these categories has gotten more complex and the lines between them more nuanced. Although people within each of these groups have different life experiences, this practice is still necessary because their lives are similarly impacted by policy that results in racialized outcomes. It is, in effect, a quiet acknowledgment of the impact of racist policy throughout American history. While there are well over five hundred Indigenous groups in the United States, for example, each with its own language and culture, their lives have been similarly impacted by centuries of federal Indian policy.

Simultaneously, some people continue to tenaciously cling to the idea that people within these racial categories share traits beyond skin color. We have been socialized to believe that people in so-called racial groups are fundamentally different from one another. Sociologist Karen Fields explained that this assumption operates invisibly in the background of American life, misperceived as an "objective reality."[25]

We are surrounded by such racist ideas. It is still common, for example, to hear people refer to the "natural" tendencies of Black people to excel in sports as a way to explain the numbers of professional football or basketball players who are Black. From there, it is a short leap to an idea less often spoken, an assumption that silently justifies the disproportionate number of lawyers, psychologists, doctors, teachers, or CEOs who are White as also being due to a set of inherited traits. For over a century, large-scale testing data have been cited as evidence for these racist ideas. Whenever someone refers to a trait as being *in their blood* because of their race or ethnicity, the statement harkens back to the time when eugenicists promoted this message. There is, of course, no difference in the blood of people who come from any so-called racial category. Yet even in contemporary society, we continue to communicate this idea. This is an example of one of many threads woven into the fabric of our society connecting us to a history of racist policy and racist ideas that are rarely discussed. Our silence allows a system of false hierarchy to retain its power.[26]

White Europeans had a reason for designing hierarchical maps of humans based on skin color. They were looking for ways to justify colonization and enslavement. The concept of Whiteness, after all, exists only to advantage White people, who declared themselves naturally worthy of leading nations. Racism was invented to support a myth of White supremacy upheld by racist thought, policy, and practice. Although the structures and rhetoric have evolved over time, and what was once overt is now more covert, America's racist legacy continues.

The veiled memory of a racist past causes many to visibly cringe when they are identified as White. This memory is alive in our bodies, but we don't often think about it. We are carefully taught to avoid the topics of race and racism for this very reason. Yet it's clear that all categories of what Wilkerson describes as the "shape-shifting, unspoken, race-based caste pyramid in the United States" were created to uphold the illusion of White superiority. Racist ideas used to justify the contemporary social hierarchy have evolved from this mythology. Understanding the history of race and racism is therefore not only relevant but essential to the analysis of any US policy or practice, including test-based policy in public education.[27]

In *Stamped from the Beginning,* Kendi points out a historic pattern in which people in power create self-serving policies, then produce racist ideas to justify them. Racist ideas act as the backdrop for a story spun to promote the idea that those in the highest caste deserve their money and their power because they earned them in a system promoted as merit-based. Their positions, in other words, are perceived as indicative of their worth, according to indicators of merit that they defined. Those at the top justify the oppression of lower-ranking groups, defined as less worthy measured by the same indicators. To those who believe in the dignity and value of all people, of course, nothing is further from the truth. Yet rhetoric can shape the collective thinking of a people, bending it in ways that allow us to perceive the justice we hope for even as a different reality plays out before our eyes.

Structure and Rhetoric

As it has evolved into the twenty-first century, test-based policy maintains upper-caste advantage, obscured by declarations of equitable intent. O'Neil helped us place the perceived value of amassing an increased volume of test scores into the context of the Big Data era. Kendi's history of racist ideas will allow us to follow the contemporary thread of Big Data, including testing's role, back to the ideologies that informed it.

Through lines from past to present show how rhetoric around race has been spun, time and again, to justify the power and economic privilege of White Americans. In this and the chapters to come, we will see how patterns of policy supported by racist ideas spiral through the historical narrative as the ideology of biological determinism intertwines with eugenic practice, morphs into the myth of meritocracy, and continues on its way. A light shone through the past can break through the opacity of present policy and illuminate a different pathway into the future.

Power and Expansion

US history textbooks often begin with what they call the age of exploration. Kendi provides information that fills the many gaps in these narratives. The story of Prince Henry the Navigator is a good example. In 1444, the ship captained by Prince Henry, a man textbooks hail as an explorer and hero, carried captive Africans to a slave auction in Lisbon, Portugal. Although the countries that funded these journeys anticipated the great wealth they might acquire from voyages like Prince Henry's, greed was not the value they wanted on display. Instead, the narrative was spun to describe the trip's purpose as evangelical. Propaganda described Africans as heathens, so their kidnapping and sale could be rationalized as an introduction to Christian masters who could save their souls. In 1452, Pope Nicholas V issued a papal bull directing the king of Portugal to "capture, vanquish, and subdue the [S]aracens, pagans, and other enemies of Christ," to "put them into perpetual slavery," and "to take all their possessions and property." The great wealth gathered along the way was apparently a convenient side benefit.[28]

Other colonizing countries picked up this rhetoric, and the trend of creating racist ideas to support self-serving policy spread to the North American colonies. Kendi's thesis reverses the commonly held theory that racist ideas prompt racist actions. Instead, Kendi contends that policy motivated by greed was implemented to serve the self-interests of those in power. His book then reveals a pattern in which racist ideas are spun to justify even the cruelest acts and conceal the self-serving motive of exploitation for profit. By claiming salvation as their goal, European empire builders are framed as heroes rather than kidnappers, enslavers, and murderers. In a story that categorizes Africans as heathens, Europeans are portrayed as saviors, and righteous intent is used to justify even the most violent of outcomes.

The kidnapping of Africans in the slave trade exemplifies how policy created to benefit the wealthy and powerful can be flipped on its head to be represented as just. In repeated examples, Kendi shows how imaginary clothes are woven from racist ideas and used to conceal or defend an emperor's naked greed. The gains of empire include power and influence as well as wealth. Kendi observed, "Racially discriminatory policies have usually sprung from economic, political, and cultural self-interests, self-interests that are constantly changing. Politicians seeking higher office have primarily created and defended discriminatory policies out of political self-interest—not racist ideas. Capitalists seeking to increase profit margins have primarily created and defended discriminatory policies out of economic self-interest—not racist ideas. Cultural professionals, including theologians, artists, scholars, and journalists, were seeking to advance their careers or cultures and have primarily created and defended discriminatory policies out of professional self-interest—not racist ideas." Racist ideas, Kendi explained, are invented to justify self-serving motives and build public acceptance for socially divided policy outcomes. Like the concept of race itself, these racist ideas gradually become normalized, intertwined into a national narrative that reframes both heroes and villains.[29]

Might Makes Right

The textbook story of the "founding" of the United States often begins with Christopher Columbus who, like Prince Henry, has often been hailed as a hero. Columbus landed on the island of Hispaniola, and racist ideas about Africans were quickly transferred to the Taino people who lived there. Taino people were brutalized as the riches of their homeland were stolen, yet the terrorism was framed as a religious crusade. By portraying the Earth's many non-Christians as subhuman, stories of colonization could be spun as the gracious salvation of those who were otherwise eternally doomed. This ideology was soon codified. Federal Indian law scholar Steve Newcomb wrote, "After Columbus returned to Europe, Pope Alexander VI issued a papal document, the bull

Inter Cetera of May 3, 1493, 'granting' to Spain—at the request of Ferdinand and Isabella—the right to conquer the lands which Columbus had already found, as well as any lands which Spain might 'discover' in the future."[30]

Justified as righteous, the pattern of violent colonization continued, and European empires spread. The navigators who initiated the exploitation of lands and peoples were honored as brave heroes. American textbooks explain or imply that these acts were just because they allowed those referred to as *us*, meaning Christians of European ancestry, to spread around the globe, including what is now the United States. Newcomb explained, "The Christian 'Law of Nations' asserted that Christian nations had a divine right, based on the Bible, to claim absolute title to and ultimate authority over any newly 'discovered' Non-Christian inhabitants and their lands. Over the next several centuries, these beliefs gave rise to the Doctrine of Discovery used by Spain, Portugal, England, France, and Holland—all Christian nations."[31]

While some events in human history are regarded as genocides, colonization by Europeans is rarely included on this list, despite evidence that clearly matches the UN definition. The racist ideas used to justify colonization were, and apparently still are, effective in alleviating any hint of guilt.[32]

The Invention of Race

As empires expanded, a few Europeans traveled to lands newly opened to them. Published travelogues were filled with racist ideas about the people they encountered. As they became ever richer, political leaders used these dehumanizing narratives as propaganda to further public acceptance of continued violence and exploitation.

The word *race* first appeared as a descriptor in a 1481 poem about hunting dogs. Kendi wrote, "As the term expanded to include humans over the next century, it was used primarily to identify and differentiate and animalize African people." Britain entered the slave trade in the mid-1500s, kidnapping Africans they called beasts. An entry for *race* was published in a 1606 dictionary. The term was defined as *descent,* and the entry explained that a person or animal could be from a "good or bad race." Right from the start, then, the concept of race was used not only to divide but to judge.[33]

Racist ideas traveled to the Americas in European minds and hearts. Pirates brought the first African captives to sell on American soil in 1619, and Virginia's governor bought twenty Angolans. For the planter class, the arrival of forced labor was perfectly timed. Tobacco was poised to become the New World's cash crop, yet the work was labor intensive. Once Britain's civil war had ended, fewer indentured servants came to the colonies. So when the African captives arrived, planters like Virginia's governor saw an opportunity for huge economic gain. Slave-owning planters carefully explained, however, that this was a benevolent step toward redeeming the souls of savages.[34]

This was a watershed moment for the American colonies. Before enslavement, people had been differentiated in terms of religion, national origin, and economic status. Both light- and dark-skinned people had arrived as indentured servants with debts to work off. Early colonial policy categorized people as either indentured or free. At that time, all free people, regardless of skin color, had equal status under the law. Up until the mid-1600s, in fact, free Africans owned land in Virginia.[35]

To gain an economic edge, however, the planter class gradually increased the time of required servitude for those indentured. They also decided to systematize the demarcation between the two classes. Laws were passed that favored bond holders and further oppressed the bonded, making it more difficult for indentured servants to ever become free. These policies, as intended, increased the wealth of the planters. As gaps between the groups widened, planters feared the possibility of revolt as indentured servants began to lose hope that they might one day be free.

In 1676, those fears were realized. White planter Nathaniel Bacon organized bonded workers of all skin colors and demanded an end to unpaid labor. The causes of what became known as Bacon's Rebellion were many and complicated. Bacon had long-standing disputes with Virginia's governor, who was trying to control colonists who had turned their anger about an economic downturn against Indigenous peoples. As a result, some Indigenous groups were categorized as "good" Indians, and others as "bad." Nonetheless, an uprising ensued, which was violently quelled by wealthy landowners. Had it succeeded, the accumulating wealth of the planter class might have been interrupted and a more egalitarian society may have emerged. Instead, the stage had been set for the United States to be organized as a society of haves and have-nots.[36]

As their wealth grew, the planter class concluded that their power ultimately relied on a social order that included "lifetime hereditary slavery." A system built on policies that attempt to dehumanize a segment of the population, however, is ripe for revolution. Bacon's Rebellion showed how powerful the masses could be when they worked together, so elite planters sought a way to disempower them. I'll note, however, the complete exclusion of Indigenous peoples, who were not even considered part of "the masses."[37]

As the number of kidnapped Africans sold in the New World increased, so did the rhetoric that portrayed them as beasts of burden. The planters learned that racist propaganda served as a powerful weapon to divide those who might oppose their rule. Racial divisions were quickly codified by laws categorizing people as either Black or White. New regulations restricted access to land ownership, a privilege reserved exclusively for White males. Their race, gender, and Christian identity opened the door of possibility for White men in the lower classes who clung to the hope that their lot might improve. Once they gained their freedom, these men hoped they might gradually accrue the resources to become planters themselves. That door to hope, however, had been slammed shut to anyone with dark skin.

The planters' strategy worked like a charm. With dark-skinned people clearly established as the lowest caste, White people perceived themselves as aligned with the planters, no matter how poor they were. Policy and propaganda worked together to convince White people that they, by virtue of their skin color, were either the "haves" or "soon-to-haves." They may have hoped that one day they, too, would be wealthy enough to own slaves. Until that time, they would do everything they could to support this new social order. Thus, a race-based caste system was established.

From the perspective of the planter class, codifying racial divisions solved two problems: economic and social. The use of forced slave labor would ensure their wealth would continue to increase. And with the lower classes now divided, the chance of overthrow had greatly decreased. Using skin color as the line of demarcation, the hierarchical order was clear to all at a glance. Once policy placed even the poorest of White people a step above Africans, supported by propaganda claiming that White people were inherently superior and therefore more deserving, the system became self-regulating. Lower-class Whites guarded these divisions in word and in deed as a way to prove themselves worthy of citizenship.[38]

Normalizing Whiteness

Racist ideas about White supremacy were used to rationalize the increasing wealth and power of the elite. The word *White* was first used as a descriptor of social status in a law passed in colonial Maryland in 1681. From that point on, colonial law increasingly advantaged those referred to as White as it stripped rights from all others, bonded or free. These policies systematized the ideology of White supremacy and planted the seeds of social and economic inequities that persist in the twenty-first century.[39]

The wealthy, people who largely identified as Christians, had to convince themselves and their fellow White citizens that these decisions were just, even as they stripped Black people of basic human rights. Kendi writes it is likely that in North America the enslavers would "rationalize their enslavement of African people in the same way that other British intellectuals did—and in the same way that Latin American slaveholders did—by considering these African people to be stamped from the beginning as a racially distinct people, as lower than themselves, and as lower in the scale of being than the more populous White indentured servants." In other words, the caste system was rationalized by racist ideas that declared Blacks unworthy.[40]

Kendi presented four theories that support racist propaganda. Each has circulated continually, one gaining favor over the others at different times. By promoting the oppressor's righteous intent, each set of ideas reverberates in the present, distracting attention away from inequities created by governmental policy.

The first theory claimed an evangelical motive for the slave trade. This ideology allowed slave traders and slave owners to claim that they were saving the souls of African subhumans by introducing them to "civilized" European values, including Christianity. Early colonial preachers like Cotton Mather reinforced the view that slavery ultimately saved its captives. Enslavement was therefore justified as a Christian mission, as if the nation's vast economic gain was just an unintended side benefit. These ideas evolved into the notion that exposure to Christianity tamed captives who were actually wild beasts, helping them to accept their place in a hierarchy ordained by God. Even today, I've heard descendants of slaveholders emphasize how well their families treated the people they enslaved, implying that they were better off than if they'd been free. This is one of many examples demonstrating the staying power of racist ideas.[41]

The second line of racist propaganda, curse theory, draws from an interpretation of the biblical story of Noah, sensationalized in 1578 by British travel writer George Best. Best explains that Noah instructed his sons not to have sex with their wives on the Ark. Noah's son Ham, whom Best portrays as "evil, tyrannical, and hypersexual," ignores this order. An angry God then decreed that Ham's descendants would be "so blacke and loathsome . . . that it might remain a spectacle of disobedience to all the worlde." According to this ideology, dark-skinned people are a preordained criminal class, cursed by God. While the curse theory is no longer in the forefront of society's consciousness, there is no denying the discrepancy in arrest records and sentencing between White people and people of color in the United States, nor the many examples of Black men shot by officers of the law. Law enforcement, too, can be a mechanism of caste.[42]

The third theory, polygenesis, appeared during the late 1700s. As the name implies, it is based on the idea that human beings are not a single species. Instead, the theory claims, subspecies of humans had different origins, and only those with European backgrounds are descended from Adam and Eve. All others are lower forms of humans, more closely aligned with apes. This established Europeans as the ruling class with the right to enslave those beneath them. Remnants of this idea also persist, evidenced by images I've seen of President Obama, for example, depicted as an ape.[43]

The fourth theory marks a turning point: the origins of scientific racism. In the seventeenth and eighteenth centuries, as religion gave way to the intellectualism of the Enlightenment, a whole new set of racist ideas emerged. Theories presented as scientific attempted to provide rational arguments for the oppression of dark-skinned people. An early example was climate theory, an idea rooted in Aristotle's teachings that was reprised and expanded during the Enlightenment. Aristotle asserted that humans naturally divide into two groups: Greeks, who ruled as masters, and the Barbarians they enslaved. Aristotle described Barbarians as creatures "by nature incapable of reasoning" who "live a life of pure sensation." These two groups differed, Aristotle hypothesized, because of climate. Kendi explained that Aristotle believed "Extreme hot or cold climates produced intellectually, physically, and morally inferior people who were ugly and lacked the capacity for freedom and self-government." As Europeans later applied these ideas to Africans, some claimed that the hot climates of Africa produced uncivilized peoples capable only of hard labor. In this view, the enslavement of Africans was just because it was based on laws of nature. As scientific racism spread, early American scholars studied Aristotle's ideas, including climate theory, at Harvard, the first university on US soil. Social Darwinists later drew on Aristotle's thoughts as they ascribed character traits to groups on a racially divided phylogenetic tree.[44]

Whether justified by evangelism or climate theory, Whiteness was perceived as superior, and all were expected to subscribe to its values and norms. These ideas influenced the founding of the United States where, Kendi wrote, Massachusetts preacher "Cotton Mather led the way in producing the racist idea of Christianity simultaneously subduing and uplifting the enslaved African. He joined with the producers of racist ideas in other colonial empires, from the mother countries in Europe, and normalized and rationalized the expansion of colonialism and slavery. Europeans were taking over and subduing the Western world, establishing their rightful ruling place as the very standard of human greatness, these racist producers proclaimed."[45]

Scientific Racism and the American Colonies

The scientific revolution swept through Europe in the 1620s, just as North America was being colonized. Although racist ideas were sometimes concealed beneath a veneer of objectivity, the assumption was that researchers were somehow able to remove themselves from the influence of social context. Scientific methodologies were viewed as rational and objective, so scientific conclusions carried ever more weight. The scientific method relies on repeated experimentation and debate as questions, methods, and conclusions are critically questioned, yet once researchers' findings are shared, they are sometimes regarded as the revelation of truth.[46]

By this time, racist ideas had been normalized across society, including academia. Racist thought therefore influenced both the assumptions and the conclusions of people regarded as founders of scientific disciplines. In 1664, for example, chemist Robert Boyle wrote that while skin color was a minor difference among humans, Black skin "was an 'ugly' deformity of normal Whiteness." Boyle was a member of a scientific organization called Britain's Royal Society, and he sat on the Council of Foreign Plantations, which made agricultural decisions about England's North American colonies.[47]

Aristotle's theory that some groups of humans are inherently worthy of being masters and others slaves was incorporated into this new science. In 1677, a Royal Society economist published a hierarchical scale of humans. Theories about mental functioning became a particular area of focus. Claiming that the minds of middle Europeans were substantially different from those of Africans, William Petty placed "Guinea Negroes" at the very bottom of his scale of human worth.[48]

In 1684, French doctor and travel writer François Bernier popularized a classification of humans he had imagined. Bernier divided people into four or five racial categories based on observable characteristics, claiming these differences were evidence that each was a separate species. His hierarchy placed most Europeans (excluding Lapps) in a group he called the "first" race, represented as civilization itself, the group that should be "the yardstick against which all others are measured."[49]

Bernier "posed the notion of two human souls: one hereditary, sensitive, nonrational, and animal-like; the other God-given, spiritual, and rational." According to his value system, Bernier declared it only natural that the beings classified as rational, those who "excel in the powers of the mind," should rule over "those who only excel in brute force." This rhetoric normalized not only White skin but White power, based on a system of values that became associated with Whiteness. Bernier's conclusions, presented in the form of a chart, were perceived as scientific and therefore objective.[50]

This is one of many examples of the problem biologist Stephen J. Gould identified, described in chapter 1. The reception of Bernier's findings demonstrates how, right from the start, the assumption of scientific objectivity has led society to accept conclusions prematurely, particularly if they match a popular ideology. Gould contends that if science has any hope of representing truth, scientists must critically question how their own bias influences the questions they ask and the conclusions they reach.

During the Enlightenment, the debate between religion and science raged, but ideologies on both sides were used to defend policies that maintained White power and the norms it established. By 1728, "Royal Society fellows had fully constructed this White ruling standard for humanity. Christianity, rationality, civilization, wealth, goodness, souls, beauty, light, Adam, Jesus, God, and freedom had all been framed as the dominion of White people from Europe. The only question was whether lowly African people had the capacity of rising up and reaching the standard." By any measure, assimilation was seen as the only path for a person to become civilized.[51]

These racist theories were not the purview of a few ignorant people. They were espoused by the intellectual community and political leaders of the time, people whose other ideas are still taught in schools and universities today. As racist hegemony was established, few questioned whether humans should be categorized by race. The illusion that there are fundamental differences among people according to their skin color was simply accepted as a given.

The scientific revolution and the Enlightenment influenced all European-based societies, including the British colonies in North America. Intellectualism, reason, and learning were spun as values to bring light to a world that, in this view, had been darkened by religious constraints. Light and dark became metaphors for juxtaposed ways of being: light stood for all that was good; dark represented everything that was not.

Power lies with those who define what is considered normal and good. The "Enlightenment ideals" of "radical individualism: rationality, objectivity, private property, market capitalism, and race" obviously influenced the laws and policies of the newly independent United States of America. These values were associated with Whiteness, further aligning White with right. The ideals were woven into stock stories that continue to define American societal norms and guide American policy and practice even in the twenty-first century.[52]

Land and labor were viewed as precious commodities in the American colonies. Propaganda had supported imagined racial divisions used to justify the allocation of resources in favor of people newly described as White. Policies regulating land ownership and market capitalism placed these treasures in the hands of a few, for their financial gain. This elite group of White people had thereby secured the power to re-create and recycle this advantage for generations.[53]

Advantaging some perpetrated losses for others. Federal Indian policy exemplifies how racist ideas were used to rationalize stealing the land that allowed the planter class to gain their wealth. While evidence shows that the ideas of the Founding Fathers were influenced by Indigenous ideas, the desire to expand the nation's landholdings led to the dismissal of Native cultural practices as uncivilized and the portrayal of Native peoples as demons. The word *civilized* became encoded with a set of White values used as a measuring stick to create a hierarchy of worth. By declaring Indigenous peoples unworthy, the US government was portrayed as righteous for opening "wild" lands for "settlers" to tame. These racist ideas were codified by courts, which referenced the papal Doctrine of Discovery.

Newcomb explained, "In 1823, the Christian Doctrine of Discovery was quietly adopted into U.S. law by the Supreme Court in the celebrated case, *Johnson v. McIntosh*." Chief Justice John Marshall opined that in winning its independence, the United States had inherited England's former right of dominion, and that as a result of "discovery," Indigenous nations had lost their rights to sovereignty. Newcomb adds, "With the Johnson decision, the Christian Doctrine of Discovery was not only written into U.S. law but also became the cornerstone of U.S. Indian policy over the next century." In 1831, the Supreme Court followed with a ruling asserting that Indian nations are "subject to the federal government's absolute legislative authority—known in the law as 'plenary power.'"[54]

Policies were enacted either to "civilize" Indigenous peoples (Indian boarding schools, the Indian Relocation Act) or to remove them by any means necessary, including mass murder. For those who view the spread of White supremacy as progress, federal Indian policy was a success. Hitler studied these policies as he contemplated ways to achieve "lebensraum" for society's most worthy by ridding Europe of Jews. The dehumanizing propaganda of racist ideas has, in fact, cycled time and again as a way for "the chosen" to gain or maintain power and economic gain.[55]

The legal precedent set in Supreme Court cases based on the Doctrine of Discovery has not been overturned. While language has changed, outcomes are much the same. Lands and peoples in "underdeveloped" nations are exploited under the guise that exposure to "Western" values will support their development. In other words, they are expected to assimilate. Cultures continue to be categorized in a hierarchy according to their adherence to Euro-American norms, as if no other value system is equally worthy.

The hegemony based on racist ideas and White cultural norms has been effective. From my vantage point as an American, it seems some are blind to possibilities offered by other worldviews. They truly can't understand why any country or culture would ever reject American aid or intervention. Viewed from the outside, however, the greed of the power grab is readily recognizable. This is, by now, an old story.

Because racist ideas have been heralded rather than hidden during much of their history, it is relatively easy to find their origins and early development.

It is more difficult to see how they play out in today's society. But by tracking these ideas and studying historic patterns, we can follow their path into a contemporary context. Here their racist outcomes might be clear, but the ideas used to justify them are cleverly spun. If the information in this chapter is largely new to you, as it was to me, perhaps it will support us on the journey to recognize the role American education plays in perpetuating hegemony.

The power structure that maintains America's caste system is built upon false racial categories and a hegemony that promotes the interests of the elite. Although the idea of race is an illusion, the impact of racist policy makes divisions a very real part of people's lived experiences. Racist ideas have become normalized to the point that they are unrecognizable to many. It therefore takes concerted effort to begin to see that a network of racist ideas operates just beneath society's surface, and they are being used to justify policy outcomes that continue to advantage White and wealthy people.

Education policy is no exception. In fact, it is a prime example. Returning to Kendi's definition of racist policy as one that "produces or sustains racial inequality," we can see that the decision to center the use of racially divided test scores clearly falls into that category. The results are also clear. In any evaluation of the US education system, racial divisions are far too pervasive to be simply the result of individual bias, no matter how frequently applied. As Wilkerson explains, the structures that hold the caste system in place are systemic. Functioning as effectively as Jim Crow laws, the racial inequities in today's educational outcomes are not due to inherent differences in groups of children. They result, instead, from the system that produces them.[56]

4

Measuring Human Worth
The Great Myths behind Large-Scale Testing

The mobilization of sham science to justify bigotry might be said to be a deep characteristic of only one culture: that of the developed West. Northern Europeans and their diaspora, having conquered much of the world, predictably sought to remake it in their image. They filled it with imagined races and subtypes, imbeciles and geniuses, primitives and civilized men. They then declared their intellectual artifice to be deeply, provably, natural.
—Charles King, *Gods of the Upper Air*

History and Legacy: The Roots of Standardized Testing

You may find yourself resisting the suggestion that ends the last chapter, that racial inequities in educational outcomes are caused by the system that produces them. Exploring such a notion might upend our vision of reality. Our socialization shapes our concept of what is normal, and it influences our expectations. Much to the delight of those at its peak, the mental model of a human pyramid predominates the collective thinking of European-based cultures. The possibility of more egalitarian social models brings on panicked cries of *socialism!* or *communism!* harkening back to the McCarthy era. Indeed, the hierarchical model has proved its resilience, although the rhetoric that supports it has adapted to the times. Chapter 3 demonstrated that religious ideas supported the myth of White superiority, which then intertwined with the Enlightenment values of individualism, market capitalism, rationality, and objectivity to influence American policy.

In short, many of us have the image of a human hierarchy emblazoned in our minds. It has become so normalized, in fact, that the US educational system was built upon this assumption. We have learned to believe it is important to assign children to their proper places within an orderly system, and we rely on large-scale testing to accomplish this goal. In turn, we are socialized to accept the verdict of test scores and the social stratification that results. We therefore tend to accept statements of test-based policy's good intent and avoid questioning a complex system and its socially divided outcomes. We have, in fact, been socialized to *expect* unequal results.

We see these results in large-scale testing, which creates and supports an educational hierarchy that transfers to the broader society. We've been told it is best that children receive an education according to their intellectual ability or level of achievement—and we assume that ability or achievement has been clearly defined and adequately measured. If we accept the idea that large-scale tests are well suited for this purpose, it means we must also accept their findings: that at all grade levels, in all subject areas, and across time, far higher percentages of White children have been more intelligent, have greater ability, or have achieved at higher levels than children of color. And there it is: the normalization of a pervasive racist idea.

Searching for the roots of this practice led to a connection that stunned me. Large-scale testing was invented during the eugenics era by eugenics practitioners for eugenic purposes. I had known eugenics ideology was behind the atrocities committed in Nazi Germany. I had no idea, however, that eugenics research had strongly influenced policies and practice in the United States. Eugenics created a framework for long-standing racist ideas. White supremacist ideology led to the passage of Jim Crow laws in the South, James Crow practices in the North, and the Immigration Act of 1924, which restricted immigration to people from northern European countries.[1]

The history of eugenics had been omitted from my schooling, and my education courses never even hinted that eugenics was the soil in which large-scale testing took root. The fact that this was new information for me, a long-time educator, got my attention. An inquiry that had stemmed from curiosity became a responsibility. This story needed to be told.

As I studied the origins of large-scale testing, I discovered that to get a complete picture of the model, I needed to step even further back—to include the moment Adolphe Quetelet decided to apply the predictive statistics of astronomers to human societies. Three profound societal shifts, based on the theories and assumptions of their time, act as theoretical markers on the trail leading to the acceptance of large-scale standardized testing as a measure of human potential. Each, however, is a myth. So what follows will explore the myth of the Average Man, the myth of Social Darwinism, and the myth of eugenics as science.

The Myth of the Average Man

Two key concepts introduced before the eugenics era of the late nineteenth century led to the development of large-scale tests: one was the idea of a statistically described "Average Man"; the other was a new application for a mathematical model called the normal curve of error, better known as the bell curve. Both are the ideas of Adolphe Quetelet, a Belgian astronomer, mathematician, and early social scientist known as a father of modern statistics. By "pioneer[ing] the technique of charting human characteristics on frequency of error curves," Quetelet became "the first person to count human activity the way astronomers measured the stars."[2]

Statistics evolved based on Quetelet's great leap: his assumption that the mathematical models of physics could be applied to the social sciences. This assumption laid the groundwork for the eventual development of the large-scale testing model. And in more general terms, Kevin Donnelly, author of a book about Quetelet, explained that even though Quetelet is "relatively unknown today . . . the current enthusiasm for Big Data and quantification in the social sciences and elsewhere" can be traced directly to his work.[3]

Quetelet loved analyzing numbers. So between 1825 and 1835, while biding his time waiting for an astronomical observatory to be completed, Quetelet began exploring the collection of birth and death records of Brussels. Having used the normal curve of error as an astronomer, Quetelet decided to try plotting births and deaths as if they were data from an astrological observation. Intrigued by a pattern that seemed to emerge, Quetelet posed a hypothesis: statistical models had allowed astronomers to discover that physical laws are at play in the universe. If he applied the same models to social data, perhaps they would reveal that natural laws also govern human society. If he discovered such laws, Quetelet reasoned, governments could use them to forecast social trends, much like astronomers can predict the movement of the stars. If politicians could anticipate human responses, Quetelet believed, they could shape policy that would improve society. This possibility inspired Quetelet to spend years applying statistical models to social data, creating a field called social physics. Interestingly, much of the research conducted in the contemporary era of Big Data is based on the concepts and models of social physics, an homage to Quetelet's work.[4]

German mathematician Johann Gauss had postulated that the predictive potential of the bell curve might be useful in fields like physics and astronomy where direct measurement is not possible. Until that time, the curve had been used to predict *how likely* something was to occur. This made it useful for gambling. When applied to astronomy, however, the curve of error was used to track *how often* a phenomenon or result occurred. Predicting the *frequency* of outcomes required collecting much more data, yet this shift eventually led to the use of the bell curve in other areas, including social theory and eventually large-scale testing.[5]

Because a bell curve distributes data in a way that highlights differences in a set of numbers, it is useful for making comparisons. A bell curve clusters half the data in a regular pattern around a mean, which is calculated by averaging the data set. The other half are distributed in a regular, predictable, descending pattern as they fall further from the mean in both directions. The shape of the resulting curve looks like a bell. While *bell curve* describes the shape of the graph, the term *curve of probable error* best describes its function.[6]

Astronomers trying to pinpoint the size, location, and movement of celestial objects knew that the best they could do was to estimate, so they understood that their calculations would contain error. There were variables they could not control, or might not even be aware of, which interfered with every attempt. Therefore, they took as many measurements as possible, from different angles and under many different conditions. When the results were averaged and charted, the resulting graph resembled a bell curve. Astronomers thought that their many trials would even out the error so the numbers clustered closest to the mean were the most accurate, and those more distant from the mean were the result of error. They referred to this as the "curve of probable error."[7]

Rather than inferring the location of a single entity like a planet, Quetelet hoped to make inferences about a collective—the human collective. He therefore proposed using the bell curve to interpret social data. Some large discrepancies exist, however, in Quetelet's leap to apply the bell curve to human populations. When charting the results of a coin toss or the location of a celestial object, each focal point is a real, potentially knowable quantity. A planet, for example, has an exact location, whether or not astronomers know how to find and describe it. Quetelet's decision to apply the bell curve to chart human characteristics "changed the game" entirely.[8]

The focus of this new application was much more nebulous than a single point. In addition, Quetelet wanted to compare disparate sets of data. He assumed that when two data points were charted and compared, the results indicated causal relationships. He believed this could give insight into the *reason* a given social trend occurred. In Quetelet's early studies, he correlated information about physical attributes like human height and weight, each of which, he found, roughly followed a bell curve. Encouraged by these findings, Quetelet then made a giant leap to propose that, given enough data to even out the inherent error, human qualities and patterns of behavior would also form a bell curve. He then postulated that these data could be correlated in ways that would allow societies to predict people's actions, and this information could then be used to create policy to support social order and stability.[9]

In summarizing Quetelet's work, Donnelly emphasized the importance of statistical correlation, an idea Quetelet had accidentally stumbled upon. "This 'advancement,'" Donnelly wrote, "may have been the most important development for professional statistics and maybe the social sciences because it allowed the field to supplant a morally fraught term (causation) with a technical one (correlation)." The two are not the same, but Quetelet's assumptions at this early stage laid the groundwork for much that followed.[10]

Quetelet's view that statistics had the potential to improve society inspired him to collect data about human qualities like courage and intelligence. That meant he had to find a way to quantify those characteristics, and he surmised that they are revealed though people's actions. Quetelet acknowledged that any tool created to measure such vague traits would be inherently imperfect. Conclusions would rely on the interpretation of meaning from correlations between data sets gathered through indirect measurement. The entire process would rely heavily on theory. Quetelet believed, however, that the potential benefits to society would outweigh any consequences resulting from flawed data or mistaken interpretations.[11]

So Quetelet began to collate and correlate statistics related to crime, poverty, and education. Although his findings were, by his own determination, less than trustworthy, Quetelet grew increasingly confident that correlations could be drawn between incongruent sets of data. Just as probability theory had led physical scientists to conclude that "seemingly inexplicable events had underlying causes," Quetelet believed that these statistical models would similarly reveal laws that regulate human behavior. Rather than predicting the course of a planet, Quetelet aimed to use probability theory and inferential statistics "to determine a projected course of society."[12]

Quetelet saw the potential for misinterpretation. He "recognized that statistics could be made to say anything with poor data." Yet he remained focused on his goal: to analyze and use vast amounts of information to create a society without crime and poverty. He believed the larger the data sets, the more accurate the conclusions drawn from them. Quetelet would no doubt be envious of the massive amounts of data collected from millions of cell phone users. He would be interested to know that this information is indeed used to predict patterns of human behavior, although perhaps not for the purposes he envisioned.[13]

Quetelet's faith in statistical modeling and his attempts to quantify human qualities led to an idea that is now so common it is part of our collective thought: the concept of the Average Man. Quetelet theorized that if statistical data were averaged across a broad range of human traits from very large data sets, the averages would depict a human norm. This idea of an average person is purely theoretical, yet it forms the basis for much of our contemporary thought. We commonly hear differentiations between *normal* and *abnormal* behavior, for example, or higher than average intelligence, or references to *the average* man, woman, or child. Our collective imaginations transformed Quetelet's statistical averages into a human portrait and brought it to life.[14]

Quetelet envisioned *average* as the human ideal. In contemporary thought, however, "the norm" is a standard people often strive to rise above. In a society where people compete to reach a predetermined definition of success, many of us carry an image of the bell curve in our minds. Through Quetelet's imaginings, the bell curve's statistical mean has come to define all that is considered normal. The mean is, in fact, commonly called the norm, and the bell curve is often referred to as the normal curve of error or, simply, the normal curve. Conversely, then, anything that deviates from the mean is considered abnormal or deviant, terms that carry negative connotations.[15]

Plotting data onto a bell curve makes it easy to establish a norm and use it to compare and categorize. The concepts of *normal* and *abnormal* are now applied so broadly that it is hard to remember they are only theoretical. They are, in fact, Quetelet's contribution to our collective consciousness.

Donnelly concluded that Quetelet's work "is central to understanding" a nineteenth-century societal shift that historian Frank Manuel described as a transformation. In this worldview, progress is achieved through competition, which removes any expectation of egalitarian outcomes. People are divided instead into winners and losers. Manuel called the shift "from egalitarian to competitive progress 'one of the most crucial developments in modern intellectual history.'"[16]

Quetelet's social application of the bell curve aided and abetted this transformation. Indeed, it opened the possibility of allowing statistical models to define what is *normal* among humans. The concept of standardization is steeped in these assumptions, and they provided the platform upon which large-scale testing would be built.[17]

While Quetelet's publications drew criticism at the time, those voices were apparently overridden by the enthusiasm of those who believed statistics could and should shape the future of society. Sir Peter Buck, a preeminent sociologist of the early twentieth century, confirmed this. "As social scientists," he summarized, "it is with Adolphe Quetelet, and not seventeenth-century natural philosophers, that we share assumptions." Western societies grasped the concepts of *normal* and *abnormal* and held them tightly. The acceptance of Quetelet's ideas marks a turning point, allowing us to draw a line from his work to the Big Data era of the twenty-first century, including the widespread use of large-scale testing. Quetelet himself might be surprised to know how profoundly his ideas continue to influence contemporary policy and practice. We can only guess at whether he would be pleased with the results.[18]

By applying the "tools of the natural sciences to the study of mankind," Quetelet created a new opportunity for exploration where direct measurement is not possible, including the inner workings of the human mind. Donnelly explains that Quetelet's work was therefore "a principal inspiration for the eugenicists Francis Galton and Karl Pearson." Using Quetelet's assumptions as a starting point, Galton and Pearson made a few more theoretical leaps to build a statistical foundation for large-scale testing. And yes, as Donnelly stated, both were proponents of eugenic ideology, and they worked to produce evidence to achieve eugenic goals.[19]

Quetelet, Galton, and Pearson were well intentioned. They truly believed their work would lead to a better world. For Galton and Pearson, however, swayed by eugenic beliefs, that required engineering a better breed of humans.[20]

The Myth of Social Darwinism

In November 1859, Charles Darwin introduced the world to ideas that guide contemporary research and practice. Without a doubt, Darwin's theories were transformational. The book that served as catalyst is titled *On the Origin of Species by Means of Natural Selection, or the Preservation of Favoured Races in the Struggle for Life*. While Darwin's studies and his resulting theories were not focused on humans, by the 1870s, other scholars forged that connection. The theory that emerged, called Social Darwinism, was infused with racist ideas. Advocates were eager to gather supporting evidence, which was eventually used to justify eugenic policy and practice.[21]

As at any crossroads, things could have gone differently. For example, researchers might have focused on discovering what factors contribute to the relative success of the human species as a whole. Instead, Social Darwinists chose to chase the illusion of White superiority, to solidify the image of a human hierarchy with groups separated by "race" on a phylogenetic tree. People from northern Europe were awarded the spot at the pinnacle, and other racial categories descended from there, closely reflecting the existing social order. Hoping to provide a rationale for their categorization, Social Darwinists assigned physical and behavioral characteristics to each racial group, claiming these as evidence of varying stages of evolutionary development. The exclusive group at the pyramid's top was considered the most evolved, while the least evolved groups were assigned spots at its much wider base. Thus, the propaganda created to justify colonization and enslavement had been definitively moved into the realm of science. This chart was used to promote the ideas that White supremacy was the natural order and that those at the top were best suited for survival.[22]

The term *survival of the fittest* was coined by Herbert Spencer, a biologist who believed that "societies, too, were engaged in a struggle for survival . . . the fight for biological superiority . . . outlined by Darwin." Spencer's interpretation of Darwin's theory led him to opine that "nature itself determined which peoples would, through their superior achievements and worldviews, dominate."[23]

Could it be that the *diagram* caused these beliefs to be accepted as science rather than seen as propaganda? Can graphing ideas resemble the work of physical scientists enough to prompt people to accept dubious conclusions more readily? Whatever the cause, we now seem acculturated to accepting charted conclusions as *research based*, without always knowing the methods used, the purposes served, or plans for applying the results.

This is certainly true in education. Philosophy drives educational practice, yet in the era of Big Data, that is not always acknowledged. There is danger, however, in ignoring that fact. If we go back to a time when the ideology was clearly visible, we might gain information useful for today, when the philosophy behind federal policy goes largely unspoken. Eugenics is an important example. Ann Gibson Winfield, author of *Eugenics and Education in America*, demonstrated the influence of eugenics on educational practice. Social Darwinists transformed Darwin's evidence-based theory to support their ideological goals. Winfield explained, "To understand the subtleties of the Social Darwinists' take on Darwin is to see clearly the launching pad of the eugenics movement." Politicians saw that the Social Darwinists' blurring of the lines between ideology and science served their interests well. If science "proved" the superiority of the elite, their battle would be won. White supremacist ideology would be normalized, securing their status. A science curriculum that teaches the nation's children that their social status is predetermined might lead those in the lower classes to peacefully accept their lot in life. Without the constant fear of being overthrown, the upper caste could then finally relax into their power. Contentious explanations of a social order ordained by God would be laid to rest, as Social Darwinists set out to prove instead that caste was an act of nature.[24]

Caste systems are enforced by policy, and policy is supported by ideology. The Nuremberg laws in Nazi Germany and Jim Crow laws in the United States were developed to create or reinforce caste systems. Those laws were justified by centuries of antisemitic and racist ideas. The entanglement of the two during the eugenics movement provided even greater support for the ruling class. Once these ideas took hold, leaders would be permanently absolved from all responsibility for societal divisions. After all, if some members of society are declared unworthy, no one would expect policy outcomes to be equitable. Politicians proposed the elimination of social welfare, explaining that because people's fates are biologically determined, welfare interrupts natural cycles of extinction.[25]

Social Darwinists were confident that their research could and should guide the separation of those who are worthy from those who are not. The all-important task, then, was for researchers to develop tools to make those determinations. In *Gods of the Upper Air,* Charles King wrote, "Science demanded moving from such surface-level observations [as skin tone] to the careful recording of measurable physical distinctions, from head shape to height, weight, and femur length, with the goal being to categorize people according to the physical features that distinguished them." New instruments were designed to calibrate these measurements. Anthropometrists used these tools to measure and compare many parts of the human body, attempting to link specific physical features with each so-called race. While the physical data were being collected, another idea hovered in the background, foreshadowing things to come. King summarized the reasoning: "Since the head also contained the brain, the cephalic index and other cranial features might well provide keys to understanding behavior."[26]

To reach that understanding, researchers aimed to generate a very large database to compare head measurements of people around the world. They knew that physically gathering all the necessary measurements would be inefficient, but Quetelet's work had opened the door to another possibility. They turned instead to inferential statistics, a model that allows data to be extrapolated from a relatively small population to one so large it is impossible to measure. Riccardo Sartori, professor of human sciences, explained that inferential statistics "are particularly powerful, valid, and reliable, when it is possible to assume normal distributions." Acting on that assumption prompted researchers to chart the collected data on a bell curve, where the data are spread, making it easier to compare that which is considered normal from that which is not.[27]

Still, measurements would need to be taken. A Swiss anatomist developed a procedure to generate a cephalic index. This formula divided the width of the skull by its length. That total was then multiplied by 100. Once measurements were gathered across a sample population, those numbers would be averaged to establish a group norm. Sets of norms from different groups were then graphed so skull sizes could be compared across populations.

The conclusions drawn from these studies claimed that biological differences did, in fact, exist among racial groups. The interpretation of meaning extrapolated from those findings was deeply rooted in racist ideas. Phrenologist George Combe, for example, after studying the cephalic indexes of a group of African people, described "African skulls as overdeveloped in the Organs of Philoprogenitiveness and Concentrativeness (accounting for the African's alleged love of children and proclivity for sedentary occupations, respectively), and underdeveloped in Conscientiousness, Cautiousness, Ideality, and Reflection." The physical findings were linked to assumptions and character traits based on the author's own beliefs. Although clearly influenced by ideology, such conclusions were widely publicized, exemplifying how evidence can become propaganda. Stephen J. Gould has warned that we should be on the lookout for this. By falsely assuming their methods ensure objectivity, Gould explained, scientists often fail to question the influence of their own cultural perspectives. Gould reached this understanding while studying the rise of large-scale testing during the eugenics movement. But we're getting ahead of ourselves. We'll follow that thought in the next chapter.[28]

As Social Darwinism caught on, researchers tried to generate additional evidence to support its theories. No longer limited to what they could learn through direct measurement, they increasingly relied on probability theory to predict how a phenomenon might play out in large populations. This opened possibilities for new areas of research that, practitioners hoped, would lead to the fields of social *studies* to be treated as social *sciences*. King explained that in fields like psychology and sociology, "the allure of quantification was irresistible. It was the surest route toward respectability." However, while inferential statistics might allow us to draw conclusions for large populations, that confidence does not transfer to extrapolating meaning from a single data point.[29]

Chapter 5 will allow us to see the interplay of theories, assumptions, and practices in the development of large-scale tests and the interpretation of test scores. First, though, we'll continue to explore how eugenicists successfully convinced the world that their ideology was, in fact, science. Although that correlation is now widely disregarded, rather than simply tossing it away, let's see what we can learn from it, staying alert for through lines we might otherwise have missed.

The Myth of Eugenics as Science

Enter Sir Francis Galton, a strong proponent of Social Darwinist ideals. The introduction on the Galton Institute website said: "Sir Francis Galton was an eminent 19th century scientist, a polymath whose life and career spanned the entire reign of Queen Victoria. He was a cousin of Charles Darwin and made significant contributions himself to subjects from meteorology to psychology, genetics, forensics and statistical methods. Many of his findings formed the basis of modern experimental methods and are still in use in science and medicine today. However, he is chiefly remembered for introducing the term 'eugenics' and for his enthusiastic advocacy of selective breeding in human populations, although this work has long been discredited."[30]

Yes, selective breeding. Like Quetelet, Galton thought government had a role to play in building a better society. He, too, wanted to end crime and poverty. As a eugenicist, however, Galton had very specific ideas about how that might be accomplished. Social Darwinist theory suggested that nature be allowed to take its course without interference, so that even in human societies, only the fittest would survive. Guided by the idea that mankind would naturally evolve toward a human ideal, many Social Darwinists believed government should take a hands-off approach, eliminating social services to allow the "weaker" human strains to gradually die off—for the good of the whole, of course.[31]

Eugenicists took Social Darwinist theory a step further, suggesting that governments could help human evolution progress more quickly and efficiently. So rather than just wait for these "weak" strains of humans to die out, eugenicists proposed that governments should oversee forced sterilization. This, Galton explained, was a humanitarian quest. He wrote, "What nature does blindly, slowly and ruthlessly, man may do providently, quickly and kindly." Practitioners believed that science and statistics would guide them in sorting and separating society's worthy from its unworthy. They believed they were following a "natural order"—which happened to align perfectly with their racist ideas.[32]

Eugenicists were convinced that they had identified and found ways to evaluate traits that served as markers of inferiority. They believed their methods allowed them to predict who would inevitably became burdens on society and who would become its leaders. Speeding up the selection process would preserve society's resources, they argued, rather than wasting them on people doomed to extinction. From this perspective, society's bounty should be used to nurture those furthest along in the evolutionary process, encouraging them to pass their "superior" traits to the next generation, giving rise to events like "Better Baby" and "Fitter Family" contests.[33]

Government intervention based on eugenics ideology played out differently in Nazi Germany and the United States. While a number of groups were treated as enemies of the state, National Socialists drew on centuries of antisemitism to focus their propaganda and policies on eliminating what they labeled the Jewish "race." Justified by White supremacist ideology, which claimed the superiority of the Aryan "race," the Nazi government murdered millions of their fellow humans.[34]

While eugenics did not lead directly to death camps in the United States, the call to heed the so-called "natural order gave way to a new form of 'social sanitation,'" drawing from centuries of racist propaganda and practice. State governments enacted Jim Crow laws, for example, and between 1865 and

1950, racial terrorists lynched at least sixty-five hundred of their fellow humans, sometimes during public events. Once eugenic ideology had reframed racist ideas, state governments further allowed the forced sterilization of Black, Indigenous, people of color, and poor White people, all considered unworthy of creating new life.[35]

Eugenicists had convinced themselves and many in the larger society that science, rather their own racist ideology, was leading the way. The arrogance of this attitude, the belief that humans can objectively define and judge the quality or worth of other humans, led eugenicists to create lines of demarcation. They believed in the findings of the tools they had created to make these determinations. In short, eugenics prepared the soil for the seeds of large-scale testing to take root.[36]

While the use of statistics is associated with science, mathematician Cathy O'Neil cautioned us to remember that quantitative models are "only primitive tools, which hammer complexity into simplicity." Yet statistics and science became intertwined with racist ideas just as US education was consolidating into a public system. Author Ann Gibson Winfield cited a number of contemporary educational practices based on eugenics ideology, including the development and use of large-scale testing. This raises a key question: could large-scale testing have been one of the first tanks to roll off the assembly line of weapons of math destruction, described in chapter 2?[37]

There are, of course, multiple ways to "cleanse" a society. One is to create a system of caste. Winfield explained that eugenicists compromised their ultimate goal of racial cleansing, settling instead for a system that separated children by tracking them into different categories according to their perceived potential. She wrote, "Eugenicists believed ability was innate and that it was the job of education to successfully sort students. . . . By matching inborn ability with the appropriate [vocational] path society would achieve a system of meritocracy where income and ability were directly correlated." Large-scale test scores created the divisions, and for more than a century, scores have been used as evidence to claim that those who are White or wealthy have superior intellect, abilities, or levels of achievement. These, then, are the students who receive educations of the highest quality. Considering that outcome, it should give us pause to learn that the people who designed and developed the large-scale testing model were motivated by eugenic ideals.[38]

Sir Francis Galton, in fact, coined the word *eugenics*, which he defined as "the science of improving stock." Galton's White supremacist views are clearly stated by author Charles King, who explained Galton believed mankind would be improved through the "purposeful perpetuation of good qualities over bad ones. . . [and therefore] the surest way to improve humanity was to encourage those racial qualities . . . of the very best kind of white people." Important among those qualities, Galton believed, was intelligence.[39]

Like Quetelet, Galton was fascinated by mathematics. Historian Ruth Cowan wrote that Galton "habitually mathematized problems that he was studying, whether or not they appeared to lend themselves to mathematical analysis." Part of the allure came from Galton's belief that mathematics enables humans to reach objective conclusions. Yet in a judgment-filled early effort to demonstrate the usefulness of quantification, Galton "constructed a map of the British Isles based on what he believed to be the objective, calculable beauty of its inhabitants."[40]

It is historic irony, perhaps, that Galton's own mathematical ability did not shine among the best and the brightest. He noticed that while his performance in math competitions was good, a few of his classmates consistently surpassed all others. Many years later, Galton would suggest that the best way to represent the intelligence of those top math students was by assuming their scores would lie in the thin margin far above the bell curve's norm. Concerned about his own natural abilities, Galton consulted a phrenologist who, based on Galton's head size and shape, concluded that his self-evaluation was correct. His skull showed that he did not have an aptitude for scholarly pursuits and was better suited for physical labor. Greatly disappointed by this news, Galton contemplated his next steps. He was lucky, however, because his family's wealth allowed him a wide range of options. In 1850, Galton set off on a two-year exploration of the southwest part of Africa.[41]

By his own assessment, this trip greatly influenced Galton's theories of biological inheritance. While in Africa, Galton took what measurements he could, hoping to get enough information to compare Africans to Europeans. He recorded data about men's strength, for example, and he went so far as to use a sextant to secretly calculate the measurements of women's bodies from afar. Ultimately, the conclusions Galton drew reinforced his view that Africans were innately inferior to Europeans. His writings make that position perfectly clear. In one account, for example, Galton wrote that the people he met "clicked, howled, and chattered and behaved like baboons." Similar dehumanizing descriptions are scattered throughout his publications. Psychology professor Raymond Fancher summarized that Galton "likened natives to pigs, dogs, or children just as easily as to baboons or barren ewes."[42]

Over time, Galton became most interested in evaluating and comparing internal traits. This eventually led to the focus that guided the rest of his life's research: studies of human intelligence. Galton believed intelligence is an inherited trait that remains stable throughout a person's life. This assumption formed the basis of much of the research that followed.[43]

As he searched for a way to prove his theory of hereditary intelligence, Winfield explained, Galton "worked from the premise that eminence and reputation in society provided a reliable indicator of inborn ability. Conversely, Galton believed an absence of eminence indicated an absence of ability and further, that social circumstance did not affect outcome in either case." Operating from those assumptions, Galton consulted a biographical dictionary and counted the number entries for men who were related to each other. From that, he drew a preliminary conclusion confirming that intelligence was indeed inherited.[44]

Galton knew he would need stronger evidence, however. So he looked to the subject he loved best. Ruth Schwartz Cowan wrote, "Since he instinctively believed that natural laws were only comprehensible when mathematized, he spent the rest of his life in pursuit of the mathematics of heredity." Given Galton's belief that physical and mental qualities are biologically determined, he concluded that the statistical models used to assess physical attributes could also be applied to mental traits like intelligence.[45]

Galton's faith rested on his belief that there is an order to every aspect of the world. This led him to trust that the bell curve represented reality. Galton wrote, "I know of scarcely anything so apt to impress the imagination as the wonderful form of cosmic order expressed by the 'Law of Frequency of Error.'" We can see that the bell curve imposes an order on data, whether it occurs naturally or not. Acting on the assumption that most phenomena naturally form a bell curve opened new possibilities for research. Cowan explained, "Galton (and other meteorologists) suspected that the normal law might be applied with profit to their science; sensing the similarity between meteorological problems and genetical problems[,] he was inspired to transfer the techniques." Quetelet had boldly applied the normal curve of error to demonstrate consistencies across human populations. Galton decided it could also be useful in highlighting distinctions among groups. This gave Galton a way to achieve his goal of demonstrating what he believed to be a naturally occurring range of human intelligence.[46]

Galton knew it would be tricky to make the leap from comparing physical characteristics to mental traits. He used the mathematical possibilities offered by the bell curve to build a model that allowed him to correlate generational trends. Galton's theory of hereditary intelligence was controversial, so he approached his experiments cautiously. He confined himself at first to physical aspects of species; the first field tests using this new model involved sweet peas. Pleased with his results, Galton moved on to correlate physical characteristics over several generations of humans, looking for hereditary trends. Once he felt he had accumulated enough data, he confirmed his model was valid.

With bolstered confidence, Galton then began to map generational trends in intelligence.[47]

There is, of course, a big difference between quantifying the concrete characteristics of sweet peas or the physical traits of humans and measuring a multifaceted quality like intelligence, which has no physical manifestation. We can only wonder why Galton felt he could make such a giant leap. Intelligence, after all, is not an object. It cannot be directly measured, and it is only presumed to exist. Inventing a way to measure a concept that cannot even be clearly defined is indeed a challenge. Galton knew that any model would rely heavily on inference to reach any conclusion. Yet he was adamant that quantification was crucial. In his mind, once a nebulous concept is quantified, it can then be visualized and treated as an object. Charles King summarized Galton's view: "If a concept could be measured, it could also be observed, and if it could be observed, it must be a *thing.*"[48]

Galton's work was a watershed. The decisions he made, based on his own assumptions about the world, established intelligence as a measurable entity and the normal curve of random error as a statistical standard. Assumptions about what is *normal* continue to guide the interpretation of data across fields of study. In fact, in research studies and in test development, the bell curve is considered the standard of accuracy. This means, as later chapters will explain, that psychometricians strive to ensure tests result in bell curve–shaped scores.

Without a doubt, the bell curve was a mathematically convenient choice that allowed Galton to easily make comparisons. Psychologist Arthur Jensen explained the process Galton used to evaluate and interpret his findings: using his African field observations, Galton "made an admittedly rough estimate of the average individual's position in the normal frequency distribution of what he conceived as general mental ability, theoretically scaled on 'Anglo-Saxons,' and suggested that Africans were 'two grades' below Anglo-Saxons on his scale, a difference equivalent to 1.33 standard deviations or 20 IQ points on present-day IQ tests." It seems to me this means he took the data he had gathered in Africa, guessed at their placement on the bell curve, and found that his conclusions matched what he had suspected all along. Jensen acknowledges that Galton's strategy amounted to not much more than a guess, but Jensen marvels that Galton's conclusions are remarkably close to the median score resulting from generations of tests of "Black IQ worldwide."[49]

Rather than raising questions about how the ideologies of Galton and subsequent psychometricians might have impacted their methodologies, Jensen and many other researchers operate on the assumption that these scores indicate something that is true. These demographic score gaps do, of course, align with the expectations of Social Darwinists. And, as Jensen said, these demographic divides in test scores have changed little over time.

At this point, it is important to say that for the sake of accuracy I will henceforth refer to these gaps as *test score* gaps. All we really know is that demographic gaps exist, and they are consistent. Any interpretation of what these gaps represent is based on the meaning assigned to a set of test scores. As we will see, the process that leads to that end is far from straightforward.

We do know that the statistical models Galton created became the foundation upon which large-scale, standardized testing was built. Jensen explained:

> Galton provided psychometrics with some of its most fundamental measurement tools and descriptive statistics, and all of these are still in use. He invented the measures of bivariate correlation and regression (further developed by Karl Pearson), the use of percentile scores for measuring relative standing on various measurements, and the use of the Gaussian or normal curve as a means for scaling variables that theoretically are normally distributed but cannot be directly measured on an interval scale or a true ratio scale. . . . Galton concluded that general ability, or intelligence, is normally distributed in the population, so measures of rank order could be converted to percentile ranks, which in turn could be transformed to normal deviates. . . . [Galton's] scale can be transformed exactly to the scale of IQ used in all present-day IQ tests. Galton's early statistical inventions were soon after further developed or supplemented by mathematical statisticians.[50]

Jensen's summary highlights Galton's theoretical leaps as one assumption led to the next. Are we to accept that these choices are somehow objective simply because they were folded into a statistical model? Cathy O'Neil warns that it is foolish to equate quantification with objectivity. She reminds us that cultural influences and ideology certainly factor into the development of statistical models. Cowan, for example, highlights Galton's beliefs as she concludes that Galton created biostatistics because he "sincerely believed that statistics could be used to construct the perfect eugenic state." Galton dreamed of producing "a truly eugenic society, a society based upon the laws of heredity . . . [which] would guide the breeding habits of men, and the evolutionary welfare of the race would become a moral criterion."[51]

As we begin the journey to explore how the large-scale testing model was created, then, we have been alerted to the eugenic beliefs of its founders. We can watch for ways in which this ideology influenced practice. As Jensen clarified, based on his assumptions, Galton built a foundation for all subsequent work in the field of psychometry. A scientific approach would expect outside evidence to corroborate each theoretical claim. If such evidence existed, it might help to wash away suspicions of ideological influences. Yet as we accumulate the necessary background to critically examine the model's conceptual framework in chapter 11, we will finally be able to trace a path from ideology to theory, and from theory to practice.

Eugenics and Education: Measuring Intelligence

Ann Gibson Winfield summarized the ideological connections that led from one line of thinking to the next. She wrote, "There is a distinct common denominator that follows hierarchicalized, racialized thinking from the Great Chain of Being Theory through phrenology, Social Darwinism, and eugenics. Each iteration was focused on sorting human beings based on their declared worth as the result of a socially constructed formula—a formula that makes sense to those wielding it precisely because the basic infrastructure is familiar, a residual part of collective memory." Proponents believe that some are born with traits that place them at the bottom of the social order, predicting lives of poverty or crime, while the inherent qualities of others predispose them to leadership. Once that premise is accepted, it follows that if schools could evaluate students' potential right from the start, the system would operate more efficiently. The nation's best resources would therefore be reserved for students destined to become its future leaders. Children with superior potential would receive a superior education. Those with less potential would be tracked and trained accordingly. By now you can see where this is headed, and you may feel the sting of familiarity at the through lines from past to present.[52]

Enacting this plan hinged on developing a tool to determine the relative worth of each child, based on a trait that could indicate human potential. Galton's conceptualized intelligence served that purpose. Quantification did, indeed, lead people to perceive intelligence as something tangible enough to be measured. Astronomers had, after all, developed ways to obtain seemingly unknowable information, so perhaps Galton, too, could make possible the seemingly impossible.

Never mind that there was, and is, no consensus about what intelligence actually is—or if it even exists outside our imaginations. *Merriam-Webster*, for example, offers five definitions of intelligence, each influenced by a different perspective. The first listing is based on the Enlightenment values of reason and objectivity. It highlights the link between intelligence and test scores, based on the dual assumptions that tests are capable of measuring abstract thought and that their results have indeed been obtained objectively.

Intelligence

1a (1) : the ability to learn or understand or to deal with new or trying situations

also: the skilled use of reason

(2) : the ability to apply knowledge to manipulate one's environment or to think abstractly as measured by objective criteria (such as tests)[53]

A statement by Nicholas Lemann, however, refutes any claim of objectivity when it comes to studies of intelligence. In his book *The Big Test,* Lemann summarized: "The study of human intelligence had always attracted people with a certain cluster of beliefs, even before there were IQ tests around for use as evidence. They thought of intelligence as being by far the single most important human trait, and therefore the one around which society should be organized; they believed it was genetically inherited; they believed that the world's darker-skinned races were inferior in intelligence to its lighter-skinned ones; and they were concerned that unintelligent people were reproducing at a more rapid rate than intelligent ones, which would ultimately bring down the IQ of the entire human species."[54]

These are the racist ideas upon which the testing industry was constructed.

Social Darwinist theory drove this line of reasoning forward as, within a few decades, thought led to action. By the latter part of the 1800s, buoyed by centuries of racist ideas, a eugenics movement swept America, the United Kingdom, and western Europe. Eugenicists acted on the beliefs that human traits and abilities can and should be measured, that these data should be regularly collected and interpreted, and that these supposedly scientific findings should be used to guide social policy and practice. In the United States, eugenics research labs were supported by the wealth of Carnegie and Rockefeller. Eugenics was taught as a science in universities across the United States and around the world. Eugenics research informed and supported racist policy in both the United States and Nazi Germany.[55]

In Berlin, followers of Galton's work established the German Society for Race Hygiene in 1905. In 1910, the Eugenics Record Office opened in Cold Spring Harbor, New York. Eugenics research led to US policies that allowed forced sterilization, prohibited marriage across racial lines, and restricted immigration. It directly contributed to Hitler's belief that racial cleansing was a way to improve society. Isabel Wilkerson explained that policies supported caste systems in both countries. In each place, proponents suggested that eugenics should go much farther. In Nazi Germany, the end point is clear. The T-4 program included six *euthanasia* centers, precursors of more than forty-four thousand concentration camps, death camps, and incarceration sites.[56]

In the United States, eugenics was the driving force behind biostatisticians' designing of large-scale tests as instruments to measure, sort, and categorize fellow human beings. How important is it for us to be aware of this context? It is the only way we can critically analyze the assumptions built into the testing model. As a practicing evolutionary biologist, Stephen J. Gould wrote *The Mismeasure of Man* to warn against accepting scientific claims of objectivity. Not only are such claims based in illusion, Gould believed, they actively oppose scientific thought. "Impartiality," he wrote, "(even if desirable) is unattainable by human beings with inevitable backgrounds, needs, beliefs, and desires. It is dangerous for a scholar even to imagine that he might attain complete neutrality, for then one stops being vigilant about personal preferences and their influences—and then one truly falls victim to the dictates of prejudice."[57]

Mathematician Cathy O'Neil agrees. "A model's blind spots reflect the judgments and priorities of its creators." She continues, "Our own values and desires influence our choices, from the data we choose to collect to the questions we ask." Nothing makes this clearer than the history of the development of large-scale testing. Yet while other remnants of eugenics have fallen by the wayside, testing is not only alive, it is kicking harder than ever.[58]

O'Neil further cautions that any attempt to simplify complexity requires "sacrificing accuracy and insight for efficiency." The chapters to come will leave no doubt that this is true of the large-scale testing model. And because evaluation of a model's success relies on how well it accomplishes the goals it was assigned, goals that are value-based, O'Neil added, "We must ask not only who designed the model but also what that person or company is trying to accomplish." In the case of those who designed large-scale testing, I'm afraid, the answer is all too clear. It is high time for vigilance.[59]

5

Evaluating Human Worth

The Rise of Educational Testing

> Once . . . [a racist] model morphs into a belief, it becomes hardwired. It generates poisonous assumptions, yet rarely tests them, settling instead for data that seems to confirm and fortify them.
>
> —Cathy O'Neil, *Weapons of Math Destruction*

While some might debate the degree to which Sir Francis Galton's ideological beliefs affected his statistical models, there is no doubt they laid the foundation that allowed the field of psychometrics to emerge. Testing advocates operate according to several underlying assumptions: that intelligence can be defined as a quantifiable entity, that tests are objective instruments that generate accurate information about an individual's intelligence, and that intelligence (and mental traits in general) naturally distribute in a bell curve. These assumptions made it possible for statisticians to gather data on a grand scale and interpret those data according to their theories.

Large-scale tests were introduced to ever broader audiences as diagnostic tools designed by experts, and psychometrics became its own field of study. Psychometricians rely on theory to refine the mathematical model and to justify the procedures used to select test content, create test items, and generate the methods for scoring, interpreting, and reporting scores. In the chapters to come, we will explore each of these processes and the theory that backs them. First, though, we will follow the evolution of large-scale testing as it intersects with public education in the United States. This background will support a more comprehensive understanding of the ideological assumptions that guide educational testing's theory and practice.

As we consider this history, it is important to separate the goals and assumptions of psychometricians from those of the policy makers who decide how test scores should be used. Psychometricians, as we've seen, strive to create models that come as close as possible to estimating quantities for mental processes that are, in reality, impossible to measure. Their role is to consider how the results of each process combine to produce the single number that we call a test score. Psychometricians know that each step inherently involves transmutation, like a funhouse mirror reflects a distorted image. So when these images combine, the results do not represent reality but instead produce an altered view. Politicians and policy makers, however, wish tests could produce something more concrete and precise. Somewhere along the line, these hopes became expectations and then blind faith as policy makers now mandate that educators treat test scores as if they are true reflections of reality. Those expectations, however, far exceed the capabilities of the testing model.

Outside the world of psychometry, there is widespread misunderstanding about what test scores mean. The reason lies with the complex model we'll examine in section 3. Misunderstanding, of course, can lead to misinterpretation and misuse, as Daniel Koretz explains. "Achievement testing is a very complex enterprise, and as a result, test scores are widely misunderstood and misused. And precisely because of the importance given to test scores in our society, those mistakes can have serious consequences." Indeed, as O'Neil demonstrates, misuse of a model can produce a weapon of math destruction.[1]

Citing other examples, O'Neil explained that "misinterpreted statistics run through the history of teacher evaluation." O'Neil specifically criticizes the twenty-first-century value-added model, which she describes as simply "bogus." If you're the teacher being fired on the basis of a bogus system, the misuse of testing data is indeed a very serious issue. And, as chapter 2 described, O'Neil explained how the entire contemporary school reform movement was based on a mistaken read of the testing data cited in the *Nation at Risk* report.[2]

Practitioners' misunderstandings can transfer to practice. For example, psychology researcher Riccardo Sartori cautioned that "psychologists often have a poor understanding that the mathematical formula of Gauss [the bell curve] is based on assumptions not often encountered in the empirical [real] world." Sartori would argue that those who decide to use the bell curve should base that decision on a clear understanding of its theoretical assumptions.[3]

As Sartori's words attest, the meaning that can be drawn from the results of a statistical model relies on the theory behind its creation. If practitioners don't understand the intricacies of the theory, it is all too easy to misinterpret, and therefore misapply, the results. We should bear this in mind as we trace the next steps in the development of large-scale testing. While psychometricians do their best to estimate scores that may be in the proximity of what they'd like to measure, we'll see that researchers, policy makers, and politicians often use these scores as if they are straightforward proxies for reality, assigning them meaning according to a political or social purpose. In those cases, test scores serve as both judge and jury, separating people along lines of division conceived in the human mind.[4]

For a deeper understanding of how a score's ascribed meaning changes from its production to its use, we'll return to a time that set the stage for testing to enter the newly consolidated system of US public education. The confluence occurred as the ideology of eugenics took hold and began its spread into both politics and academic fields. To that end, we'll pick up the story at the time Sir Francis Galton partnered with mathematician Karl Pearson.[5]

Eugenics and Statistics

Although Galton's ideas were used as the platform, his younger partner, Karl Pearson, provided the building blocks for testing's development. Statisticians consider Pearson one of the field's founders. In his first book, *The Grammar of Science*, published in 1892, Pearson emphasized the importance of data collection and statistical analysis in the biological and social sciences. Pearson's work made significant contributions to the development of statistical models that were later applied in large-scale testing. Pearson introduced the term *standard deviation* to indicate a consistent measure of distance from a bell curve's norm. Pearson also created the mathematical framework for correlation coefficients, a critical component of the testing model. Pearson knew correlation would be especially important in the social sciences, where direct measurement is difficult or impossible. Correlation coefficients instead allow researchers to draw indirect conclusions. To Pearson, the inference involved would be acceptable to researchers in fields like psychology, sociology, anthropology, and craniometry, which were not at the time considered sciences. He wrote, "The statistician does not think a certain x will produce a single-valued y; not a causative relation but a correlation . . . somewhere within a zone. . . . Our treatment will fit all the vagueness of biology, sociology, etc. A very wide science." Although the word *vagueness* hints that Pearson himself did not seem convinced these fields should be considered sciences, he knew that the use of statistics might allow them to be perceived that way. If that was the case, the evidence produced through their research might be taken more seriously, which was important to him for ideological reasons.[6]

You see, Pearson, like Galton, was an enthusiastic proponent of eugenics. Pearson was guided by his belief that "superior and inferior races cannot coexist; if the former are to make effective use of global resources; [*sic*] the latter must be extirpated."[7] Let that sink in. Karl Pearson, like Hitler and the Nazi Party, considered entire groups of people unworthy, and he thought they should be eliminated in order to preserve the world's resources for those most deserving.

For that reason, Pearson set out to design methods to provide evidence that demonstrated the relative value of human worth. Delzel and Poliak wrote that one of Pearson's goals "was to apply numerical and statistical rigor to the sociological investigation of eugenics," particularly regarding the "racial problems in man."[8]

Pearson was awarded positions of power and prestige, positioning him to work toward his goal. Early in his career, he was named director of a biometrics laboratory devoted to the measurement and statistical analysis of human characteristics. In 1906, Pearson advanced to become director of the Galton Laboratory for National Eugenics at University College in London. The Galton Laboratory merged the work of Pearson's lab with that of the Eugenics Records Office Galton had founded. This gave the two men opportunities to apply statistical models that would ensure eugenics theory translated into practice. In 1909, Pearson gave two lectures that were published as the book *Groundwork of Eugenics.*[9]

Pearson hoped his research would influence social policy. In 1910, for example, he and a colleague, Margaret Moul, conducted a study of Polish and Russian Jewish students who attended the Jews' Free School in London. The resulting article, "The Problem of Alien Immigration into Great Britain, Illustrated by an Examination of Russian and Polish Jewish Children," was published in the *Annals of Eugenics.* The article's title makes it clear that the researchers hoped to influence British immigration policy. Using a scale Pearson had developed, they evaluated the health, cleanliness, and intelligence of six hundred students. The conclusions drawn from this small study were applied to the Jewish "race" as a whole in Pearson and Moul's conclusion. "Taken on the average, and regarding both sexes, this alien Jewish population is somewhat inferior physically and mentally to the native population." And although the results were not as decisive as Pearson and Moul had hoped, they nonetheless found a way to argue their case, based on their ideology. The article concluded, "We have to face the facts; we know and admit that some of the children of these alien Jews from the academic standpoint have done brilliantly, [but] whether they have the staying powers of the native race is another question. No breeder of cattle, however, would purchase an entire herd because he anticipated finding one or two fine specimens included in it."[10]

Sometimes, after reading a sentence like that, you just have to pause and take a breath.

From the distance of 2013 Delzel and Poliak examined the experimental techniques used in this study, which were criticized at the time of its publication. After citing several examples of the original critiques, the authors wrote, "It would seem that even given the standards of the day, Pearson and Moul's study lacked the rigor necessary for the strong conclusions of Jewish inferiority they make throughout their work." Delzel and Poliak cited a number of problems with both the statistical analysis and scientific methods, concluding, "Pearson and Moul exhibited in their work an amazing lack of caution and humility in their inference, especially considering the ramifications of their recommendations." One of those recommendations was that race should be used as an exclusionary criterion in immigration decisions.[11]

Despite critiques of its methodology and interpretation, the Galton Lab had a wide-reaching influence. Students who studied there later held posts and published papers that shaped many fields of study, including the social sciences. As Pearson later reviewed the work of his former students, however, he worried when he saw how frequently they misapplied the bell curve. He "found that many of the distributions that had been cited in the literature as fitting the normal curve were actually significantly different from it." His former students' key assumption, in other words, was wrong. Those errors, of course, impacted the results and ultimately the researchers' conclusions. Yet those studies had already made their mark.[12]

Pearson felt partly responsible for these errors. Upon reflection, he explained that he must have inadvertently normalized use of the bell curve. Pearson's models used the bell curve to demonstrate frequency of error, and in his publications, he had referred to it as the normal curve. Pearson regretted that choice of words as he saw the bell curve being misused. He explained, "Many years ago [in 1893] I called the Laplace-Gaussian curve the normal curve, which . . . has the disadvantage of leading people to believe that all other distributions of frequency are in one sense or another abnormal." This suggests that Pearson did not believe the bell curve should be used as a standard; instead, each use should be carefully considered. Unlike the many researchers who thought they were following his lead, Pearson did not consider the bell curve a naturally occurring norm. As Sartori explained, Pearson "concluded that 'the normal curve of error possesses no special fitness for describing errors or deviations such as arise either in observing practice or in nature.'" In short, Pearson didn't mean to normalize use of the bell curve; it was an accident of word choice. Yet the ramifications of that mistake reverberate many generations later.[13]

Despite Pearson's regrets and his criticism of the fact that the bell curve was treated as a norm in both research and practice, the normalized use of the bell curve continued. This is certainly clear in large-scale testing, where, as section 3 will clarify, the quality of a test is measured by how closely its scores follow a bell curve pattern. We'll see that tests are, in fact, designed to ensure their scores produce this outcome.[14]

Other researchers subsequently backed Pearson's assertions of misuse. Wechsler in the 1930s and Cronbach in the 1970s, for example, concluded that the bell curve should not be assumed to be the natural order in all areas, especially in the social sciences. Sartori summarized their shared view that "psychological phenomena are not somehow inherently normally distributed." Yet these critiques seem to have been largely ignored. Sartori surmised that perhaps "the absence of any other criterion" allows the myth of the bell curve to hold sway in the social sciences. There may be no other way to do what they're trying to do. Yet once a phenomenon is normalized, the burden seems to fall on critics to *disprove* it. It leads me to wonder if such common application of the bell curve might sometimes be justified by citing the frequency of its application rather than providing evidence validating its theoretical application.[15]

While the bell curve is used throughout the social sciences, Ted Goertzel concluded that "the misuse of the bell curve has perhaps been most frequent in the field of education." This should give us pause. Given that a misinterpretation of data was used to justify an entire school reform movement, there is reason to raise questions. What if the entire system of test-based policy is based on false norms and assumptions? And the questions must go far deeper than that. The fact that testing outcomes continue to accomplish the ideological goals of the eugenicists who built the model, paired with the fact that policy has now embedded the use of test scores throughout the educational system, should surely sound an alarm.[16]

To heed the danger this alarm portends, we must learn to recognize how all these pieces fit together and operate in the system as a whole, from inception to outcomes. We must critically examine the rhetoric used to justify policies that determine the course of our children's futures. This responsibility requires us not only to critically examine testing's methodologies, but also to finally confront the context that gave rise to them.

Evaluating Mental Capacity

The first large-scale tests used in the United States were created by Henry Goddard, superintendent of the Vineland Training Center for Feeble-Minded Boys and Girls, which operated in Vineland, New Jersey. Goddard was determined to find a way to evaluate which students were, in fact, *feeble-minded*. In 1908, he learned of the test developed by Alfred Binet. Although Binet himself stated that his test was not an adequate measure of intelligence, Goddard translated it to English and created a scale for ranking student scores. Influenced by eugenic ideology, Goddard believed feeble-mindedness marked a person who was genetically predisposed to a life of poverty and crime. He claimed it was therefore important to diagnose low intelligence as early as possible and to remove those people from the larger society. Despite Binet's caution about testing's limitations, Goddard promoted the use of the Binet and Simon Tests of Intellectual Capacity, named for Binet and his collaborator, Theodore Simon. By 1911 the test was used as a diagnostic tool in doctor's offices and public school classrooms.[17]

In the early twentieth century, American eugenicists warned that people with superior traits were increasingly "breeding" with their inferiors, including African Americans, poor White people, and immigrants who were not from northern Europe. They fanned flames of fear that the gene pool of upper-class Americans of northern European ancestry was becoming diluted, which would precipitate an increase in feeble-mindedness across the nation. They also worried that people in the so-called lower classes were having more children than the elite.[18]

Goddard, like Pearson, hoped the conclusions drawn from his test results would influence immigration policy. In 1912, Goddard tested a small number of people entering the United States at Ellis Island, hoping to detect "mental defectives." His preliminary results, although "meager" by his own account, were enough to secure funding for the Vineland laboratory to conduct a larger study the following year. Even at the time, Goddard explained, "We were in fact most inadequately prepared for the task . . . the Binet-Simon Scale was so new as to be still largely in the experimental stage."[19]

Goddard decided it was better for his team to do their best, however, rather than miss an opportunity that might not come again. So two of the laboratory's staff spent two and a half months evaluating 165 immigrants identified as "Jews, Hungarians, Italians, and Russians." They tried a number of different tests, all newly developed. Goddard claimed his staff could recognize "mental defectives" on sight. Their goal was to evaluate how well using the tests for this purpose would compare. It is important to note that all the tests had to be given through an interpreter, with one exception. They found a Jewish psychologist among the immigrants, and they recruited him to work with the Jewish population, which was treated as a distinct racial group. Those were the only tests given in the native language of the test takers.[20] Although these data were collected in 1913, the results weren't published until 1917. Goddard explained, "We have waited more than three years to present the results, because not until recently have we had standards by which we could make even a tentative evaluation of the data."[21]

The test scores were used to assign test takers mental ages and people were then categorized as normal, borderline, feeble-minded, moron, or imbecile. The results of this first large-scale use of the Binet-Simon test concluded that in a group of thirty Jews, 83 percent were feeble-minded. Even the team was surprised by this high number, so they doubted the accuracy of their results. They decided to try other tests and techniques, adapting the procedures as they practiced. Ultimately, however, Goddard concluded, "While we may not be very well satisfied with the results of our study of the data furnished by the Binet-Simon examination by either of the methods employed, we cannot escape the general conclusion that these immigrants were of surprisingly low intelligence."[22] One table in Goddard's report defined 79 percent or greater of the Italians, Russians, Hungarians, and Jews tested as feeble-minded, with IQs lower than a "normal" twelve year old. While Goddard acknowledged they selected people they suspected had low mental functioning and the team's findings would therefore not allow them to claim these percentages as accurate reflections of entire groups, his summary nonetheless expressed his confidence that the "tests can be successfully used on immigrants," with the caveat that "much study is still necessary before a completely satisfactory scale can be developed." Despite that qualification, Goddard's next sentence read, "One can hardly escape the conviction that the intelligence of the average 'third class' immigrant is low, perhaps of moron grade." In other words, the nation could expect that those people poor enough to arrive by steerage, would, on average, be categorized as morons.[23]

From there, Goddard's report moved on to the question of what the nation should do with this information. He wrote, "Assuming that they are morons, we have two practical questions: first is it hereditary defect or; [sic] second, apparent defect due to deprivation? If the latter, as seems likely, little fear may be felt for the children. Even if the former, we may still question whether we cannot use moron laborers if we are wise enough to train them properly." Train them, in other words, to serve the needs of their superiors.[24]

Linking his findings to policy recommendations, Goddard wrote, "If [the results are] accepted, they furnish important considerations for future action both scientific and social as well as legislative." Despite Goddard's qualms about the quality of his data, the results of his study were apparently accepted wholeheartedly. Goddard explained that "due to the untiring efforts of the physicians who were inspired by the belief that mental tests could be used for the detection of feeble-minded aliens . . . the number of aliens deported because of feeble-mindedness (not insane or epileptic) increased approximately 350 percent in 1913 and 570 percent in 1914 over what it had been in each of the five preceding years." Never mind that even the primary investigator had said the data were flawed. Never mind that he said the physicians making these evaluations were "inspired by [their] belief" about the information mental tests could provide. It appears America's upper castes had found just the evidence they had been looking for to uphold their ideology.[25]

Goddard's account of his team's struggles on Ellis Island is a good illustration of the tension between acknowledging a model's limits and the desire to use test scores as if they represent truth. In general, eugenicists believed the government had a moral duty to create policies to protect its citizens from a genetic threat they feared would impact the nation's future. They believed that this would require immigration restrictions. They believed the United States should adopt sterilization policies to prevent the mentally deficient from having children. They believed that enacting restrictive marriage laws would deter those with superior "blood" from having children with others considered their genetic inferiors. The introduction of testing only served to reinforce the lines of race and class that divided those who considered themselves superior from those marked inferior.[26]

Eugenics enthusiasts launched a public campaign to educate people about these perceived threats and to convince them of the need for protective policies. Madison Grant's 1916 book *The Passing of the Great Race,* for example, and Stoddard's 1920 book *The Rising Tide of Color: Against White World Supremacy* reached a broad audience. Eugenics was taught in science classes across the country, and grassroots volunteers went door to door handing out information asking "thoughtful people . . . to do what [they] can to raise the hereditary endowment of the human race . . . [so they] may become happier." In *Eugenics and Education in America,* Ann Gibson Winfield summarized how racism and elitism were embedded in this propaganda campaign. "Among eugenicists there was wide acceptance of the idea that national and racial identities were equated and that behavioral characteristics were determined by race. Like heredity, the construct of race difference was so ubiquitous in eugenic thought that it is difficult to discuss eugenic beliefs about race separately from other of their programmatic imperatives. Furthermore, eugenicists believed in a hierarchical construct of *worth* that superseded race to include class, habit, and behavior."[27]

This confluence of identities, norms, and behaviors lead Isabel Wilkerson to conclude that it is therefore more accurate to refer to the American hierarchy as a caste system. When eugenicists promoted a policy of sterilization for those considered genetically inferior, for example, they were referring to those relegated to the lowest caste.[28]

Americans commonly react with horror when they learn that what was called race science and racist ideology were infused throughout the curriculum in Nazi German schools. John Simkin explained, "Children learnt about 'worthy' and 'unworthy' races, about breeding and hereditary disease." Yet in the last century, eugenics was not only taught as science in American schools, racist propaganda was also delivered directly to people's front doors.[29]

At the turn of the twenty-first century, President Clinton announced the findings of the Human Genome Project, which discredited eugenic beliefs with finality. Clinton explained, "We are here to celebrate the completion of the first survey of the entire human genome. Without a doubt, this is the most important, most wondrous map ever produced by humankind. . . . I believe one of the great truths to emerge from this triumphant expedition inside the human genome is that in genetic terms all human beings, regardless of race, are more than 99.9 percent the same. What that means is that modern science has confirmed what we first learned from ancient faiths. The most important fact of life on this earth is our common humanity."[30]

Nevertheless, the propaganda about race so widely disseminated during the first half of the twentieth century continues to influence American thought. Because the eugenics movement is a concealed story, Americans often do not recognize why they talk about human bloodlines—as if all human blood is not the same. This harkens back to the one-drop rule, which declared that if a person had one drop of "Negro blood," they were relegated to the bottom rung of the caste system. Hitler's agents, who carefully studied American racial policy, ultimately decided that the one-drop rule was too extreme even for use in Nazi Germany.[31]

Propaganda drummed up fear, and fear led to action. For example, a 1921 headline in the *Boston Sunday Herald* screamed: "Danger That World Scum Will Demoralize America." The article warned that America was becoming "Mongrelized." Propaganda was plentiful and effective, as many US states adopted policies that allowed forced sterilization and laws restricting marriage across racial lines. James Whitman, author of *Hitler's American Model*, wrote that race-based policies "culminat[ed] in the Immigration Act of 1924, [which] conditioned entry into the United States on race-based tables of 'national origins' . . . [which] Hitler praised in *Mein Kampf.*" Whitman summarized, "In the 1930s the United States, as the Nazis frequently noted, stood at the forefront of race-based lawmaking." This means that on the eve of the Nazi Holocaust, based on the same racist ideology, the United States enacted immigration restrictions that prevented many of Europe's Jews from finding safe haven.[32]

Winfield connected the history of racist ideas with the success of eugenic propaganda: "Using heredity in combination with older hierarchical versions of race theory eugenicists successfully convinced the public that race, ability, and essential human worth were correlated." This is how the lines of caste are drawn in the United States.[33]

Using the power of persuasion and "scientific" evidence that reinforced age-old racist ideas, policy makers extended the reach of eugenic ideology. They began to act on the idea that poverty and criminal behavior indicated low intellectual capacities. This bypassed even the need for test score evidence. In the mountains of Appalachia, poor people were rounded up and taken to be sterilized. And all it took was a signature on an official form to declare the mental incompetence of Black and Indigenous Americans, causing them to be institutionalized and/or forcibly sterilized. These actions were supported by public policy and enacted by doctors and psychologists around the country. In the 1927 case *Buck v. Bell,* for example, the US Supreme Court upheld the right of state governments to forcibly sterilize people because, as Chief Justice Oliver Wendell Holmes declared, "three generations of imbeciles are enough." The ruling in *Buck v. Bell* remains on the books, although it has largely been discredited by subsequent court rulings.

Law professor Jasmine E. Harris explains its contemporary relevance, which lies "not in its doctrinal deployment, but in its *expressive value* and how it continues to shape public norms and legal interpretations about the humanity and dignity of Black, Latinx, Indigenous, and disabled bodies and minds." To clarify, Harris cites a longer passage from Holmes's ruling that was supported by all but one of the justices: "We have seen more than once that the public welfare may call upon the best citizens for their lives. It would be strange if it could not call upon those *who already sap the strength of the State* for these lesser sacrifices . . . in order to prevent our being swamped with incompetence. It is better for all the world if, instead of waiting to execute degenerate offspring for crime or to let them starve for their imbecility, society can prevent those who are manifestly unfit from continuing their kind." "In other words," Harris summarizes, "**some lives matter more than others,**" a stance that lingers in American systems and in American minds.[34]

Eugenic propaganda connected the construct of race with specific attributes and behaviors so effectively that if we are aware, we can find its widespread influence. For example, in an article published in *Inside Higher Ed,* Colleen Flaherty cites the work of Joseph Graves, a biology professor at the University of North Carolina who examined the fields of medicine and biology regarding studies of complex human traits. "Graves said it was a mistake to think that race science ever went away." Flaherty continued, "The majority of biomedical researchers still think that humans have biological races, and race differences are still taught in medical schools, [Graves] said. To understand why that's wrong—why our geographically based genetic variations can't be 'unambiguously apportioned into biological races'—requires a specific sort of training, in evolutionary and population genetics. The majority of graduate students who exit Ph.D. programs in biology never receive that training."[35]

The point is that racist ideas have permeated American society. Once we recognize that, it is less of a surprise to learn that, as Winfield contends, the legacy of eugenics can still be found in American education. In fact, she explained, there is "a deeply intertwined relationship between eugenic ideology and the educational philosophy that defines our current system." Her book *Eugenics and*

Education in America provides evidence, including the unapologetic use of test scores to sort and separate children. The public inclination to perceive this as not only acceptable but necessary is an indisputable part of this legacy.[36]

In America's twenty-first century, the higher test scores of White people and wealthy people continue to be used as evidence to justify the fact that they are offered greater educational opportunity. While the debate continues as to whether test score–driven claims of superiority are a result of nature or nurture, the efficacy of these test score–based verdicts is simply accepted as truth. Kendi warns that our willingness to accept that test scores indicate real differences among groups shows the degree to which we are influenced by racist ideas. After all, any line drawn to divide the human species has been drawn by fellow humans. If we believe that demographic divides in test scores makes sense, it means we have been persuaded to accept the racist idea that White students and wealthy students truly *are* consistently higher achieving or more intelligent or possess greater potential to contribute to society. If we step back to consider that each human group has a similar genetic makeup and that the same blood runs through our veins, we can see that the test score divides make no sense. There is no biological reason that tests should show differences in intelligence or ability or achievement. If there are social reasons for divisions in test scores, *that* is what needs to be fixed. And that is a complex issue.[37]

The rhetoric of education policy, however, claims that the cure for inequity lies solely in raising teaching standards. Meanwhile, the tool developed by eugenicists for eugenic purposes continues to deliver its verdict of inequality. Kendi explains things this way: "Racism is a marriage of racist policies and racist ideas that produces and normalizes racial inequities." As we have seen, test score–based policy favors people who are White and who are wealthy. Treating the tests as if they are beyond question contributes to the normalization of these racial and class discrepancies. Despite the social inequities, which are clear in policy outcomes, America continues to operate under the assumption that whatever a test score is presumed to indicate, we can bank our nation's future on it. In the discussion to follow, we will tease apart ideology from practice as we consider how we have reached a place where these ideas, like the test scores themselves, go largely unchallenged.[38]

Eugenics, Education, and the Rise of Large-Scale Educational Testing

The substantial influence of the eugenics movement on American public education in general, and large-scale testing in particular, is a story that has not often been told. Goddard's efforts to put eugenic theory into practice through intelligence testing not only impacted immigration policy as he had hoped, it led to the rise of testing in America's system of public education. Since that time, educational testing has broadly influenced educational research as well as school policy and practices.[39]

The meaning of data produced by any mathematical model relies on how those data are interpreted. While Quetelet had proposed a model he used to predict trends in human communities, Goddard relied on Galton's assumptions as he chose to treat test scores as if they had actually measured the fixed mental abilities of each person. This allowed him to justify using the results to categorize people according to the "amount" of intelligence they were assumed to possess, according to their test score.

In 1913, the same year Goddard's Ellis Island study was conducted, Stoskopf wrote that Goddard "was hired as a consultant by the New York Public Schools to advise on the placement of students into specialized learning tracks, which the city was already pursuing. Goddard's . . . IQ tests could help determine which students belonged in special classes and which students should be sent to separate schools." The views of eugenicists were vindicated when, according to Harry Bruinius, "the *New York Times* announced that Goddard had found that over fifteen thousand pupils were in fact feeble-minded." Test scores had "successfully" been used to establish a child's position in the nation's social hierarchy.[40]

Although Goddard introduced the idea of using intelligence tests in education, it was Lewis Terman who widely promoted their use. Terman served as a professor at Stanford from 1910 to 1942. His beliefs about intelligence are revealed in the title of his doctoral study: "Genius and Stupidity: A Study of the Intellectual Processes of Seven 'Bright' and Seven 'Stupid' Boys."[41]

Like Goddard, Terman championed eugenics philosophy and practice, and he was a stanch advocate of social engineering for eugenic purposes. In fact, he unabashedly voiced his belief that people from inferior groups "should not be allowed to reproduce," especially because, he claimed, they showed a propensity toward "unusually prolific breeding."[42]

Early in the eugenics movement, Terman didn't think the public was ready to accept the overt enforcement of mandatory separation and sterilization of those categorized as feeble-minded, a group with a high prevalence of "Indians, Mexicans, and negroes." Eugenics propaganda needed time to do its work. Terman's interest in testing led him to propose a subtler approach. He understood that if test results strategically guided educational practice, testing might also be a tool that could shape the nation according to the tenets of White supremacy. "There is no possibility at present of convincing society that [feeble-minded people] should not be allowed to reproduce," Terman wrote, "although from a eugenic point of view they pose a grave problem. . . . Children of this group should be segregated in special classes and be given instruction, which is concrete and practical. They cannot master abstractions, but they can often be made efficient workers, able to look out for themselves." Terman knew that if test scores drove the practice of tracking, separating those students deemed worthy of a high-quality education from those who were not, it would ultimately impact the whole of American society. Terman understood that education policy defines the contours of the nation.[43]

This was a breakthrough for the eugenics movement. As eugenic ideology intertwined with practice, test scores would justify grooming the highest-ranking students as future leaders without resources being "wasted" on low-scoring students fated to occupy the lowest tiers of society. Bruinius concluded, "The advent of mental tests would transform the science of eugenics. First born from this quest for better breeding and the need for more reliable data, the idea of intelligence testing would later change the course of American history, reshaping ideas of equality, merit, and heredity, as well as revolutionizing access to higher education. These tests seemed to reify an elusive human trait and allow it to be quantified and measured. They then could place everyone where they belonged on a great curve of intelligence." Thus, large-scale testing became an instrumental tool to perpetuate the American caste system, and it continues that work to this day.[44]

Goddard's hierarchical tiers of intelligence created for his Ellis Island research were ready to be implemented. He had invented the new category of *moron,* a term he coined, to demarcate the highest-functioning members of the lowest tier of intelligence, those declared to be feeble-minded. Goddard explained, "The moron is a person [with a] mental level of from 8 to perhaps 12 years. He is capable of earning a living under favorable circumstances . . . [if] someone looks after him and manages his affairs." The other labels dividing that lowest category—*idiot* and *imbecile*—had been in use much longer.[45]

Testing and Tracking

Contemporaries, Goddard and Terman clearly had similar ideas. After contemplating how society should handle people categorized as feeble-minded, Goddard's conclusion sounds much like Terman's: "The real problem with the moron lies with his training. The moron boy and girl requires a radically different treatment from the normal child. . . . Perhaps after all it is a superficial view of that problem to say, we will eliminate them all as fast as we can. It may be vastly wiser, more scientific, and more practicable to say, we will accept the moron, discover him as early as we can, train him properly and use him as far as his limited intelligence will permit." We should, however, note Goddard's reference to the possibility of eliminating those in the lowest castes "as fast as we can." Clearly, this idea had been raised, but Goddard believed that it would be more acceptable or advantageous to society to "properly train" the moron class, which might then be of great service to the upper classes. Wilkerson explained that this expectation of servitude is a common marker of a caste system.[46]

Goddard and Terman agreed that educational tracking was the perfect form of social engineering. The practice would allow society to properly train students according to intellectual levels defined by the test and place them in the categories Goddard had created. Never mind that Binet himself did not believe his test, which Goddard had put into service, could measure innate intelligence. In the view of eugenicists, this physical segregation of these groups would accomplish two goals. First, separation would reduce the chances that feeble-minded people would weaken the gene pool of those considered most intelligent. Second, eugenicists hoped that if children were indoctrinated as to their social status at a young age, they would simply accept their placement at the bottom rungs of the social pyramid. Furthermore, by ensuring they received no more than the "proper training" for their rank, eugenicists knew they would have little chance of escape.[47]

In the eyes of the nation's leaders, testing also offered the advantage of economic efficiency. In an era when assembly lines had allowed US industries to boom, categorizing students imposed an order that ultimately saved time and money. Educator John Dewey tried to carefully explain the differences in outcomes between a school system where all students are nurtured to reach their full potential and a factory model where students are treated as cogs in a societal wheel. In *Democracy and Education,* Dewey wrote, "Were all instructors to realize that the quality of mental process, not the production of correct answers, is the measure of educative growth something hardly less than a revolution in teaching would be worked." A process is only efficient, of course, if it meets its goals. School administrators actively pursued the economic advantages of standardization nonetheless.[48]

With economic efficiency as a top priority in US education, Terman saw his opening. He began to promote testing and tracking as a way to achieve greater productivity. Based on a small norming group of middle class, native-born, White, Protestant children, Terman revised the Binet-Simon scale. He called his newly scaled test, published in 1916, the Stanford-Binet. In only its fifth edition after more than one hundred years, the Stanford-Binet is still in use.[49]

The original Stanford-Binet testing manual made lofty claims, summarized thus by education professor Jonathan Plucker: "The new Stanford-Binet scale. . . would allow for the scientific diagnosis and classification of children to be placed in special classes; bring tens of thousands of high-grade defectives under the surveillance and protection of society; reduce delinquency; help the schools respond to children of superior intelligence; assist in assigning children to school grades; help determine vocational fitness; and serve as a standard for research." Who would reject a tool that could do all that?[50]

Terman then teamed with Robert Yerkes and Henry Goddard, who revised the test to be used by the US Army during World War I to channel recruits into career paths from officer to grunt. The researchers saw this as an opportunity to generate evidence to support eugenic assumptions. Garland Allen wrote, "This unprecedented sample offered the hope of being able to draw statistically significant conclusions about the relationship between innate mental capacity and ethnicity, race, socio-economic status and many other social and cultural parameters." And it did just that. Allen wrote, "The data showed that the average American-born recruit had a mental age of 13 years, just above the level of a 'moron.'" Nicholas Lemann added, "On the Army IQ tests, Nordics scored higher than Alpines, who scored higher than Mediterraneans. The test results as a whole were like a photograph of American culture, so faithfully did they reproduce the social order. Officers scored higher than enlisted men, the native-born scored higher than the foreign-born, less recent immigrants scored higher than more recent immigrants, and whites scored higher than Negroes." Army recruits were tracked into military roles according to these scores.[51]

Two factors determine what meaning is attributed to test scores: the test's content and the way scores are interpreted. Allen wrote that Goddard, Terman, and Yerkes "believed these scores measured genetically determined differences in mental function . . . the tests proved to be highly bound to American culture, asking the subject to identify commercial products, sports figures, or to point out what was missing in the drawing of an object such as an old-fashioned Victrola phonograph." The test content, in fact, influenced the results to such an extent that even the test's designers were skeptical of them. For example, Allen shared one clear correlation to content: "The longer the immigrant had resided in the USA, the higher the score they received on the test."[52]

The power of interpretation, however, is mighty. So, too, is the power of social position. In 1923, a book called *A Study of American Intelligence* was published. Its author was Carl Brigham, a professor of psychology at Princeton whom Lemann described as "an ardent eugenicist." Allen wrote that Brigham's position on the results of the army test "preserved the objectivity of the test and the inferiority of the immigrant." Rather than encouraging researchers to question the test's content and closely examine testing procedures, Brigham simply claimed the scores as proof that the intelligence of immigrants was low. Given that interpretation, eugenicists could use the data to justify their calls to further restrict immigration. Clearly, interpretation can be influenced by ideology and purpose. And unless there is a demand for corroborating evidence to back their claims, such verdicts often stand.[53]

Inspired by the perceived success of allowing test scores to track army recruits into "appropriate" jobs, Terman collaborated with Edward Thorndike, an educational psychologist at Columbia University, to adapt the army test for use in schools. Terman marketed the result, which they called the National Intelligence Test, as a tool for educational efficiency while Thorndike convinced the nation's leaders that they should rely on the advice of "experts" like himself and Terman rather than teachers or administrators.[54]

The marketing campaigns were highly successful. The educational use of test scores caught on quickly and the nation swore allegiance to them. The results pleased both eugenicists and businessmen. By 1920, schools across the nation had purchased four hundred thousand copies of Terman's National Intelligence Test, and those test scores determined who would receive the highest-quality education and who would not.[55]

Carl Brigham agreed with Terman's argument that racial mixing would cause not only a decline in American education but the genetic decline of the population at large. Their elitist ideas further delineated who would be considered worthy. For example, in *A Study of American Intelligence,* Brigham wrote, "The army mental tests had proven beyond any scientific doubt that, like the American Negroes, the Italians and Jews were genetically ineducable. It would be a waste of good money to even attempt to try to give these born morons and imbeciles a good Anglo-Saxon education, let alone admit them into our fine medical, law, and engineering graduate schools."[56]

As the use of testing caught on in K-12 education, Carl Brigham invited Terman to help him once again adapt the army test, this time as a tool for making college admission decisions. The resulting test is the now famous Stanford Achievement Test, commonly known as the SAT. Brigham's words make it clear that he thought the SAT would ensure that society's resources would never be wasted on those whose scores declared them ineducable, instead ensuring that only the worthy would receive the "good Anglo-Saxon education" provided by the nation's colleges and universities.[57]

With their racial and class divides, test scores across the board aligned with the eugenic ideology that swept the nation. By the time tests were used in education, generations of propaganda had promoted the false notion of a racial hierarchy as the natural order. This illusion had been championed so successfully that when scores showed racial and class divides, no one questioned these results. Instead, the nation's elite received the news only as evidence that the tests had done their job well.[58]

Terman's conclusion about how society should use these test-generated data display an unsettling lack of humanity. Stoskopf, quoting Terman, wrote: "Due to the prevalence of deficiencies among 'Indians, Mexicans, and negroes' . . . the whole question of racial differences in mental traits will have to be taken up anew. . . . No amount of school instruction will ever make [the feeble minded] intelligent voters or capable citizens in the true sense of the word." In other words, Terman thought there was no hope of schooling darker-skinned segments of the population, so why even try? This from a professor of education at one of the nation's leading universities.[59]

If we take a step back at this point, knowing, as we do, that Terman's assumptions about categories of racial differences are false, that humans are, in fact, 99.9 percent genetically similar, we can see there is every reason to question test scores that show stark racial divisions. Testing outcomes that show demographic divides should raise questions. Those questions should lead us to critically examine testing procedures and the assumptions that led to their development. These, then, are the topics of the chapters to come.

But first, let's take a moment to focus on the increased use of the term *expert* and the role it played in silencing the voices of critics. Because right from the very start, testing did have its detractors.

6

"Experts," Opposition, and Obfuscation

I hate the impudence of a claim that in fifty minutes you can judge and classify a human being's predestined fitness in life. I hate the pretentiousness of that claim. I hate the abuse of the scientific method which it involves. I hate the sense of superiority which it creates and the sense of inferiority which it imposes.

—Walter Lippmann, "The Great Confusion"

The Experts

Eugenic beliefs were able to spread because of the privileged status of those who promoted them. In education, Terman, Thorndike, and Brigham, for example, declared themselves to be educational "experts." Edward Thorndike championed the idea that experts alone should wield the power to influence policy when in 1920 he wrote, "Wherever there is the expert . . . should we not, in fact, let him do our thinking for us in that field?" Thorndike was not talking about practitioners; he did not consider the teachers who spend their days working directly with children the experts in education. Instead, Thorndike considered experts to be people like himself, based on advanced degrees that had allowed him to become professor of educational psychology at Columbia University. Based on his social status, that avenue had been open to him, even as it was blocked for others. During his long career, Thorndike had fifty books and 450 articles selected for publication. His ideas were therefore able to spread, even as others were silenced. Similarly, Lewis Terman was editor of six research journals, and in 1922, he was elected president of the American Psychological Association. In addition to Carl Brigham's teaching and publications, his legacy is the SAT, a test that continues its reign.[1]

With this level of influence, the educational research, theory, and practice of these three men, self-declared experts, helped shape the philosophies of generations of educators and policy makers. Like Galton's and Pearson's before them, the views of these men impacted the nation through their publications and also through the many students they influenced. Eugenics researchers and scholars aimed to ensure that eugenic ideals were so deeply embedded in policy and practice that they would continue to be carried out by the nation's future leaders.[2]

Goddard had suggested that the country's system of public education was fertile ground for both promoting and practicing eugenics, and Terman agreed that testing and tracking was a form of social engineering the public would most likely accept. Terman's next task was to convince the nation that large-scale tests were trustworthy enough to guide the separation of so-called morons, idiots, and imbeciles from those children deemed "normal." Those selected as "natural leaders" would receive the best education of all. It just so happened that, on the whole, the scores used to justify these decisions also categorized people by the color of their skin and by their socioeconomic status. This enactment of eugenic principles was so successful that perhaps Terman's most significant legacy is summarized in this short statement: "As far as intelligence is concerned, the tests have told the truth."[3]

From that moment on, American society has been shaped by this fallacy.

Terman's words supported a grand illusion whose impact still matters. His social position and self-declared expertise allowed him to make this grandiose statement and trust it would have influence. Clearly, it did, as the verdict of test scores continue to influence the social structure of the United States well into the twenty-first century.

The Detractors

Large-scale testing had its critics then as now. Researcher and professor Alan Stoskopf connected past to present when he wrote that "current critiques of testing and the calls for more authentic forms of assessment have been built in part upon the pioneering work of African-American intellectuals in the 1920s and 1930s." It was clear to them that educational testing was being used to support a racist system.[4]

W. E. B. DuBois, for example, wrote, "It was not until I was long out of school and indeed after the (first) World War that there came the hurried use of the new technique of psychological [IQ] tests, which were quickly adjusted so as to put black folk absolutely beyond the possibility of civilization." During Reconstruction, some Black people, like DuBois, broke barriers that had previously barred them from professions and political offices. DuBois understood that test scores were being used to exclude even those willing to successfully assimilate. Excluding Black minds from a high-quality education would, in turn, limit the trajectory of their lives. Wilkerson explained that, in any caste system, the top priority is to keep the lowest caste firmly in its place.[5]

DuBois could also see what Goddard and Terman understood: testing and tracking in schools would serve White supremacist purposes. Test-based tracking would limit access to educational opportunity in an attempt to prevent voices like his from gaining an audience. Like the eugenicists, DuBois understood that those who control the narrative have a far better chance of controlling society.

Other testing critics also sounded alarms. In his role as professor and educational leader, Horace Mann Bond took a strong stance against the use of testing in schools. The title of his first professional paper, published in 1924, was "Intelligence Tests and Propaganda." In what Winfield called a "scathing article decrying the abuse of testing in American education," published in 1927, Bond wrote, "Ever since the 'measurement of minds' became a popular field in which to pursue investigations, the testing of Negro children has easily ranked as a major indoor sport among psychologists. . . . The rules of the game are simple and seem to be standardized throughout the country with but few exceptions." Bond described the negative impact of evaluating students of color within a school system standardized to ensure the success of White children. Today, critics echo Bond's cry that American education has still not focused on how it might best serve children of color.[6]

Ann Gibson Winfield explained, "Bond was clear that the intent behind the increasing use of tests to determine ability belied a deeper racist imperative. He ridiculed the claim of fairness so often uttered by proponents of testing." Bond wrote, "Only one conclusion is to be drawn. If Negro children make lower scores than White, they are inferior, they were born that way and though we had a sneaking suspicion that this was the fact all along, we are now able to fortify our prejudices with a vast array of statistical tables, bewildering vistas of curves and ranges and distributions and the other cabalistic phrases with which we clothe the sacred profession of Psychology from the view of the profane public."[7]

Clearly, Bond understood that testing's opaque statistical model played a role in leading the public to simply accept the meaning experts and politicians attributed to test scores. Stoskopf explains that after carefully studying how tests were constructed, Bond "dismissed the claim that these tests were objective. Instead, Bond called them 'funds for propaganda' and encouraged each African-American student to '. . . be in possession of every detail of the operation, use, and origin of these tests, in order that he might better equip himself as an active agent against the insidious propaganda which seeks to demonstrate that the Negro is intellectually and physically incapable of assuming the dignities, rights, and duties which devolve upon him as a member of modern society.'" Whether laws endorsing sterilization and restricting so-called interracial marriage passed or failed, Bond understood that the eugenicists' goal of upholding the racial caste system could be achieved through test-based education policy.[8]

In 1933, Berea College– and Harvard-educated historian Carter G. Woodson added his voice to the conversation with the publication of *The Mis-Education of the Negro*. Woodson, editor of the *Journal of Negro History*, maintained that any critique of social and educational inequality in the United States must be viewed through the lens of race. Woodson's work afforded a multi-layered view of African American life, in contrast to the single dimension represented in widespread propaganda. He asked educators to take a hard look at the many ways in which schools institutionalized inequality, including destroying Black children's motivation and denying their aspirations. Woodson's critique echoes loudly today among critics of mandatory, scripted, standardized educational programming prescribed for schools with low-scoring students.[9]

Stoskopf explained that the works of these and other African American scholars challenged the accepted myths that were held as scientific truth by most of their White counterparts. These included:

- Test scores proved that African Americans and other "lesser strains" were innately inferior to Northern European Whites.
- Environmental conditions had little to do with performance on IQ tests. Intelligence was essentially fixed and unchangeable.
- Exceptionally intelligent children were rarely found among African Americans.
- Children of mixed White and Black ancestry had a higher intelligence than "pure Negro" Blacks. (This was known as the "mulatto hypothesis" at the time.)
- Better educational opportunities made little difference in helping children succeed.[10]

Racism also affected whose work got published and whose did not. The views of Black scholars were largely restricted from reaching mainstream America. At a time when "black inferiority was near universal convention in American culture," as Isabel Wilkerson describes the eugenics era, racist power could belie the expertise of even Harvard-educated scholars like Woodson because they had been born with dark skin.[11]

Testing had White detractors as well, and their critiques sometimes reached a larger audience. As we saw in chapter 5, Alfred Binet, the man who made the first attempt to evaluate mental capacity, was one of them. As the tests' initial designer, he understood their many flaws. To the end of his life,

Binet criticized psychologists for misusing his tests based on the mistaken claim that they actually measured intelligence.[12]

Binet died in 1911, knowing his admonitions had fallen on deaf ears as tests continued to be lauded as revelatory tools. In 1922, for example, Lothrop Stoddard's book, *The Revolt against Civilization: The Menace of the Underman*, reprised the rhetoric that the "average" American had a mental age of about fourteen, based on the results of the army tests. After Stoddard's book was published, journalist Walter Lippmann could no longer stay silent. Heeding his inner call to action, Lippmann wrote a series of six articles published in the *New Republic* in 1922. The articles debunked testing procedures and decried the way scores were interpreted. Lippmann hoped that once the public learned how test-based conclusions were reached, they might be rejected. He therefore began the series by highlighting the arbitrary decisions and assumptions in the procedure Binet had created to establish a child's "mental age."[13]

Lippmann wrote:

[Binet] . . . turned his attention to the practical problem of distinguishing the "backward" child from the "normal" child in the Paris schools. . . . For Binet concluded, quite logically, that the standard of a normal child of any particular age was something or other which an arbitrary percentage of children of that age could do. Binet therefore decided to consider "normal" those abilities which were common to between 65 and 75 percent of the children of a particular age. In deciding these percentages he thus decided to consider at least twenty-five percent of the children as backward. He might just as easily have fixed a percentage which would have classified ten percent of the children as backward, or fifty percent.

Having fixed a percentage which he would hence-forth regard as "normal" he devoted himself to collecting questions, stunts and puzzles of various sorts, hard ones and easy ones. . . . Binet then gave these tests in Paris to two hundred school children who ranged from three to fifteen years of age. . . . Thus a mental age of seven years was the ability to do all the tests which sixty-five percent of a small group of seven year old Paris school children had shown themselves able to do.[14]

Lippmann explained that Terman had found that the scores of American children differed from their French counterparts, so he followed Binet's procedure and created new age-level norms for the United States. Then, in a leap of faith, Terman invented the measure of IQ. He decided that if he simply divided test takers' mental ages, represented by test scores, by their actual ages, he could claim that the result revealed the children's intelligence quotients, or IQs.

As a result of the ambiguity in these methods, created nearly a century ago, Lippmann cautioned us not to simply accept what we are told tests scores mean. He wrote, "The puzzles which this average child among a hundred Californian children of the same age about the year 1913 could answer are the yardstick by which 'mental age' is measured in what is known as the Stanford Revision of the Binet-Simon Scale." In other words, an entire test was calibrated using the age-level norms established by about a hundred children per group, following a process Lippmann questioned from the start. He railed against claims that these procedures were in any way scientific. He was incredulous that practitioners would believe that this series of steps could reveal something as complex as a person's intelligence. Those who draw conclusions based on IQ scores, however, apparently accept the credibility of these methods, because since the Stanford-Binet test was introduced, people around the world have used IQ scores as if they accurately indicate human intelligence.[15]

Scientific historian Garland Allen added another example to show this ambiguity continued long after Lippmann's criticism. Allen explained that when the Stanford-Binet was given in US schools and the results consistently showed that the scores of Black students were below those of White students and girls' scores were lower than boys', in 1936 the test was revised and "'standardized' so that male-female means became identical; not so, however, for black-white differences, which remain 15 IQ points apart to this day."[16]

Lippmann had begged readers to critique the many assumptions and inferences involved in producing a score. "If the impression takes root that these tests really measure intelligence, that they constitute a sort of last judgment on the child's capacity, that they reveal 'scientifically' his predestined ability, then it would be a thousand times better if all the intelligence testers and all their questionnaires were sunk without warning in the Sargasso Sea."[17]

Clearly the tests are still afloat, buoyed by the public impression Lippmann feared. "Unfortunately," wrote Paul Houts, author of *The Myth of Measurability*, "little attention was paid to Lippmann's warning. He was regarded merely as a cranky critic of the tests . . . and by 1929, more than 5 million tests were being administered annually."[18]

Despite the best efforts of testing's detractors, its trajectory continued to rise, even after Carl Brigham, designer of the SAT, had a change of heart. In his later years, Brigham renounced much of his own work, including the conclusions he had reached in *A Study of American Intelligence*. Like Binet, Brigham finally concluded that there is no universal measure of human intelligence. Nicholas Lemann, author of *The Big Test*, summarized Brigham's belief: "The enthusiasm of the leaders of the IQ-testing movement had led them to make an unwarranted and dangerous leap. They assumed that because they could produce a reliable test result, what the test measured must be a biological trait of the brain, although there was no physical evidence for the truth of this belief."[19]

In a letter to Charles Davenport, director of the US Eugenics Record Office, Brigham faulted both psychometricians and practitioners for this "dangerous leap." "I feel we should all stop naming tests and saying what they measure . . . if we are to proceed beyond the stage of a psycho-phrenology." A test's name, after all, carries implications. "The more I work in this field," Brigham wrote, "the more I am convinced that psychologists have sinned greatly in sliding easily from the name of the test to the function or trait measured." Brigham contended that by simply ascribing meaning to test results practitioners have been led to false conclusions.[20]

Brigham became increasingly concerned by the bold claims of testing advocates. In an unfinished manuscript he wrote, "The test movement came to this country some twenty-five or thirty years ago accompanied by one of the most glorious fallacies in the history of science, namely, that the tests measured native intelligence purely and simply without regard to training or schooling. I hope nobody believes that now. . . . The 'native intelligence' hypothesis is dead."[21]

Yet, as we will see, testing's key assumptions rely on the concept of native intelligence, and therefore, so does the model. Brigham, like DuBois, was disturbed by the speed at which test-based practice accelerated. Brigham wrote, "Practice has always outrun theory . . . this is a new field and . . . very little has been done which is right. As new information comes in and new methods are developed, practically everything that has gone before seems full of errors." Nonetheless, few have seemed much interested in finding the source of those errors by revisiting the model's basic assumptions.[22]

The stakes of test-based decisions increased when the SAT became a factor in determining college admission. Brigham's biggest concern was in the consequences of using test scores as if they reveal something true when, in fact, the model "seems full of errors." It was one thing to put tests to use during wartime, Brigham explained, when "emergencies demand the sacrifice of individual ambitions," and quite another to apply them in educational settings where the results impact the trajectory of people's lives. Brigham wrote, "A college being a humanitarian institution cannot afford to make mistakes against the individual." As designer of the SAT, Brigham could foresee what lay ahead. A few years later he cautioned, "If the unhappy day ever comes when teachers point their students toward these newer examinations, and the present weak and restricted procedures get a grip on education, then we may look for the inevitable distortion of education in terms of tests." It's as though he had predicted the future. Although he didn't live to see it, that unhappy day arrived with the passage of No Child Left Behind.[23]

As he watched testing gain prestige, Brigham also strongly advised against the formation of the Educational Testing Service, which had been proposed as a national agency to house testing research and development. Lemann explained that Brigham believed "any organization that owned the rights to a particular test would inevitably become more interested in promoting it than in honestly researching its effectiveness."[24]

For a time, Brigham's objections stalled ETS's formation, yet all the pieces for scaling up the testing industry, including computer scoring, were already in place. With Brigham's death in 1943, Lehmann wrote, "the roadblock was removed," and by 1948, ETS was established as the home of America's testing industry. Lemann concluded, "The ironic result was that Carl Brigham's test was hitched to a test promotion and administration structure he disapproved of, built by people he had no use for."[25]

The Advocates

The rhetoric drummed up by testing advocates allowed the tank of educational testing to roll right over Brigham's objections. The zeal of possibility overshadowed any doubt, just as it had when Quetelet and Goddard expressed their reservations about the use of procedures they had designed yet knew were inadequate. The objections of testing's detractors, and even of its founders, were ignored as testing advocates pledged their loyalty.

Eugenicists justified the use of test scores because they believed that tests revealed objective truth. This belief was rooted in the fact that tests delivered the outcomes they expected. The meaning attributed to the test scores was driven by eugenic ideology and used to conceal social engineering that benefited the elite. Despite a few falters along the way, the testing industry is not only alive but thriving in the twenty-first century. From No Child Left Behind onward, the stakes attached to test scores have never been higher. Testing's racist tracks have been swept away by declarations that the past is irrelevant as we now live in a post-racial society. The racist outcomes of "color-blind" policy are hidden beneath promises of educational equity.

How could this have happened? What factors allow a mirage to be perceived as truth?

In the case of test-based policy, we might look for answers by following a thread of racist ideas regarding achievement. In *Caste: The Origins of Our*

Discontents, Isabel Wilkerson explained, "Achievement by those in the lowest caste goes against the script handed down to us all. It undermines the core assumptions upon which a caste system is constructed and to which the identities of people on all rungs of the hierarchy are linked. Achievement by marginalized people who step outside the roles expected of them puts things out of order and triggers primeval and often violent backlash." The policies of Reconstruction had opened opportunities for Woodson, Bond, and DuBois to gain notoriety as intellectual leaders. Although viewed as exceptions, their achievements, among many others, had threatened the racist ideas that uphold the illusion of caste.[26]

This threat was enhanced by the fact that by 1918, compulsory education laws had been passed in every state. This coincided with the Great Migration, as many African Americans moved north, fleeing racial terror and dreaming of opportunity. By 1920, "over 90% of American children between the age of 7 and 13 were reported as enrolled in school." As they gained access to public education, it was increasingly obvious that people of color could indeed excel. But as Wilkerson explained, this threatened a system in which White power had been justified as the natural order. The veneer of natural hierarchy, you see, requires constant polishing so that the image reflected back to those in the upper classes depicts kind and generous actions that contribute to the good of all. That reflection is maintained by ongoing propaganda that dehumanizes those in the lowest caste in ways that make it appear that they alone are responsible for their circumstances. If that carefully constructed veneer were to crack, the common humanity of all people would be exposed for all to see, which could trigger a seismic societal disruption.[27]

The illusion of natural points of separation among castes is reinforced by physical segregation, reducing the possibility that people from different racial and economic categories might touch each other's hearts. While physical segregation limits direct interactions, further gatekeepers have limited access to the humanity that shines through the work of Black and Indigenous and poor White writers, artists, and musicians. Segregation allows propaganda to tell its false stories without the danger of disruption.

This propaganda continues to play an important role in upholding its narrative of unequal worth. Absent that narrative, the entire social structure comes crashing down. After all, if people are seen as equally worthy, leaders would be held responsible for ensuring equity throughout society.

In the days when racism was overt, a social hierarchy was expected. No one was surprised by policies created to support it. In fact, the hierarchy was staunchly, often violently, defended. Historians describe a pattern of White rage prompted by any threat that might disrupt the racial status quo. Wilkerson points out that this rage was often triggered as Black people claimed their rights as US citizens and Black communities excelled. Early in the twentieth century, there was "a wave of anti-black pogroms in more than a dozen American cities, from East St. Louis to Chicago to Baltimore, as black southerners arrived north during the Great Migration and many tried to make their claims to citizenship after risking their lives in the Great War." In 1920, sixty Black people were murdered for trying to vote in Ocoee, Florida. In 1921, White people perpetrated a massacre in Black Wall Street, Tulsa's affluent African American community. In these and many other acts of terrorism, Black people were murdered, and their homes and businesses were burned to the ground.[28]

Wilkerson explains, "One thing those rampages had in common: the mobs tended to go after the most prosperous in the lowest caste, those who might have managed to surpass even some people in the dominant caste." The mobs, in other words, were out to destroy any evidence that might disprove eugenic claims that the social order was dictated by nature. Such evidence would reveal the illusion that White people alone deserved their place at the top. Each act of violence was therefore justified to the White community as self-defense.[29]

Violence, it turns out, is a shape-shifter that can take on many forms. This fear that those in the lowest caste might prove their ability to achieve leads us to consider test-based policy in a new light. It's clear that the groups assigned the lowest ranks in society also collectively receive the lowest scores on large-scale tests. Combined with the idea that children should be sorted and taught according to the perceived level of their ability, the outcomes of test-based tracking are predetermined. In short, tracking denies low-scoring students the very opportunities that might allow them to thrive. This sets up a cycle that ensures that most of the people in society's lower ranks will remain there. The exceptions, people from low-scoring groups who test well, are cited as examples to support the claim that the tests are indeed objective, and the scores have accurately indicated those who are most deserving of opportunity. After all, the argument goes, if there were barriers stacked against these groups, no one would be able to break through. We've been socialized to think about racism and elitism as binary—either they exist or they don't. If the negative effects do not impact everyone in a group in the same way, we take that as evidence that it doesn't exist at all. Instead, the effects of racism and elitism operate more like a continuum, either singly or collectively, and many other parts of our identities also come into play.

Instead of acknowledging exceptions as just that—that a few people have managed to break through a system stacked against them—their success is woven into a narrative asserting that with enough effort on the part of any individual, the exception could become the rule. In fact, the exceptions allowed the SAT to be marketed as a path toward greater equity compared to the legacy enrollment then practiced by universities. At least some who were previously excluded would be offered a chance. This led to the widespread belief that anyone could be admitted to college if they just worked hard enough. Twenty-first-century education policy strongly reinforces the message that testing actually creates equal opportunities for success, despite all evidence to the contrary.

That narrative is socially destructive. It says that, as a group, people of color and people with low SES have just not tried hard enough. For over a century, lower group norms have been cited as evidence that people in these groups have not taken advantage of the education they've (so generously) been offered. This message is delivered, over and over, in the form of test scores. Imagine the rage you would feel in receiving this verdict after decades of working toward your goal, overcoming many other social barriers along the way. This is the message my students Ronald, Roxanne, and Jocelyn received. To the shame of our nation, many of those assigned to society's lower ranks do not have to imagine; this is their lived reality.

Early testing advocates understood that the way this system operates makes it nearly impossible to disprove test scores' efficacy. After all, when score-based tracking is used to deny opportunity to low-scoring students right from the start, it's anyone's guess as to how those children might have fared if they'd had equal access to high-quality education. In other words, there is no way to tell if scores have sorted students "correctly." And while it's true that a test-based caste system must accept a few disruptors, those exceptions actually work in its favor; they are part of its disguise. All in all, eugenicists could rest assured that within this closed system, the impact of testing would have a long reign. And it has.

So it seems testing was another form of backlash to Black success. Test-based tracking may have been put into place to preclude the rise of another Black Wall Street. However it was justified, the fact is that testing took off; the 1.5 million copies of the SAT sold in 1925 had risen to over 5 million by 1929, and its meteoric rise continued. By guarding the gate to higher education, test scores would assuredly limit the access of those assigned to lower classes, and eugenicists would have achieved their goal.[30]

Large-scale testing had become a tool of hegemony, used to both perpetuate and conceal a caste system. The meaning associated with test scores became a stock story, rarely questioned. The cycle of dominance was set to spin like this: "Experts" told teachers what test scores mean. That assumed meaning influenced teacher expectations about each student's abilities. Alan Stoskopf explained that, as a result, "teachers learned to apply terms like *moron* and *defective learner* to children who scored low on the tests, separating the feeble-minded student from 'normal' learners." Based on categories assigned by the scores, students were allocated into tracks which either granted or denied them educational opportunities which, in turn, impacted the trajectory of their lives.[31]

Just as Goddard and Terman had predicted, long-term evidence shows that test-based policy can indeed shape American society in very intentional ways. The high scores of White males from elite families were hailed as verification that society's leadership lay just where it should—with its most intelligent people. The generational wealth had apparently followed naturally, as long as you ignore the fact that generations of policy, including an entire system of enslavement, had been designed to produce that outcome.

As the eugenics movement faded, testing moved into a context where overt racism was less socially acceptable. A new narrative was needed to explain the hierarchy produced through the use of test scores, and somehow it had to be cloaked in a mirage of equity. Yet while the rhetoric used to justify the use of test scores has shifted over time, the resulting social stratification has not. Over one hundred years later, the outcomes of test-based policy reflect the racist ideals of those who initially devised the testing model.

7

Shifting Rhetoric

Meritocracy and Education as the Great Equalizer

Meritocracy is not the solution to rising inequality but rather its root.
—Daniel Markovits, *The Meritocracy Trap*

Galton, Terman, Thorndike, and Brigham were, of course, products of their time, as all of us are. During its reign, eugenics ideology was widespread among the upper caste. Some testing advocates might consider it is safe to ignore the belief systems of testings' founders, assuming it did not influence their work. Others including some closest to the work recommended careful scrutiny. Because the testing model rests on the foundation of the ideas of these eugenics practitioners, it seems prudent to reconsider testing's key assumptions in a contemporary context. To do this, we must follow the progression of ideas as they evolved from one generation of psychometricians to the next and the lines of thought that maintain the public's acceptance of large-scale testing. They, too, have changed over time.

If we follow the rhetoric from the racist ideas of eugenics, it may shed light on why contemporary tests continue to produce outcomes favoring those who are White or wealthy. If we find that the test-based system of policies produces outcomes that uphold the values of eugenics, we have some hard choices to make. If we intend to disrupt the American caste system, regulations will need to change in many different areas, including education. Reimagining an entire system is hard work indeed. But in a nation of innovators, these are not impossible tasks. The work will, however, require opening our minds and hearts to a broad range of perspectives. We will need to ensure that our practice and its outcomes match our true intent. And that, of course, means collectively deciding what that intent should be. Up to now, it seems, we have allowed those decisions to be made for us.

Viewing the United States through a wide-angle lens will help us understand the role testing plays as part of a larger system. Professor and author Wayne Au, for example, demonstrates how large-scale testing and the school-to-prison pipeline, two seemingly separate systems, in fact operate in concert. Outcomes of one system sometimes feed right into another, compounding their impact. Rather than "classical racism of our forefathers' era," Isabel Wilkerson describes such examples as a "mutation of the software that adjusts to the updated needs of the operating system" that maintains the American system of caste.[1]

Most testing advocates today would deny racist intent. When questioned about the racist impact of test-based policy, the argument often defers to the myth that test scores reveal truth. This allows advocates to throw up their hands and exclaim, "Yes, the racial divides are terrible, but what can we do?" They go on to confidently explain that the tests are a scientific and objective form of evaluation, and it can't be helped if the results break down along lines of race and class. Social differences, they would argue, do not factor into the results of an objective, inherently color-blind system. Testing advocates maintain that the results prove there must *be* racial differences in every area large-scale tests measure, and somehow White and wealthy people always rise to the top. The base assumption is that the meaning assigned to test scores, whatever it is and however it was obtained, is beyond question.

Yes, some leaders may be unaware of the history of racist ideas that has brought us to this point. Yet that does not change the fact that test score evidence continues to grant opportunity to some and deny it to others. Our practices align with a paradigm that rests on racist beliefs many in our nation no longer support. Although support for eugenic ideology may have faded, US policy supports the use of tests for the purpose eugenicists intended—to sort and to separate—and testing outcomes continue to maintain a hierarchy that reflects eugenic goals. On the basis of test scores, students are assigned their ranks early and become indoctrinated with the idea that they earn the placement they deserve. All the while, they are told the goal of such separation is to help them reach an arbitrarily assigned standard. Just as in the time of eugenics, however, once labeled, students tend to remain in the same tracks throughout their school careers. And even those who manage to overcome the barriers of those labels remember and are affected by them over the course of their lives.[2]

"Caste is insidious and therefore powerful because it is not hatred," Wilkerson explains. "It is the worn grooves of comforting routines and unthinking expectations, patterns of a social order that have been in place for so long that it looks like the natural order of things."[3]

When we step back to see the larger picture, we can see the arrogance of a stance that claims people have found a way to objectively sort and judge other humans. As Walter Lippmann pointed out, the notion is absurdly arrogant, yet the practice continues. Once Americans saw eugenics carried out in Nazi Germany, they tried to distance themselves from the ideology and the practice. Yet eugenics had been large-scale testing's driving force. In order for testing to continue, its advocates realized, a new ideology had to take its place. Calling on a phrase often used by Kendi, the idea of meritocracy arrived just in time.

Meritocracy: A Dystopian Vision

After World War II, the word *eugenics* faded from daily conversation in the United States, and its history seemed to vanish into thin air. It gradually became less fashionable to talk about weeding out people once considered to be idiots, morons, or imbeciles. Yet sorting and tracking students had become standard practice in schools, hailed for efficiency. The labels of these categories may have changed, but the practice continued to quietly produce the results eugenicists hoped it would.

There are, of course, many educational alternatives to test-based practice. Yet in the twenty-first century, testing advocates feign shock that anyone would suggest such a possibility. Any mention of abolishing testing is met with questions about what would replace it, reinforcing the false notion that large-scale testing serves an essential educational function. Teachers striving to nurture each child's potential find themselves working around policy obstacles, because standardization has the opposite effect. While twenty-first-century education reform tries to speak the language of racial and class equity, anyone attending to outcomes can see they are exactly the opposite. While this puzzles some, others suspect that equity was never the policy's goal. In any case, it is clear that the high-stakes use of large-scale test scores is not the road to educational equity. The most troubling thing is that this should have been obvious from the start.

Segregationists had decades of practice adjusting the spin used to justify their actions. Ann Gibson Winfield, for example, explained how two reports were interpreted in a way that allowed a North Carolina school district to ignore, in full or in part, the 1954 *Brown v. Board of Education*–mandated desegregation of schools. A 1954 University of North Carolina report to the governor argued, "If local authorities could demonstrate that pupils of one race in a given grade could *not* be expected to participate and keep up with the students of the other race in the same grade level, then it is arguable that immediate integration of the two classes would be unreasonable and delay justifiable." In other words, until low-scoring students were "ready," meaning they had "caught up" to their peers, they should be segregated. If racial and class segregation is your goal, the demographic divide in test scores proves to be quite useful.[4]

Another document from New Hanover County referenced a report concluding that test scores had demonstrated "that 70% of African Americans were moronic or imbecile." This finding was used to raise the question: "Shall we integrate only those negroes who show mental ability with the Whites at the White standard of scholarship?"[5]

As these North Carolina documents show, racist ideas had not suddenly vanished; they remained an ongoing force in American society. Because of their demographic divides, test scores were used to justify continuing segregation. Winfield concluded that racial segregation was the goal, and testing was used as the tool used to obtain—and seemingly justify—that result.

The next important question, then, is how the continued use of large-scale testing has been sold to the public in the post-eugenic era.

For those looking to justify and maintain the American hierarchy while concealing White supremacist ideals, the notion of meritocracy was just the ticket. Its language was used, for example, to support the segregationist goals outlined in those North Carolina school documents. Meritocracy rests on the idea that people achieve the social rank they deserve through a combination of ability, self-discipline, and hard work. The word *merit* implies that an honor or position has been earned. Meritocratic ideals have become so embedded in our national narrative it seems they have always existed. Yet the term was not introduced until after World War II, by an author of a dystopian novel intended as satire.[6]

Sociologist Michael Young coined the term *meritocracy* in his book *The Rise of Meritocracy*, published in Britain in 1958. It described a society ruled "not so much by the people as by the cleverest people." Young's vision of the future is portrayed as his protagonist looks back from the year 2034, reflecting on a society that had been structured around test scores perceived as precise measures of intelligence and used as predictors of a student's future economic productivity. Students with the highest test scores were highly valued, nurtured, and educated in ways that would allow them to achieve their anticipated potential. The superior education and special opportunities these students received welcomed them into an elite class. This obvious inequality was considered just, based on the assumption that each person had an equal opportunity to achieve these heights. Young's novel follows the impact of this inequality as it grows wider and eventually leads to revolution.[7]

Young had focused his career on researching ways to create a just society. *The Rise of Meritocracy* was based on studies of historic patterns precipitated by the use of test scores. Examining these data allowed him to see through the illusion of equity often associated with testing. Young saw that despite the rhetoric, the social consequences of using tests as sorting mechanisms resulted in the same social structure that had always existed. Children disadvantaged by other social policies would wind up at the bottom of a test score–based hierarchy as well. According to journalist Margalit Fox, Young had concluded that "though the test-based system of advancement emerging in postwar Britain appeared to provide opportunity for all, it was . . . simply the centuries-old class system in sheep's clothing."[8]

And why not? The basic framework of the model that produced these scores had not changed since the time of eugenics. Nor had the interpretation of the scores' meanings. The only difference was the explanation used to promote the need for large-scale testing. As social ideology changed, tests were hailed as arbiters of equity, even while testing's divided outcomes told an entirely different story. People began to speak about test scores as if they were earned, rather than as products derived from a statistical model.[9]

Young did not seem to question the testing model itself or the results it produces. Yet he observed that most of the students receiving high scores continued to be from society's elite families, which he attributed to their access to better schools. No matter the reason, Young could see that a system that granted or limited opportunity according to the use of educational tests had inequality built into its framework.

Young's book predicted that a system of test-based "wholesale educational selection" would emerge in which test scores were used as indicators of merit and test-based systems became self-fulfilling prophecies. It follows that children would begin to believe what the test scores implied about their worth to society, and if their scores were low, quietly accept their lot in life. This would prevent uprisings, therefore benefiting those in power. Buying into this illusion of their own unworthiness, Young imagined, those disenfranchised by test scores would lose their will to protest and would simply give up. Meanwhile, those in society's upper echelons would find new peace, believing their positions had been rightly earned, putting their consciences at ease. Young explained that the elite might one day come to "actually believe they have morality on their side." Young hoped his social commentary might prevent what he considered a ridiculous and dangerous scheme from coming to pass.[10]

As you might have guessed by now, in the United States, the reaction to Young's book countered his intent. Meritocracy attracted the attention of the nation. If Young's story feels strangely familiar, it's because rather than heeding it as a warning, it seems US policy makers took a different perspective. Whereas Young believed "it is good to appoint individual people to jobs on their merit," Lemann explained, "the central principle of this modern American meritocracy was different: it was that people should be chosen not for their suitability for specific roles but for their general worth. . . . Hence it seemed right to select them by their grades and test scores . . . and to grant the high scorers a general, long-duration ticket to high status that could be cashed in anywhere." American leaders grabbed hold of Young's vision and spun it so that citizens would see an entirely different aspect of the issue than the one Young had intended to expose.[11]

In *The Big Test: The Secret History of the American Meritocracy,* journalist Nicholas Lemann continued: "In the United States, the appearance of *The Rise of Meritocracy* was duly noted by the key figures in education and testing, not so much with alarm over its dire predictions as with an appreciative chuckle over its wittiness. . . . These American men believed . . . that they were building an American meritocracy that would be much more stable and sustainable than the one in Young's book—a meritocracy that couldn't be toppled in a revolt. In fact, they believed . . . that a meritocracy, their meritocracy, could bring about a truly good and just society."[12]

Whether or not it is true that these men believed a test-based system could be just, they must have known they had to divorce testing from eugenics. Meritocracy was just the angle they needed. Their tests could be sold as the perfect instruments to accomplish the educational selection a meritocratic system relies on. Who could be opposed? It seemed everyone had a chance to win. People who could not have previously imagined themselves as part of the elite might now have reason to entertain dreams of working their way to the top. And those already there would feel vindicated by a test score's assurance that they had earned their positions.

The Great Equalizer?

It is true that test-based meritocracy granted access, including college entry, to some who had been previously denied opportunities. Some of those people have worked their way into positions of power. We can presume that opening opportunity to some is better than providing no chance at all. If social equity is the intended goal, meritocracy may seem a step in the right direction, but it is surely not an endpoint.

The social divisions inherent in test-based meritocracy were clear from the start. Yet meritocracy is used to reinforce the idea that America is a land of opportunity, where anyone can work their way up the economic ladder. That narrative fails to mention, however, that first they have to do well on the test.

And therein lies the challenge. Whatever rationale advocates use to justify large-scale testing, it doesn't change the fact that the test score divides exist, just as they always have. In fact, we've seen how segregationist ideologies have relied on these gaps to justify inequality. Test scores have been used to set people who are White and who are wealthy apart from all others. Accompanying policies have then enabled them to get much further ahead in a race for wealth and power than everyone else. No matter how the need for large-scale testing is explained, test scores place people in rank order. What that order is presumed to signify relies on interpretation. The test results once used to organize a society according to eugenic ideals have played an equally important role in a new story that touts education as the great equalizer. The language of meritocracy has simply flipped the script. While the divide in test results had not changed, politicians claim that tests give every person an equal chance to succeed. Open conversation about hereditary intelligence quieted, as did the language promoting eugenic ideals. Equal opportunity became the catchphrase that replaced them.

In a test-based meritocracy, even the most marginalized members of society are encouraged to view education as their opportunity to raise their social status. The propaganda promoting meritocracy's ideals leads us to believe that individuals control their own destiny, and that social policies have little or no influence on our lives. This effectively releases policy makers from responsibility in an ongoing system of caste.

Between the end of the eugenics movement and before the *Nation at Risk* report was released in 1983, there was little talk about demographic score gaps. With the advent of No Child Left Behind in 2002, however, politicians changed course and decided to address these gaps head-on. Rather than ignore their existence, NCLB policy showcased them. Politicians used them to blame teachers for what they suddenly called achievement gaps. This strategic move effectively silenced questions about the many possible reasons test score gaps exist, including questions about the model that produces the scores. Instead, test scores are treated as revealed truth, used to guide educational decisions every step of the way. Educators are expected to simply follow suit.

Much to his dismay, this move to test-based policy and its illusion of equity resonated eerily with Young's dystopian vision. Young saw it coming as early as 1991, when he wrote, "Much that was predicted has already come about. . . . A social revolution has been accomplished by harnessing schools and universities to the task of sieving people according to education's narrow band of values. . . . The new class has the means at hand, and largely under its control, by which it reproduces itself. . . . [Societies] have been deprived by educational selection of many of those who would have been their natural leaders . . . a standing opposition to the rich and powerful. . . . As a result, general inequality has been becoming more grievous with every year that passes."[13]

The mechanism of educational selection Young refers to is, of course, large-scale testing. We should be alarmed by his contention that score-based selection has intentionally prevented the rise of the very leaders who might liberate us all. And Young is not alone in warning there is danger ahead.

Daniel Markovits, author of *The Meritocracy Trap*, concurs, explaining that we have been seduced by the idea of meritocracy. Young and Markovits each cite meritocracy as a cause of the growing inequity in the United States rather than its solution. Like Young, Markovits understood how the rhetoric of meritocracy serves to benefit only the elite. Both authors agree that the rest of us have been hoodwinked. Markovits concluded, "The meritocratic achievement commonly celebrated today, no less than the aristocratic virtue acclaimed in the ancien régime, is a sham."[14]

Markovits explained that meritocratic ideals call for social and economic rewards to be based on a person's achievement, ability, effort, or output. This seems a different angle of the idea eugenicists promoted—which also presumes that people end up in the social position they deserve. Each paradigm claims that some are more deserving of society's wealth than others. Both assume a hierarchical social order that is decided through a competitive process. The difference is in the thinking behind how social worth is determined. Eugenicists proposed organizing society around intelligence, a trait that, in their view, was biologically predetermined. Meritocracy also included traits like effort and output, which are under an individual's control. In a meritocracy, some acknowledge that biology may still be at play, but personal responsibility is added to the mix.[15]

NCLB legislation focused not on intelligence but on student achievement. Achievement is determined by whether or not a child has met predetermined academic standards associated with each grade level. Furthermore, because large-scale testing was chosen as the instrument of measurement, the standards were limited to those that could be evaluated in that format. Testing therefore became the driving force behind education reform, and large-scale test scores became the measure of educational achievement. This legislation not only buoyed the testing industry, its demands for testing at every grade level opened whole new markets, this time at taxpayer expense. The public at large is at the mercy of decisions made by policy makers who promote the efficacy of scores that may have advantaged their friends and families for generations. This is yet another example of the self-serving policies Kendi described, and the racist ideas used to justify them, all based upon the false assumption that test scores reveal truth.

At this point, we can see how the strands of meritocracy and testing, science and statistics, are stitched together. Young predicted that inequality would grow in a test-based meritocracy, and so it has. Yet that prediction directly contradicts the rhetoric of twenty-first-century education policy, which claimed no child would be left behind. It also opposes the rhetoric of meritocracy, promoted as a competitive system in which everyone has an equal chance of success. After all, the only way to consider unequal outcomes fair is if you are convinced the playing field is even to begin with.

It is likely that some testing advocates continue to believe that demographic test score gaps are the result of biological determinism. The test results may match their expectation that White people and wealthy people will score above all others. Those who also believe that test scores adequately measure a mental trait that should be used to organize society would therefore have no concerns about test-based education policy. From this perspective, testing does the work society asks of it. As long as you can comfortably attribute the demographic differences in test scores to group differences in mental capacity, there is no contradiction; the tests are differentiating as they should. This requires, of course, ignoring the fact that biological evidence shows there is more genetic variation within racial groups than between them.

If, however, you do not believe that racial and class differences in test scores are caused by biological differences among groups, testing outcomes are harder to reconcile. In that case, given that we can predict a student's score range simply by knowing a test-taker's race and/or class, some may assume that the gaps indicate that something about the field of competition is uneven. Once we accept that there is no biological reason to expect mental traits to adhere to culturally designated divisions, we are left with two possibilities. One is to explain the demographic divides as evidence of racism and elitism in society. This view accepts the verdict of test scores, but attributes differences to the fact that the playing field of people's lives has never been even, and the inequities are often differentiated by race and class. For this reason, you might reject a test-based system even if you believe tests are objective measures of mental traits or achievement.

Another alternative is less often considered. As a teacher, I saw daily evidence of discrepancies between test scores and student performance. What if test scores don't actually mean what we're told they mean? What if educators are asked to base life-altering decisions on evidence we should not trust? What if, in fact, the model exacerbates test scores gaps? Given the societal damage caused by the high-stakes use of test scores, it is surely worthwhile to evaluate whether these tests can actually measure intelligence, ability, or achievement. Or should we, instead, heed the warnings of psychometricians who advise us not to take their meaning at face value? What if all along we have been persuaded to believe that test scores indicate something they don't?

Given the rhetoric of meritocracy, we are presented with a conundrum. If the competition for a place in the hierarchy plays out in a context where the outcome is rigged, meritocracy itself, as Markovits claims, is a sham. With meritocracy as the ideal, testing as the chosen measure of merit, and educators scapegoated and blamed for creating the test score divide, political leaders have seemingly absolved themselves of any responsibility for policies that not only reinforce but reproduce the long-standing social hierarchy. These factors work together to create the illusion that responsibility for economic success or failure lies solely in the hands of individuals. Racist outcomes are excused through use of a model whose promoters have declared it to be objective, its evidence therefore irrefutable.

Thus, we find ourselves in Young's dystopia, a place where testing has increased and the gaps of inequality have grown wider. Yet tests are embedded in a system widely considered to be just, even as the highest-quality schooling continues to be awarded to the highest-scoring students, whom we still define as the best and the brightest.[16]

Markovits contends, "The concept of merit is the taproot of the wrong." Kendi and other race scholars have helped us see that this root thrives due to soil conditioned by racism and elitism. It has, after all, been used as propaganda to convince people that there is actually a hierarchy of human worth. Markovits warned, however, "What is conventionally called merit is actually an ideological conceit, constructed to launder a fundamentally unjust allocation of advantage. Meritocracy is merely the most recent instance of the iron law of oligarchy." Hubris, along with racist ideas, led to the creation of the testing model. A test-based meritocracy, then, intertwines two "ideological conceit[s]," based on the idea that people are not equally worthy.[17]

The continued use of test scores to sort and separate students presumes that large-scale testing is the appropriate gauge for determining merit. Untangling the practice from its historic rationale reveals that while the social engineering goals of the eugenics movement are no longer stated outright, they continue to impact society.

Our next task, then, is to examine the processes used to create large-scale tests and the ideological framework used to interpret the results. This will allow us to decide for ourselves whether the tests are up to the task policy makers demand of them, and whether we actually want to live in a society organized by test results. To critique these opaque processes, we must open the black boxes in which they are housed and expose them to the light of day.

A Culture Framed by Illusions

8

Establishing a Culture
The Testing Model

There seems to be a widespread faith in the wizardry of psychometrics, a tacit belief that no matter what policymakers and educators want a test to do, we can somehow figure out how to make it work.

—Daniel Koretz, *Measuring Up*

Data

People's circumstances and life experiences bring them to see the world from different perspectives. This is certainly true for advocates and opponents of meritocracy as an ideology, hierarchy as an organizational structure, and large-scale testing as a sorting mechanism. At the outset of these chapters about standardized testing procedures, allow me to clearly state what may be obvious: I am not a statistician. I do not easily speak the language of numbers, and I admire those who are fluent. Because this way of conceptualizing the world taxes my mind, I need to pull away from the statistics from time to time to take a broader view. Each pause provides an opportunity to refocus on my interest: evaluating the relationship between a test score and its presumed meaning.

The power of test-based policy is, after all, in its social impact. Our acceptance of test-based outcomes is based on our faith in the veracity of test scores. Taking a broad view allows me to examine the assumptions behind each procedure and consider how they work together to define a score's meaning from conception to impact. As I break each procedure down into its simplest terms, my goal is to explain it clearly for those who, like me, may not be fluent in the language of psychometric culture.

I was introduced to psychometrics as a result of the cognitive dissonance I experienced after reading a pair of straightforward statements. Harvard psychometrician Daniel Koretz explained that "test design and construction entail a long series of trade-offs and compromises." This results in scores that do not fully reflect reality. And researcher Terry Hibpshman confirmed that interpreting a test score's meaning relies on a "chain of inference" to establish valid use. These statements raised a thousand questions as I considered them alongside policy that treats scores as accurate representations of the meaning ascribed to them. American society has placed its trust in testing, and that trust is shaken by words like *trade-offs, compromises,* and *inference.* As well it should be, it turns out.[1]

Questions have long been raised about the meaning of test scores. When asked about inherent inaccuracies in large-scale testing, proponents commonly reach for statements like *The system is not perfect, but it's the best we can do* and *Don't let the perfect get in the way of the good.* Koretz, for one, points out the absurdity of this stance. He explained it is like saying that "worrying too much about the accuracy of the data (or, to be more precise, the accuracy of the inference based on the data) stands in the way of gleaning useful information." But of course inaccurate information is *not* useful. Its application can, in fact, be downright dangerous. Yet twenty-first-century policy proceeds as if compiling mountains of data should take precedence over carefully studying what that information actually indicates.[2]

The risk in losing focus on the meaning is contained in the adage *Data don't lie.* What qualifies as a lie, however, depends on interpretation, which history clearly shows is a human—and often contentious—endeavor. As we learn how large-scale tests are produced, then, we'll return often to the question of meaning. This focus is difficult to maintain, but without it, it is far too easy to become lost in a statistical vortex. We'll begin by exploring some basic questions about testing.[3]

Test Basics

What Is a Test?

Assessment is critical to the process of teaching and learning. Paper and pencil tests are one of many ways to gain information about what students have learned. They can be far simpler than the complex series of steps required to produce large-scale, standardized tests. A test is simply a collection of carefully selected *items,* or questions, that test takers are asked to respond to.

The most straightforward way to summarize a test taker's responses is to compare the number of items answered correctly to the total number included on the test. This score lets you know the number of items the test taker got "right" or "wrong" according to the test's creator. This cumulative score is the reported result. When the score of a classroom test is shared with students and their families, everyone understands that it indicates a student's performance on a certain set of items tested on a given day in a specific context. All are aware the outcome is influenced by variable factors like a student's health, level of motivation, the temperature of the room, and other external and internal distractions. That score is not seen as an end point. It is understood, instead, as an estimate of a student's learning at a given moment in time.

And while a teacher may survey the responses of the class as a whole to get an idea of where a number of students might continue to struggle, or to temporarily group students to reteach a concept using a different strategy, the most useful information comes from studying individual responses. While a classroom test can give some insight about what each student knows and doesn't yet know, its scores don't contain any information about *why* test takers responded as they did. Yet that is the information most helpful to educators, and it can only be obtained in direct communication with each student.

For the purpose of evaluating learning, we can envision any score as a point on a continuum. While benchmarks are sometimes assigned to track a student's progress, in reality, learning has no end point in any subject area. Nor does it have a timeline or even a particular order. Many years of experience show me that learning looks different for different students. Therefore, the best information comes from assessments that are flexible and open-ended so students can demonstrate their learning in different ways.

The goals of standardization, however, are quite the opposite. It intentionally removes teachers from the direct contact necessary to gain such rich information. Therefore, large-scale test scores simply did not provide the data I needed to guide my teaching. I didn't understand this as the source of my frustration until I learned, as previous chapters explain, that these tests were developed for a different purpose entirely.

To summarize, early social statisticians imagined the possibility that a test might evaluate something much broader than, say, memorized multiplication facts. By using inferential statistics, they hoped to draw generalized conclusions about human mental capacity, not only for entire populations but also for individuals. This information could then be used to engineer society to operate more efficiently. Giant conceptual leaps eventually led to a testing model designed for this purpose.

To this end, a collection of items on a large-scale test is presumed to represent a much broader range of knowledge and skills than what is actually found on the test. This is called the test's *domain*. A domain might include overall mathematical ability, for example, or generalized literacy skills, or the nebulous idea that became known as intelligence quotient, or IQ. A domain might also include the specialized bundle of knowledge, skills, and dispositions a doctor, lawyer, or teacher might need. Of course, such domains are far too large to be tested directly. But demands for efficiency led the testing industry to develop models that would appear to report performance for domains that are difficult even to define, let alone measure.

As a result, when a student responds to a relatively small sample of test items on a large-scale test, psychometricians interpret the resulting score as an *estimate* of the score the student *might* have gotten *if* the entire domain could have been tested, and *if* the trait being measured (intelligence? achievement?) could have been accurately represented. Psychometricians are well aware that this is the best they can do.[4]

As test takers, we've all experienced how a sample domain can distort truth. We might, for instance, be asked to name the location of a particular mountain range we don't know, even though we would have been able to identify many others. We recognize that not knowing answers to that and other specific items will be interpreted as if we don't know much about geography— or even about social studies in general. We become frustrated because we understand that we know much more than the limits of the test allow us to demonstrate. We therefore correctly understand that the test is an inadequate measuring tool. And yet, somehow we continue to accept the use of test scores to determine the course of our futures, as individuals and as a society. Perhaps each of us thinks we are the exception—believing that perhaps the scores accurately represent achievement or intelligence for everyone else. Or perhaps we believe we are just not smart enough to grasp why we should rely on test scores.

But our intuition about what is happening is correct. Generalizing results from a small domain to a large one is no easy task. It is an indirect measurement that requires statistical manipulation and conceptual extrapolation. The mathematical model used to make such generalizations is complex, and it relies on inference at every step. When scores are used as if they actually indicate intelligence, achievement, or career readiness, these facts are obscured. Some testing advocates explain that the quality of the data is sacrificed in the name of efficiency. Yet surely a practice is only efficient if it effectively accomplishes its goal.[5]

Large-scale testing does not involve wizardry; nor is it the way of the universe. Many decisions go into the process of creating a large-scale test score: the breadth of the domain, which items are selected to represent it, how each item should be written, tested, and selected, and how results are scaled, reported, and interpreted. As with any model, each step was invented, tested, revised, and eventually standardized. Ultimately, of course, people assume the power to decide how test results should be interpreted and how scores should be used. Despite claims of objectivity, these decisions are all the result of human choices, shaped to meet the requirements of a model designed for a political purpose.

What Is a Test Score?

We can see, then, that the answer to "What is a test score?" depends on how a test is designed and how a score's meaning is interpreted. Psychometricians perceive a score's meaning quite differently from those who are impacted by policy built around this result.

Psychometricians understand a large-scale test score as "a proxy for a better and more comprehensive measure that *we cannot obtain.*" Take a moment to let that sink in. Because so many critical educational decisions are now based on use of these scores, this definition disturbs our thinking. Surely these conclusions should be drawn from information that we *can* obtain.[6]

Yet despite clear statements from those who create the tests, policy makers require educators to treat scores as if they are revealed truth. The problem here is a disconnect between the kind of solid evidence policy makers *wish* we could gather and the information the testing model is actually capable of producing. Koretz explains, "In most cases, the consumer of test scores—a parent learning about the performance of a child, a superintendent looking for strong and weak areas of performance in schools, a politician who wants to criticize schools or bask in the glow of their improvement—wants to draw conclusions about students' mastery of a large range of knowledge and skills. In the case of an end-of-course test, this might be something like the mastery of the concepts and skills of basic algebra. In other cases, the range of knowledge might be far broader . . . for example . . . the cumulative mastery of mathematics over many grades." Or, I would add, generalized academic achievement.[7]

This is a big ask. The testing industry does its best to meet policy makers' requests, but psychometricians' thorough understanding of statistics allows them to also know its limits. The history of test development clearly shows that psychometricians have always known that the best they can do is produce scores that *estimate* the mental capacity they are attempting to measure.

Whether policy makers share this understanding or not, No Child Left Behind declared that tests must be used *as if* they reveal truth, no matter how imperfectly scores match the meaning assigned to them. Yet declaring something to be truth doesn't make it any truer. Whatever policy makers hoped to accomplish, one thing is clear. Over twenty years later, test-based policy reinforces lines of racial and class division in American society. And that leads some of us to wonder what tests are truly for.

The Purpose of Testing: Conflation and Confusion

Clearly, there are different purposes for testing. While educators need assessment information to guide their teaching, previous chapters show that, historically, large-scale testing data have backed politically motivated social policy. Those policies relied on test score evidence that could be used to sort and separate people. The information gained from these tests is categorically different from data gathered to assess learning. Tests designed for these different purposes, then, should differ in scale, design, and interpretation.

The meaning of a large-scale test score is determined by its point of comparison. We've seen that scores from large-scale tests are reported according to their distance from a preestablished norm, represented as the highest point on a bell curve. This way of interpreting a score's meaning is called norm-referencing. Meaning is derived only through the scores' relationships to each other. The statistical model's procedures are designed to rank-order scores, not to provide nuanced information about what students have learned or are able to do.

In the early 1960s, educational psychologist Robert Glaser introduced a new paradigm as a stark alternative to norm-referencing. He suggested scores could be measured according to their proximity to a given standard or criteria rather than by their distance from a statistical average. This method of calibrating scores is called criterion-referencing. As we will see, large philosophical differences divide these two ways of interpreting scores.[8]

Yet in the twenty-first century, confusion abounds about the theoretical and practical differences between these interpretive frameworks. Many people don't even realize there *are* different ways of interpreting scores. Yet grasping these ideological discrepancies is critical to understanding how meaning is assigned to a score. Let's take a closer look at each framework to clarify our own understanding.

Norm-Referencing: Conceptual Assumptions

Chapters 4 and 5 explored the development of a norm-referenced testing model that serves as a framework for the development of large-scale tests. At this point, we'll add a further layer of complexity. If norm-referencing prioritizes placing scores in order according to a valued attribute, what exactly, in this day and age, is that attribute? If we no longer assume that most large-scale tests are measuring intelligence, what do they measure?

As you recall, the large-scale testing model rests on the premise that mental traits can be measured and quantified, and humans can be ranked accordingly. Galton imagined a broad intelligence that he believed to be inherent and stable throughout a person's life. In the early 1900s, Charles Spearman investigated Galton's concept and dismissed his use of the term *intelligence*. Instead, he conceptualized what he named the g-factor. The g stands for general. In this vague term, the testing model found its theoretical ground.[9]

What is the g-factor? Well, it's hard to explain, because no one really knows. Spearman thought of it as a kind of cerebral milieu that controls every aspect of our mental functioning. He described the g-factor as a "native capacity" far broader than intelligence, yet similarly inherent and stable throughout a person's lifetime. In 2000, an abstract of an article by Arthur Jensen called it simply a "property of the brain."[10]

We'll return to this notion of g later as we home in further on the concepts and assumptions used to assign meaning to scores. For now, though, let's follow the idea that norm-referenced tests are produced to detect differences in g among the human population. The order of the scores, then, represents what is assumed to be the natural variation in people's mental abilities.

Tests designed for norm-referencing focus on highlighting differences among scores. The abstract of Jensen's article states that "g cannot be described in terms of the tests' content, or even in psychological terms. It is actually a property of the brain." Therefore, as noted earlier, large-scale tests were not designed to detect differences in *learning* but rather to depict presumed differences in people's innate capacities *to* learn.[11]

Testing's statistical model was constructed around the use of the bell curve to chart this variation. By adding the g-factor to this equation, we now understand that scores from the norming group are assumed to depict how g exhibits in the larger population. This norm serves as a point of comparison.

The bell curve exaggerates the spread of scores to clarify their sequence and standardizes communication about the order of scores, which are reported according to their distance, or deviation, from the norm. The unit used to gauge and communicate this distance is called standard deviation (SD). When scores from any test are plotted on a bell curve, 34.13 percent of the scores will fall between the norm and a SD of +1 or −1; 13.59 percent of scores will lie between +/−1 and +/− 2 SD; 2.14 percent of scores will fall between +/−2 and +/−3 SD; and 13 percent are between +/− 3 and 4 SD. Thus, no matter how many items are on a test or what scale a test uses, when scores are placed on a bell curve, they can be reported as percentiles, which makes comparisons possible among tests, over time, and across contexts. [12]

To summarize, norm-referencing is based on this series of assumptions: the g-factor exists as an inherent trait; large-scale tests depict its expression; and its variance is significant. These assumptions, however, are open to question on many fronts.

Criterion-Referencing: An Ideological Shift

Criterion-referencing was, in fact, an ideological shift away from the assumptions of norm-referencing. Rather than focus on the order of the scores, the goal of criterion-referencing is to gain specific, accurate information about student learning. There is no need to generalize the meaning of test results, and therefore no reason to debate the g-factor's existence. In the model's purest form, the scores' sequence is irrelevant. As UCLA professor emeritus James

Popham wrote, criterion-referencing is "regarded as the most appropriate assessment strategy for educators who focus more on *teaching* students than on *comparing* them."[13]

The philosophy behind criterion-referencing grew from Robert Glaser's interest in how the theories of psychologist B. F. Skinner might apply to education. In the 1950s, Skinner introduced behaviorist theory, which holds that people respond in similar, predictable ways when exposed to the same stimuli. This led Glaser and other researchers to propose that once a set of teaching methods was proven effective, it could be standardized for use across the nation and all students would be successful in school. Sounds simple, right?

To achieve this goal, researchers needed a test that would accurately evaluate student learning. Then, as a teacher followed a specific protocol, frequent testing would measure student progress over time. Successful teaching would be indicated by test scores clustered around a mark selected to indicate achievement. In that case, that specific sequence of teaching methods would be documented, published, and widely distributed in what became known as *programmed instruction*.[14]

The problem was, as Popham wrote, "to support actionable instructional decisions about how best to teach students, norm-referenced inferences simply don't cut it." Large-scale tests were not built to evaluate learning, so they couldn't provide the data researchers needed. Researchers were watching for scores to cluster as a sign that most students had learned the information. They soon realized that placing scores on a bell curve had the opposite effect. Even if raw scores are clustered, the bell curve's function is to spread them out again. Therefore, even when all students achieve at a high level, when scores are placed on a bell curve, it doesn't appear that way. They are instead depicted as a normal distribution. In the chapters to come, we'll see that the assumption behind the testing model's processes values maintaining the order and spread of the scores over what they might tell us about what students have learned.[15]

Instead, these researchers needed a testing model designed to focus on test content. Yet no such model existed to test on a large scale. Rather than the broad domain needed for testing generalized mental ability, Glaser and his colleagues needed tests with narrow, specific domains.

So Glaser proposed producing tests in which scores would be referenced to a "clearly described cognitive domain or body of knowledge" rather than to a norm. This testing framework became known as criterion-referencing.[16]

The theory behind criterion-referencing might sound familiar. It echoes through twenty-first-century education policy's common standards, programmed instruction, and frequent testing. The stated goal was to ensure that all students succeed.

So why hasn't it worked?

Well, there are at least two reasons. One is the disconnect between the hopes of standardization and the reality of human variation. The other involves how policy translates into practice.

Problems

Standardization

The goal of standardization is uniformity. Some believe that if the playing field is leveled, people can make fair judgments about the varying traits or abilities of others. Therefore the primary objective of test design is to create conditions in which test takers "face the same tasks, administered in the same manner and scored in the same way."[17]

The problem, however, is that people are not standard. Nor are the conditions of their lives. So despite every attempt to standardize the context, a multitude of variables cannot be controlled. Education cannot be treated as a simple science experiment because children vary in so many ways that researchers could never account for them all, let alone control for these variables.

So experienced teachers take a different approach. We understand that ambiguity requires flexibility. Few would expect one method to be effective for all learners, so we tailor classroom instruction and assessment to the context of our teaching. We know we must draw from a variety of approaches to serve individuals who learn differently from one another. Our daily experiences lead us to understand, as parents do, that that each child is unique. Despite rhetoric to the contrary, teachers have always been accountable—to the children, families, and communities we serve. They, of course, are not uniform. They do not respond to the same stimulus in the same ways. To meet their varying needs, educators draw from experience and rely on professional judgment, just as doctors and lawyers do. That is, we did . . . until policy mandated a behaviorist approach.

Standardized testing flatlines the dynamics of human relationships. Of course the complexities of learning cannot be magically transformed into a single number. In contrast to the rich, nuanced information gleaned from daily classroom interactions, large-scale testing data are one-dimensional. Yet since the time of eugenics, we have been socialized to believe that testing data are more valuable precisely *because* they are removed from a human context. Dehumanization is hailed as the hallmark of objectivity, as if such disconnect is possible. While previous chapters reveal a testing model influenced by the values of the people who created it, educators are expected to treat testing data as pure, and parents are to accept uniform, policy-based judgments as worthy of their trust.

With the advent of No Child Left Behind, policy rhetoric shifted to the ideology of criterion-referencing. Yet accountability models simultaneously reinforced the use of scores to make comparisons. To make valid comparisons, data must be statistically equivalent over time and context. This demand for uniformity circumvented the invention of an entirely new testing model that would prioritize content over the order of the scores. In coming chapters, we'll see how this choice affects the quality of the information gained. Its impact is greatest when the meaning of scores derived from this standard model is interpreted as if the scores are criterion-referenced.

Standards-Referenced Interpretive Framework

If that last sentence raised questions for you, you're not alone. Once I grasped the significant differences between norm- and criterion-referencing, I was even more baffled by the Praxis exams. Scores are reported in norm-referenced ways, as percentiles, yet the exams are used as minimum competency tests, which implies criterion-referencing. I wondered how policy makers' ideological pivot had impacted large-scale test design and interpretation.

It took some digging, but I finally reached the source of a problem that lies at the intersection of policy and practice. It seems that rather than create a new evaluative tool designed to measure student learning, psychometricians simply adjusted a few parts of the existing model and policy makers called it good. The model with a few additional procedures is the standards-referenced interpretive framework.

Michael J. Young and Sasha Zucker, authors of a 2004 report for the testing company Pearson, explained this new adaptation. "The standards-referenced interpretive framework, a recent innovation in assessment design that incorporates elements from both the norm- and criterion-referenced frameworks, has emerged as a solution to the increasingly complex requirements of a series of educational reform initiatives." What the authors don't say is that the complexities result from conflicting ideologies. Instead, they tout the benefits of merging "elements from the two traditional interpretive frameworks thereby yielding more information than either framework alone."[18]

The testing industry had again rallied to meet policy that required districts to report scores referenced to both norms and state learning standards, which served as the criteria. But does this adapted model actually yield more or different information? And what is the quality of that information?

While large-scale tests had previously been designed to make local, national, and international comparisons, districts now had to report student progress on standards specific to each state. It seems this would be a daunting task for the testing industry. In practice, however, the tests given in each state remain largely similar. Young and Zucker describe two relatively small modifications that were made. One affects the norm-referenced interpretation of scores, the other the interpretation presumed to be referenced to state standards.

You'll recall that norm-referencing requires a norming group to establish the bell curve's highest point, which represents the mean, median, and mode. These groups were traditionally drawn from test takers across the nation. The standards-referenced framework, however, limits comparisons "to the students of the state for which the assessment was designed." Young and Zucker explain that norms are established by those who take the test the first year it is given in a state. These students' scores establish the norms to be used as points of comparison for all who take the test from that point onward.[19]

The second modification addresses how scores are referenced to state standards. Criterion-referencing, remember, requires that test content aligns with what was taught. When tests were created for nationwide use, psychometricians developed test content by drawing from a "national consensus curriculum" they had created. This document listed standards states held in common. While adoption of the Common Core Standards would have been helpful to them, variations in standards are still relatively minor, so test developers continue to use this national consensus curriculum as a starting point. Then they study each state's standards and make any necessary adjustments. Discrepancies are "resolved by augmenting the test with additional items that match any content standards not covered by the original test." Because this was the only change in content, large-scale tests remain remarkably similar nationwide.[20]

According to Young and Zucker's report, that is pretty much the extent of the changes made to a testing model designed to prioritize the rank-ordering of scores that are now also interpreted as if they are criterion-referenced. So few changes were made, in fact, that the standards-based interpretive framework is described as an *augmented norm-referenced test*. Indeed, it appears that the primary shift is not in the model but in the rhetoric used to justify how scores are interpreted.[21]

Young and Zucker clearly accept claims based on the premise that the resulting scores can be interpreted as standards-based. In their view, these tests can be used not only to compare scores but also "can potentially provide a more complete, efficient understanding of a student's educational achievement and progress . . . which can be used for a broader range of purposes." Note that by adding the word *potentially*, they are hedging their bets. Nonetheless, they explain that the US Department of Education concurred, accepting these scores to meet NCLB and subsequent policy reporting requirements. And although the content of Praxis exams does not vary from state to state, each state sets its own cut scores, a process we'll soon explore.[22]

The difference between norm- and criterion-referencing reminds us that the meaning ascribed to a test score is always a matter of interpretation. Yet given the juxtaposition of ideology and purpose, how is it possible to accept that simply augmenting a norm-referenced model means the scores can also be interpreted as measures of student learning?

In short, it's possible because government regulators have accepted the testing industry's adjustments. When so few people understand how the model works and the assumptions behind it, there are relatively few informed skeptics. And to the great relief of administrators, the standards-based interpretive framework makes it possible for districts to comply with federal and state reporting requirements. Yet if the model has changed only slightly, how can we assume the meaning of the information has changed so dramatically?

The answer, of course, is that it hasn't. Once again, it seems we are flying on faith. And because large-scale tests continue to be built on a model designed for norm-referencing, it's time to explore the series of procedures that produce a score and the assumptions that assign it meaning.

9

Test Design

Mathematical models, by their nature, are based on the past, and on the assumption that patterns will repeat.

—Cathy O'Neil, *Weapons of Math Destruction*

Components of Test Design

Young and Zucker's report makes it clear that the interpretation of a score's meaning has once again been bent to the will of policy. As a teacher-educator whose students were forced to adhere to conclusions delivered by a Praxis exam score, I saw firsthand how test-based policy impacts the lives of individuals and communities. No one at Berea College or in its teacher education program was consulted about the decision to base admission or certification on scores from this test. It was instead a decision made by someone in a distant government office, explained as a way to improve teacher quality. The practice disempowers every person involved in the educational process.

As the previous chapter clarifies, test scores result from a model that assumes it can discern people's natural mental abilities and rank them accordingly. If at this point, the procedural details have not convinced you this is true, or your value system dissuades you from believing it is necessary, you may feel compelled to raise critical questions. Those questions will be strengthened by gaining more information about how the test design process works. So using the Praxis series as a representative example, the next few chapters will take a close look at how a test is produced for large-scale use and how meaning is assigned according to the model's assumptions. Like me, you may find the information hard to believe.

The ETS website briefly outlines its test development process. To create a test, it explains, ETS employees define criteria, form committees of professionals to determine content domain, write and review test items, pretest those items, find and delete unfair questions, compile the test, and then, once the test is in actual use, check to be sure each item is functioning as expected.[1]

The Praxis II exam, remember, strives to name and evaluate the entry-level knowledge and skills necessary for candidates to be considered *classroom-ready*, a broad domain indeed. The art and science of teaching demands such a complex, interwoven set of skills, knowledge, and dispositions that it is daunting to try to even try to name them, let alone tease them apart and represent them as test items. Yet a passing score is interpreted to mean a candidate has met that standard.

Clearly, for a criterion-referenced score, the process of determining the content domain and selecting test items is critical to interpreting a score's meaning. In fact, the Praxis technical manual explains, "the main source of validity evidence for licensure tests comes from the alignment between what the profession defines as knowledge and/or skills important for safe and effective practice and the content included on the test." The test development process begins, then, by establishing this alignment.[2]

Job Analysis and Test Content Selection

In creating the Praxis exam, ETS conducts a *job analysis* to determine factors practitioners define as "important for safe and effective practice." Tests that focus on curriculum standards rather than job performance follow a similar procedure called a *curriculum analysis*. Knapp and Knapp, creators of the job analysis procedure, describe it as "the systematic collection of data describing the responsibilities required of a professional" that is used to determine a test's domain. Psychometricians and policy makers accept job analysis as "the foundation upon which to build a viable and legally defensible licensure examination."[3]

The *Technical Manual* for the Praxis series outlines three steps in creating a job analysis: describing a domain of knowledge and skills, reviewing and revising the domain descriptions, and using the resulting list to survey a range of professionals. Early in the process, ETS convenes a National Advisory Committee (NAC), described as a panel of experts, to support this process.

ETS conducts separate job analyses for the many specialized tests that make up the Praxis series, and a NAC is convened for each one. Committee members can be nominated by professional organizations, superintendents, deans, or colleagues, or educators can self-nominate.

The goal is for each NAC to consist of "approximately 15 experts in the field—practicing teachers, teacher educators, and administrators." The ETS manual states that "the committee that is formed: Is diverse with respect to race, ethnicity, gender; is representative of different practice settings, grade levels, and geographic regions; and reflects different professional perspectives." This statement is made matter-of-factly, but with such a small committee size, it must be difficult to achieve this range of diversity. Yet ETS relies on this presumption, as the committee's approval is cited as evidence that the test development process is "fair and reasonable to subgroups of practitioners and test-takers."[4]

For a job analysis in professions in which there are wide-ranging views about "theoretical orientation or professional practice," Knapp and Knapp considered fifteen participants "barely enough." Certainly that is true of education, a field guided by many different philosophies. These differing perspectives often evoke lively discussion and debate among educators.[5]

Because the job analysis is critical to establish valid use, you might expect that, given the diversity of views, the NAC's work would center around in-depth conversations about what beginning teachers should know and be able to do. This, after all, ultimately defines what a Praxis score is supposed to *mean*. In most states, passing scores are used to determine certification, a determination that a candidate is adequately prepared to enter a classroom.[6]

Despite its importance, however, the Praxis manual does not describe an invitation to energetic debate. Quite the opposite, in fact. The manual outlines a process streamlined for efficiency, with ETS employees guiding every step to ensure that test design specifications are met. These requirements, in fact, dictate every step of the testing model; that is the nature of standardization. So, although the word *advisory* is in the committee's title, the Praxis manual explains that the first part of the NAC's role "is basically to review and revise the draft domain so that it adequately defines the knowledge and/or skills important for safe and effective entry-level practice."[7]

Before the NAC even holds its first meeting, ETS employees create this "draft domain" by reviewing the literature and listing the knowledge and skills deemed important for entry-level teaching. Testing parameters require limiting the list to "observable work behaviors and tasks and work products . . . as opposed to personality and other individual characteristics that are not directly observable." Those individual characteristics are also critical to successful teaching, however, and teacher education programs have long emphasized their importance. It is true that they cannot be measured on a large-scale test, which makes the evaluations of mentor teachers and education faculty all the more valuable. Yet when a test serves as the gatekeeper for professional entry, these critical qualities are left out of the equation entirely.[8]

When the NAC convenes for the first time, then, its role is simply to approve the list of knowledge and skills produced by ETS employees in accordance with the test's limitations. The committee's responsibility is simply to consider each statement to determine whether it is clearly written and important for the "safe and effective practice" of entry-level teachers. If a statement does not meet those criteria, committee members can recommend its elimination. That completes the NAC's first round of work.[9]

Once there is an approved list, ETS sends it to a larger sample of practitioners. Respondents are asked to rate, on a scale of 1-4, each item's importance for entry-level teaching. An example of such a survey of elementary teachers and teacher educators included two broad categories: knowledge areas and critical thinking. The critical thinking section included items like "adaptive reasoning: applying existing information to new situations." The educators were to ask themselves: on a scale of 1-4, how important is it that entry-level teachers can apply adaptive reasoning? Knowledge areas were then broken into subject areas like math and social studies, each further divided into subcategories like "major concepts in political science," followed by a narrower topic such as "nature and purpose of government."[10]

Once ETS collects these surveys, it reports the mean rating of each item. Then the NAC meets a second time. Its members review the outcomes and, "under the guidance of ETS test developers . . . construct the test content specifications." This does not mean they write the items that will appear on the test. Far from it. Instead, the committee approves language that will appear on the documents describing a test's parameters, including, for example, purpose and audience; the major categories of knowledge and skills a test will include; a detailed description of each category; the length of the test; the kinds of items that make up the test (multiple choice, constructed response, and so on); and ways in which the test complies with ETS *Standards for Quality and Fairness*.[11]

Reading about the role of the NAC shatters any illusion about meaningful educator involvement in establishing test content. I wondered why ETS would go to the trouble and expense to hold NAC meetings when members have so little opportunity to influence test content. The Praxis manual led me to understand that the existence of the NAC allows ETS to claim that educational experts are involved in test development—a factor they say is critical to establishing the valid use of test scores.[12]

The Praxis manual also states, "The involvement of various subgroups of experts also is part of the process of developing a test that is considered fair and reasonable to subgroups of practitioners and test-takers." This is code to say this is one way they can claim that test items are not biased to favor any group. Apparently if the few committee members representing "subgroups" are willing to say all is well regarding fairness, then all must *be* well.[13]

Test Item Development: An Overview

Once I learned how categories of test content are established, I wondered about the process of writing the actual test. The ETS website "How Tests and Test Questions Are Developed" states that "dozens of professionals—including test specialists, test reviewers, editors, teachers and specialists in the subject or skill being tested—are involved in developing every test question or 'test item'" to ensure they meet the "highest standards of quality and fairness in the testing industry."[14]

Let's look beneath the surface of this statement, at least insofar as we are able. Because while ETS manuals share guidelines and standards for test item development, they share little of the actual process. The website states that test items are written by "ETS staff or item development committees" following a "rigorous set of guidelines," a phrase hot-linked to the *Standards for Quality and Fairness*, which we'll return to shortly. The website explains that during an internal review, items are accepted "only if they meet . . . criteria for the standard being measured, have excellent technical qualities, [and] have appropriate difficulty and cognitive levels."[15]

While it's true that each test item is carefully considered, the primary focus is to select items that produce scores that clearly divide test takers. Harold Berlak, an independent researcher, explained, "Test makers attempt to compose test items so there will be a suitable ratio of correct to incorrect responses." The "suitable ratio" is represented by the bell curve. In other words, *psychometricians purposefully produce items to ensure test takers' responses follow a normal curve of error.* For individual items and for the test as a whole, this result is considered the mark of high quality, based on the assumption that the bell curve represents the "natural" order of human mental functioning. Tests are created to produce the result psychometricians assume is "correct."[16]

Therefore, items are not designed to evaluate whether students have mastered test content. They are instead created to differentiate test takers according to the presumed g-factor. Berlak explained, in fact, that if a large number of test takers respond to items correctly, they "would be revised or abandoned *even if there was unanimous consensus that the items tapped an educationally significant body of knowledge or set of skills.*"[17]

This focus directly counters a criterion-referenced interpretation of scores, as described in the previous chapter, in which items should closely represent what is taught and success is marked by scores that cluster around a correct response. The model's test item selection process has not changed, however. It is built to ensure there will always be a spread of scores. Each time these scores are interpreted as if they are criterion-referenced, it makes it appear that teaching goals have not been met.

Scores produced by this model should not, in fact, be treated as if they are criterion-referenced. Just the opposite. The model is designed to *preclude* a direct correlation between scores and test content. This presumably allows scores to represent a meaning far beyond what could ever be demonstrated by a single set of items.

This profound disconnect illustrates why Popham and Husek, writing in 1969, explained that while they could imagine how scores produced by a test designed for criterion-referencing might also be interpreted in reference to a norm, they could not imagine how the situation could ever work in reverse. Yet as the last chapter explained, that is just what is happening. Policy makers accept an interpretation of scores that, although based on an augmented norm-referenced testing model, claims to achieve both goals.[18]

Item Analysis

To find out which items produce bell curve–shaped results, large testing companies field-test them in an unscored portion of a test. Then psychometricians evaluate and rate each item according to its difficulty and quality. Items are carefully selected to act in concert, so item selection shapes the results of the test as a whole. It's important, then, to know how psychometricians define difficulty and quality.[19]

Item Difficulty

The goal of rating items according to their difficulty is to assemble a collection of items that produce a "normal" curve. When a test or an item is rated "too hard" or "too easy," it means it didn't create the expected spread of scores. Psychometric theory interprets that to mean that the item didn't successfully differentiate among the varying aptitudes of test takers.[20]

Item difficulty is rated by comparing correct and incorrect responses. It is often communicated as the p-value: the proportion of students who answer the item correctly is expressed as a decimal between 0 and 1. An item with a p-value closer to 1 is treated as a relatively easy item; a ratio closer to 0 is considered a more difficult item. This simple average can be misleading if an entire group happens to be very high or low scoring, but much of the time, the p-value serves to estimate item difficulty. If an item performs differently than expected, it might be flagged for further review.[21]

Item Quality

A second aspect of item analysis is evaluating each item's quality to ensure the test maintains a consistent level of difficulty from year to year and across all versions. Like item difficulty, quality is defined by how well the item discriminates among test takers, but in this case, a point of comparison is added using a process called biserial correlation or point-biserial correlation.[22]

In general, correlations express the strength of the association between two variables guided by the question: how likely is it that one influenced the other? Biserial correlation was developed by Karl Pearson (see chapter 5) to estimate the strength of correspondence between test takers' overall scores and their abilities. If a test item is performing as designed, psychometricians expect the most able test takers to answer the most difficult items correctly, while test takers of lower ability would not. Given the goal of differentiation, this seems to make sense. Admissions test expert Jay Rosner explained, "If you are a psychometrician designing a test, you want the students who are adept at the test to tend to answer the questions correctly, and the students who are not adept to answer incorrectly." Theoretically, this outcome indicates that the collection of items is able to accurately discriminate among the differing abilities of test takers. This, of course, is based on two big assumptions: that the items accurately evaluate the trait being tested, and that there is value in ranking test takers accordingly.[23]

The tricky part is that to make this comparison, psychometricians need a way to determine a test taker's *ability*. For an intelligence test, for example, they would want to know how intelligent each test taker actually is. For an achievement test, they would presumably need to determine which students are "naturally" the most able. If this seems confusing, it's because the only measure of such nebulous domains has been produced by the large-scale tests themselves. This left psychometricians in a conundrum.

In any field of study, researchers are expected to publicly define their terms. Explaining how you assign meaning to a word like *ability* is called *operationalizing* the term. Once operationalized, that definition is taken as a given, an assumption upon which the study or model is based. In short, researchers can choose how to define any term they use, as long as they share these basic assumptions.

Within a given profession, operationalized definitions of frequently used terms tend to become normalized. Everyone within a field is trained to understand and accept how concepts are communicated in the context of that profession. We saw in previous chapters, however, that operationalized definitions can cause confusion when commonly used words are defined differently than in normal use. When that happens, people outside the field sometimes gain a skewed understanding of what a study's results or a model's outcomes actually mean, which can lead to misuse of the data. The resulting misunderstandings also make it more difficult, but critically important, for those outside a field to carefully analyze standard practices.

Returning to the question of how psychometricians should operationalize the term *ability* reminds us that early on, Galton used social status to indicate ability. He simply assumed that those in the highest ranks were in those positions *because* they were more able than others, and that the inverse was also true. Later, ETS psychometricians made a different, yet still troubling, choice. Psychometrician Nancy Cole explained that ETS has "for good reasons reduced the very word ability to mean operationally 'test score.'"[24]

Yes . . . test score: the overall score on the test for which they are analyzing the items.

Psychometricians decided that people with high scores on the test overall must have the highest abilities relative to the trait being tested; those with low scores are assumed to have the lowest abilities. Put simply, psychometricians chose to operate as if the scores produced by the tests they create equals truth.

Cole, who served as president of ETS from 1994 to 2000, recognized that this was likely to cause problems. She acknowledged the "very central public concern that test scores may not adequately reflect ability" in the usual sense of the word. Cole explained that while test scores may *not* reflect test takers' abilities, psychometricians had little choice but to treat them as if they do. Little choice? This makes it sound like psychometricians forged ahead with creating a model regardless of whether it produces accurate information or not. To be clear, I use "accurate" to mean the test correctly measures what it says it measures.

Apparently, this was a practical decision. When the term *ability* is operationalized as *test score,* it allows psychometricians to group test takers according to their cumulative score. Point-biserial correlation can then measure the strength of the association between a group's scores on the test as a whole and that group's performance on each specific test item.[25]

Because this is one of many examples of how a score's meaning becomes lost in the trade-offs required for the model to function, it's worth further exploration. Let's consider this definition of *ability* in terms of the statistical processes used to assess the quality of a test or item.

First, test takers are separated into groups *according to their scores on the test as a whole.* Within each group, the number of correct and incorrect responses is tallied for each item. If the correlation between performance on the test overall and performance on an item is high (indicated as near +1), psychometricians determine that the item matches the difficulty level of the test overall. Such an item is evaluated as high quality and is considered a good fit for the test. If the correlation is low (−1), the item is considered to be of low quality and is most often excluded from use on the test. Remember the assumption associated with this practice is that this correlation shows the test has truly discriminated in ways that match the test takers' actual abilities.[26]

By now, alarm bells may be sounding. Because when a test score is assumed to indicate a test taker's *ability,* we understand that psychometricians are operating under the assumption that the test has quantified the trait of interest. The ramifications of this practice are that test items are selected to match the abilities of those who are good or poor test takers. As upcoming chapters will clarify, we really have no idea how that correlates with their level of mental functioning. We do know, however, that far higher percentages of White people and wealthy people have received higher test scores since testing's origins, and now we *also* know that each test item is calibrated and selected to match, and therefore maintain, those results from year to year. We can only wonder how far back that repetition extends.

Outcomes of Test Item Selection

As we begin to understand that test item selection treats a test's results as truth, we are left to wonder about the impact of this practice. Could this be a reason tests continue to produce score gaps that mimic the results eugenicists expected? Jay Rosner wondered, too. "These gaps have been constant for decades . . . [and] there are well-known external factors that contribute to these imbalances." Yet he pursued an additional—and critical—question: "*But what if test design is also to blame?*"[27]

Rosner's search for the root cause(s) of testing's consistent demographic score gaps led him to examine test item selection. He managed to purchase two years of data from ETS, which allowed him to analyze the items selected for use on the 1988 and 2000 versions of the SAT. ETS has since redesigned the SAT, but Rosner assures us that score gaps continue. In 2016, for example, he found "boys outscore girls by a few points on the verbal section (recently renamed reading and writing) and by more than 30 points on the math section. We also know that whites outscore blacks and Latinos on verbal (by 98 points and 80 points, respectively) and on math (by 106 points and 76 points, respectively.)"[28]

The SAT data allowed Rosner to correlate the demographic information of test takers with each test item selected for use on the math and the verbal sections of the SAT. From there, he calculated the percentage of students from each demographic group who had responded correctly to each item and labeled it accordingly. Items answered correctly by higher percentages of White test takers, for example, were labeled *White*. *Neutral* items were those answered correctly by an equal percentage of, say, Hispanic and White test takers. Rosner had planned to also assign labels to items answered correctly by a higher percentage of African American test takers . . . except *there were none.*

Rosner found that *every single question selected for use on both the verbal and math sections of the SAT had been answered correctly by higher percentages of White test takers than African American test takers*—on all sections of the test and for both years Rosner studied. Not one question was even categorized as neutral.[29]

The implications are astonishing. No wonder there are demographic gaps in test scores. The SAT was introduced during the eugenics era, in 1926. Then, test items required familiarity with European-American culture and experiences available only to the wealthy. (A copy is linked in the notes.) Although there is much debate about what, if anything, SAT scores indicate, they were, and often still are, used in college-entry decisions. The items have changed, of course, but for those aware of testing's history and the item selection process, perhaps Rosner's findings aren't surprising. Certainly at the time it was developed, the test performed exactly as expected, producing results that matched its creators' beliefs. What do we make of the fact that twenty-first-century policy exponentially *expanded* the reach and consequences of tests that continue to produce these results?[30]

Rosner correlated information for other demographic groups as well. In each instance, he found the items selected advantaged higher-scoring groups. Comparing results for women and men on the math portion of the test, Rosner found only *one* SAT question answered correctly by a higher percentage of women. Comparing results of White test takers with those who identified as Hispanic, Rosner found *one* neutral question and *one* question answered correctly by a higher percentage of Hispanic test takers.

Rosner calls the advantage that results from test item selection procedures a "head-wind." You might wonder about the results of further research. Yet on that question we are left to wonder, because although ETS claims that the new SAT is more transparent, the College Board keeps a "vice grip" on item-level data.[31]

We do know, however, that test score gaps are holding steady, and policy has exacerbated the divided destruction of score-based decisions. This leads us to view affirmative action measures in a new light. Far from being an "extra leg up," affirmative action is a step toward balancing a system that favors White test takers. It is, in fact, a course correction that compensates for at least some of the score gap created by testing procedures. Opponents call affirmative action unfair when in fact exactly the opposite is true. It is the rapid demise of affirmative action that returns us to a skewed system.

No one explains this, however, and many are left with the false impression that institutions have "lowered their standards" when they admit students from lower-scoring groups. Imagine the damage that causes. Furthermore, no such adjustments are made at the K-12 level. Believing the scores to be true, educators lower their expectations for lower-scoring students right from the start, and those children lose confidence in their own abilities. Whenever the illusion of objective, accurate tests is preserved, those marginalized by the system are, as usual, left to take the hit.[32]

Rosner's findings also explain why score gaps appear on every type of tests. In a 2013 email, Rosner shared that the correlation among scores on "bubble tests" is so high that scores from one test often reliably predict a test taker's score on any other test. This makes sense once we understand that large-scale tests are all built from a model that builds score consistency into every test it creates. Yet, in an endless cycle, psychometricians interpret this built-in consistency as evidence of the test's high quality, believing it means each test has measured the g-factor.[33]

Research is also impacted by this belief. Because of the strong correlation among tests, the results of one test are used to "prove" the efficacy of another. In a policy report for ETS, for example, Drew Gitomer claimed that the strong relationship between SAT and Praxis scores demonstrated that the Praxis exam was indeed filtering out candidates of lower ability. His basic assumption, of course, was that candidates' abilities were adequately defined by their scores on the SAT.[34]

The twenty-first-century's test-based mandates have turned what Rosner called a headwind into a hurricane. The legacy of eugenics persists in the system's outcomes, and that should have been clear from the start. Leaders have asked nothing of the testing industry except to keep producing tests for ever broader application. Given how these pieces fit together, you may wonder how, exactly, policy makers expected that No Child would be Left Behind when they attached rewards and consequences to demographically divided scores. That is a question of intent, and while we may not find a definitive answer, this question serves as backdrop for the next chapter.

10

Collateral Damage

The assumptions which are intrinsic to the technology of standardized and most criterion-referenced tests are untenable.
—Harold Berlak, "The Need for a New Science of Assessment"

Intent versus Outcome

When civilians are killed during a military strike, the loss of life is sometimes referred to as collateral damage. Their deaths may result from error in the system or because they were, unfortunately, in a targeted area. Before a strike is launched, military leaders weigh the costs, often measured in human lives, against the perceived gain. In evaluating the success or failure of a mission, civilian deaths are accepted without consequence unless they greatly exceed expectations. So, while collateral damage is anticipated, the term implies innocence on the part of the aggressor. The deaths of innocents are considered incidental, an unfortunate twist of fate. No one is considered at fault, so no one is held accountable. But for those caught in the line of fire, intent makes no difference. The consequences are the same; dead is dead.

This analogy helps us consider two important aspects of test-based policy. One is that once a harm is rendered, the question of intent is a moot point. To those on the receiving end, it simply doesn't matter whether an act was intentional or not. Outside a court of law, the consequence is all that matters. The other parallel is a question of proximity. If those inflicting the harm cannot directly see the results of their actions, it makes things a little easier for them. It is hard for a feeling, caring person to live with the knowledge you have hurt or killed someone. But if you can't see the details of the destruction, your imagination can downplay the degree of harm.

When it comes to racial discrimination, the US legal system has adopted a line of thinking similar to that of collateral damage. Lawyer john a. powell explains that to bring a legal claim of racial discrimination, a plaintiff must prove the defendant's racist *intent*, regardless of the impact that results from the action. Intent is an internal quality, so, of course, it is nearly impossible to prove. This may be why, even outside of court, our attention is drawn to questions of intent rather than policy outcomes. Yet whether intentional or collateral, damage is only visible in the final result. A cost-benefit analysis must therefore consider the system as a whole, from outset to impact, as anticipated harm is considered alongside potential gain.[1]

The possibility of error, and therefore of collateral damage, increases with distance and complexity. In a military setting, the computer modeling of targets offers a layer of separation that must be helpful in making what might otherwise be heart-wrenching decisions. Facing a row of graphics that *represent* people is surely easier than looking into the eyes of people suffering as a result of your actions.

Statistical modeling also involves both distance and complexity. Cathy O'Neil explains that algorithms now guide decisions that impact many areas of our lives. As we consider the benefits of such practices, we must also be aware of the costs. It is true; the context of human relationship affects our decision making. In cases of evaluation or judgment, we have been socialized to view that influence as negative, in light of our potential for bias. Because bias is perceived as a detriment, quantification was introduced as an attempt to remove it. Now, however, we've studied a detailed example of how bias enters even systems driven by algorithms.

The real danger lies in forgetting that bias can also work for the good. Compassion, for example, is a form of bias that leads us to act humanely. But in our thwarted attempts to remove negative bias by basing decisions only on what can be quantified, we have made it impossible to enact compassion. Like the saying about throwing the baby out with the bathwater, we are, quite literally, tossing out students, families, and communities along with their test scores. As the nation fractures in the first part of the twenty-first century, we are, I'm afraid, living with the result.

Where classroom teachers were once able to make decisions inside of relationships, often in consultation with colleagues, students, and families, these decisions are now based on test data alone. In the name of fairness, those in power have chosen to standardize the criteria and the instrument that produces the data used to make these decisions.

Inside this system, administrators and policy makers interact with numbers rather than people as they decide which schools they will order closed or which students will be barred from an opportunity. Substituting numbers for individuals makes it all too easy to forget the people and communities the numbers are supposed to represent. A test score is not a student. So the people who worked at Kentucky's Department of Education, for example, couldn't register the despair as Roxanne, Ronald, and Jocelyn read their test scores and realized the consequence of the verdict. Nor did these state administrators witness the moments that had shone so brightly as these pre-service teachers worked with children in classrooms. All they saw was a row of test scores interpreted to mean that these teacher candidates had failed.

In contrast, those of us on education's front lines experience the joys and sorrows of our students' lives on a daily basis. We learn to read our students' faces. We come to know them as people and yes, we often grow to love them. Our teaching is guided, most of all, by those relationships. So our hearts ache as we witness the results of decisions based on data that miss each student's richness. When students lose access to opportunities, educators also feel that loss. And when gifted teacher candidates are rejected, the damage compounds to include the generations of children they would have taught.

This use of test scores is not inevitable. It is simply a choice made by a group of people empowered to make this decision. When my research helped me understand that Ronald's, Jocelyn's, and Roxanne's race, ethnicity, and/or economic status placed them in the very groups the eugenicists intended to exclude, in decisions justified by scores produced by large-scale tests, I could not simply stand by. In a system based on dehumanization, we all lose.

Since test-based policy was implemented, the damage has only intensified. When Ronald, Jocelyn, and Roxanne were in elementary and middle school, NCLB hadn't yet taken a firm hold. If it had, testing's nets might have caught them much sooner, denying them the opportunity to attend Berea College. The intent of early test-based policy was, after all, to reserve the best resources for those considered most deserving.

Just as the intent of those who order a drone strike is meaningless to those who die, so, too, is the intent of a policy that effectively kills students' dreams and limits their futures. In the end, the impact is all that matters.

So if some individuals are motivated by racist or elitist ideas, that form of bias is one matter to deal with. Anti-racism can be taught and learned. But it is another matter entirely to have those ideas kneaded into an entire system that continues to treat test results as unquestioned truth. The impact of that choice is as clear now as it was during the time of eugenics.

When policy demands score-based judgements, consistent demographic patterns predict whose dreams will be deferred or forced into abandonment. Yet policy makers move ahead as if these consequences are happenstance, as if every child has an equal opportunity to succeed.

I can still see the tears of frustration as Ronald, Jocelyn, Roxanne, and far too many others experienced the reality of a system set to work against their interests. Their stories illustrate the costs, for each of them and for the nation. It is left to us to evaluate whether the inevitable damage caused by the high-stakes use of test scores is worth the cost.

Cut Scores

Cut scores determine these lines of division. Their purpose is baked into the word. A cut score is a mark on a test's scale intended to separate those who are worthy of whatever reward awaits from those who are not. When test scores are referenced to cut scores, the disproportionate impact of test-based policy becomes even clearer. To understand why, we will weigh the presumption that cut scores represent educational standards against the reality of the cut score–setting process. Then we will consider the impact of this practice.

When any presumption of meaning is stripped away, cut scores are simply numbers chosen to serve as dividing lines. In Goddard's time, the marks presumably divided those considered "normal" from those called feeble-minded morons, idiots, or imbeciles. Today, they separate categories like qualified or unqualified; or advanced, proficient, nearing proficient, or novice. We refer to these as performance levels and respond as if cut scores are connected to meaning in some significant way. As theoretical proxies for learning standards, cut scores provide the point of reference by which meaning is interpreted.[2]

Cut scores are, of course, *not* learning standards; they are simply preselected marks on a bell curve. In practice, a cut score is a percentile mark that policy makers have chosen as a line of separation used to determine what percentage of the tested population will be allowed to "pass" or occupy a given category. As in other parts of the testing model, any further meaning associated with a cut score is theoretically constructed. We categorize people for reasons considered practical, yet we've seen how these divisions can serve a political purpose. As chapter 5 explained, the cut scores Goddard chose to separate those who were "normal" from the lower-scoring sectors of the population he called "feeble-minded" had no inherent meaning. Goddard set those marks on the bell curve's scale according to his guess at what percentage of the population each category might encompass. Each category's meaning is delineated by how differently people are treated as a result, and by the rewards or consequences assigned accordingly. Our responses to categorization, then, create the social order.

In the twenty-first century, we treat cut scores as if they divide levels of performance relative to specific learning standards. Those whose score at or above a given mark are presumed worthy of categorization as proficient, for example, or classroom-ready. That meaning comes from our willingness to believe that scores are measured against a collection of critical learning standards, and that a cut score demarcates a test taker's success or failure at meeting a specific level of performance.

Koretz explained, however, that in reality "there are only trivial differences between students just above and just below a standard, and there can be huge differences among students who fall between two of the standards and who are therefore assigned the same label." So, while policy may treat cut scores as significant, the associated meaning is simply assigned. Koretz clarified that "the process of setting standards, while arcane and seemingly 'scientific,' is not a way of revealing some underlying truth about categories of student achievement. The methods used are just a very complicated way of using judgment to decide which score is high enough to warrant the label 'proficient.'" Here, then, is another example of human judgment influencing a system falsely championed for its objectivity.[3]

Because large-scale tests follow the dictates of a model designed according to norm-referenced theory, the topic of chapter 11, cut scores create an illusion of standard setting. We behave as if we believe that if we set a cut score higher, the standard of quality has been raised. Some universities, for example, have been assigned greater prestige because they admit only the highest-scoring students. Yet this level of selectivity was achieved simply by deciding what percentage of test takers will be accepted and setting a mark on the bell curve accordingly. The assumption that the mark ensures the students selected are "the best and the brightest" depends entirely on the meaning we assign to those scores.

Adding cut scores to a test's scale makes it appear as if scores are criterion-referenced even after they have been artificially spread to create a bell curve. We might recall that criterion-referencing requires test items that are clearly related to a narrow set of standards corresponding to what was taught. Yet the processes of job or curriculum analysis and item selection were not created for that purpose. So, even if the model is augmented by a surface-level alignment with state standards, as we saw in chapter 8, the model's processes do not achieve this outcome. Yet these are the practices that assign meaning to a score.[4]

As I learned more, my skepticism about the processes used to produce a test score grew to the point that I no longer accept what I'm told a score represents. It is an understatement to call the process unscientific. When it comes to setting cut scores, Harvard psychometrician Andrew Ho, for example, described it as "arbitrary, determined by an overwrought, judgmental, and ultimately political process."[5]

For an in-depth look at why Koretz and Ho judge this process so harshly, let's return to the context of the Praxis series. To set cut scores for the multiple-choice sections of the Praxis tests, ETS follows a procedure called the modified Angoff method. ETS again claims the process involves the input of practitioners. In this case, though, all responsibility is left to each state. It begins when a state nominates potential candidates to serve on standard-setting panels for each subject area. ETS recommends that those panelists are practicing, certified educators who reflect the state's diversity, but the state decides whether or how to follow those guidelines. Once completed, that list of potential candidates is sent to ETS, where its employees select ten to fifteen people who match their criteria, whatever that may be. Sometimes ETS determines there are not enough qualified candidates on the list, so the process proceeds with fewer than ten panelists.[6]

Once these selections are made, ETS returns the list for state approval. As a reminder, these panels are important to ETS because they claim the panelists "reconfirm the relevance (validity) of the test content for teachers in the adopting state." As long as panelists fulfill the role ETS lays out for them, their compliance is apparently interpreted as "the profession's" approval of both the process and the results.[7]

During their first meeting, subject-area panelists take and score the test they will be working with. ETS employees then help the group envision baseline characteristics of a borderline candidate: a person they imagine would only barely have the level of knowledge and skills needed to begin teaching. The Praxis manual explained, "This method necessitates that each panelist review each test item and *judge the percentage of a hypothetical group of 100 minimally qualified test takers who would answer the item correctly.*" I quote here, so you will know I am not making this up. It continues: "For each item, panelists record the percentage (e.g., 10%, 20%, . . . 90%) of the 100 hypothetical test takers who they *feel* would answer the item correctly."[8]

Take a breath and let that sink in.

Clearly, this is nothing more than a guess; how could anyone estimate how many people in a hypothetical group would answer any test item correctly? Nonetheless, ETS gathers each panelist's estimates and averages the results to produce a mean score called the *passing score study value.*[9]

Yes, the process used to set the criteria that ultimately determine the futures of millions of test takers is *this* absurd. It serves as an important example of why we should study the testing model, focused especially on how meaning is assigned.

Some states offer a slight variation called a multi-state approach. The process is much the same, but it improves the chances that ETS will find ten to fifteen panelists who meet their qualifications, which may lead to greater diversity. In some cases, two panels are formed, and their results are compared to increase statistical reliability, a concept we'll soon explore.[10]

Whichever process is followed, ETS compiles the data, and six weeks later the state receives a report that verifies the names of the panelists, describes the procedure, and shares its recommendations for a passing score. Protocol dictates that the score ETS suggests should be "within one and two standard errors of the panel's recommendation." That leaves ETS broad leeway indeed and once again, the cursory role played by the panel is enough for ETS to claim that practitioners were involved.[11]

Having little else to go on, states rely on ETS's recommendations as they select marks to delineate pass/fail divides for each test. As in Goddard's time, cut scores predetermine what percentage of test takers will pass and fail, based on a hypothesis that only a certain percentage could or should meet this mark perceived as a minimum standard.

The final score-setting decisions are, however, the state's responsibility. Presumably, this means that ETS is exempt from legal liability for the results of their use. This is not a glowing endorsement of ETS's confidence in the process. Instead, it acknowledges the organization is aware of the potential for outcomes to be challenged.

Then again, if charges of racial discrimination are presented in court, test developers and states are covered by the legal precedent requiring plaintiffs to prove racist intent. In addition, the Federal Code of Regulations, Title 29, contains what is known as the "Four-Fifths" rule. It reads, in part, "A selection rate for any race, sex, or ethnic group which is less than four-fifths . . . (or eighty percent) of the group . . . will generally not be regarded by Federal enforcement agencies as evidence of adverse impact."[12]

There it is: inequity written right into law. If the passing rate for lower-scoring groups is only 80 percent of the rate for the highest-scoring groups, the law declares that no adverse impact has occurred. This regulation builds a 20 percent advantage for White and wealthier test takers right into the system. To make matters worse, researcher Terry Hibpshman adds that "the courts usually give test administrators a great deal more latitude" than that![13]

Yet ETS still hedges its bets. It's odd that the organization shows this level of doubt while also understanding the important implications of setting cut scores. An ETS research brief explains that standard setting is "a critical part of educational, licensing, and certification testing . . . [because] unless the cut-scores are appropriately set, the results of the assessment could come into question." After learning the process they use, I see why they might worry.[14]

How can this be considered acceptable? Is it because it's viewed as the best we can do, or because many policy makers don't know what, exactly, they are accepting? The reason matters less than the effect because either way, the decisions are based on the priorities of those empowered to determine an appropriate way to set standards. In any case, we are left with a testing model that gives no more than a procedural nod to criterion-referencing and therefore yields test results that offer little information about student learning. Absent an emphasis on test items that reflect significant and specific content, it is impossible to set meaningful criteria. And if cut scores do not represent meaningful criteria, even ETS concurs that we should question test results—and their use.

Fairness

By now, it is clear that those who cling to the belief that testing removes human judgment are only fooling themselves. Jay Rosner invites readers to imagine the outcry if people of color rather than White people or women rather than men had been advantaged for a century by a model that consistently produces demographically divided results. In that case, he wonders, would people so willingly accept the rhetoric that large-scale tests are objective and unbiased? And I wonder: have cries of injustice been silenced because those advantaged by the system gain leadership positions where they set laws and establish precedent and policies that allow the cycle to continue?[15]

From testing's inception through the civil rights movement of the 1960s, score gaps reinforced ingrained prejudice and were used to justify discriminatory regulations. By the late 1960s, however, ETS and other testing organizations were called to respond to accusations of cultural bias in test items. We can now see that is just the tip of an iceberg.

Yet as a result of that outcry, Michael Zieky of ETS explained, "From the 1960s onward . . . fairness has become a major concern in the design, development, and use of assessments." Testing companies began implementing what they call fairness reviews. These are not, however, system-wide evaluations spanning from procedures to outcomes. Instead, most fairness review guidelines focus on the careful use of language and the avoidance of controversial topics.[16]

The ETS website explains that its guidelines require each of its testing programs to develop fairness plans based on the model published in the *ETS Standards for Quality and Fairness (SQF)*. The first few pages of this document state that while the ETS standards draw from the *Standards for Psychological and Educational Testing*, "the contents have been tailored to meet the specific needs of ETS." Furthermore, the *SQF* document continues, "The application of the standards in the SQF will depend on the judgements of ETS staff and external evaluators. . . . ETS does not intend the use of any of these standards to stifle adaptation to appropriate new environments, to slow the adoption of useful new technologies, or to inhibit improvement."[17]

In other words, ETS customizes recommended guidelines to meet its own needs and gives its employees latitude to apply them or not, as they see fit.

Apparently, the organization is willing to try to make their tests more equitable as long as changes are not too disruptive, and they alone will determine what that means. The statement also reveals that the organization fears that striving for fairness will "inhibit improvement" rather than understanding it as the *way* to improve.[18]

Zieky explained the problem is that testing culture is loyal to its model and has not agreed what fairness would look like or how it should be applied. As we've seen, power lies with those who define testing's terms. The fairness statement on the ETS website says the "Educational Testing Service is committed to producing tests and other products that acknowledge the multicultural nature of society and treat its diverse populations with respect. Further, ETS is committed to ensuring that test takers and others who make up our increasingly diverse customer base enjoy equal access to our products." So part of ETS leaders' commitment to fairness is that they respect the rights of all consumers to be able to purchase ETS tests![19]

Zieky, however, took a broader view. He claimed that a fairness review should "identify any construct-irrelevant factors in tests that might plausibly prevent the members of a group of test-takers from responding to the tests in ways that allow appropriate inferences [to be drawn] about the test-takers' knowledge, skills, abilities, or other attributes." He concluded, "The driving force behind fairness review is validity, not political correctness." It's true that a test score is not valid if incorrect inferences are drawn. The testing model, however, presumes valid inferences are drawn from scores that consistently appear in the "correct" order, presumed to align with test takers' abilities.[20]

So in the end, ETS checks fairness in two ways: through its use of language and in a statistical analysis of items selected for use. Sensitivity reviews focus on the wording and cultural context of each written document ETS publishes, including test items. ETS explains that this review is conducted by assessment specialists who "receive specific training and certification, ensuring that they can recognize and eliminate the use of discriminatory language or content and bias in assessment items."[21]

The statistical procedure used to evaluate fairness is called differential item functioning (DIF). As the name implies, its goal is to indicate whether a test item performs differently for different groups of test takers. Ideally, no aspect of test takers' identities should influence a test score, so if an item produces a discrepancy, it signals a potential problem with the item. Yet testing outcomes have always shown demographic correlations, which has long puzzled those who believe humans are humans, no matter how they are politically grouped. Rosner's research indicates that these divided outcomes are, at least in part, related to test design.

So let's see how DIF works and why Rosner found that, despite its application, items selected for use on tests are still skewed to favor White and, in the case of math, male test takers. In the last chapter we learned that psychometricians categorize test takers according to their rankings on the test as a whole and assume they have grouped by ability. The demographic information test takers provide also allows ETS to create subgroups within each "ability" group.

To test DIF, psychometricians track responses to each item. They assume that individuals within each "ability" group should respond to each item similarly, answering it either correctly or incorrectly, regardless of social identity. The model demands that each item be carefully calibrated to produces consistent results, so when that is the outcome, psychometricians believe the item is performing as it should. This is the theoretical basis for the DIF procedure.[22]

If, however, an item's results differ according to demographics within an "ability" group, that is "a sign that the item may be measuring something other than the intended construct and may be unfair." Those items are flagged as potential problems. Zieky described this method as "straightforward and sensible" . . . as long, I might add, as you accept the model's basic assumptions.[23]

Once DIF values are established, items are sorted into three categories: those that exhibit a small degree of difference in the way an item functions among subgroups, a moderate degree, and a larger than moderate degree. Zieky explained, "If DIF data are available before tests are assembled, items in the first category are selected first. If items in the secondary category are needed to meet test specifications, they may be used . . . [and] items in the third category are to be avoided unless they are judged to be fair and are required for valid measurement." As if to emphasize the fact that the process relies on human input, Zieky adds, "The judgements should be made by people with no vested interest in retaining the items."[24]

So what do we make of the fact that Rosner found such stark racial disparities in item performance even after these two fairness checks were applied? The bottom line is that psychometricians select items that will produce consistent results, and this trumps all other considerations. As long as ETS selects items based on how well test takers' responses align with their results on the test as a whole, the demographic divides will stand, as they have for over a century. When they assume that test scores indicate ability, psychometricians end up evaluating the results of the tests they created against the theory they invented to back it. Of course they match. With no external point of comparison, this creates a closed system in which test results of the past determine the results of the future.

Defining Fairness

In the epigraph to the previous chapter, O'Neil explained that mathematical models assume their patterns will repeat. Repetition can lead us to perceive these patterns as reflections of reality.

As we learn more about the theory behind the testing model, we'll gain an ever deeper understanding of why DIF does little to disturb such long-standing correlations. But the definition of fairness also comes into play. After all, how can an instrument be perceived as fair when we can predict the range of test takers' scores simply by knowing their race and social class? Two separate questions emerge from this situation: is the test itself fair? and are its results applied fairly? One answer lies with psychometric theory, the other with policy. In each case, however, the answers are based in ideology and belief.[25]

Chapter 6 showed that there has always been a faction of critics who reject the divided results of large-scale tests because humans are, in fact, "of one blood" (Acts 17:26). We've seen that the human genome shows more genetic differences within demographic groups than between them. All members of the human race are made of the same basic genetic material; the same blood runs through our veins. This fact alone should lead us to question, rather than expect or accept, demographic differences in scores.[26]

Here we reach the heart of the issue. Kendi claimed that "our faith in standardized tests causes us to believe that the racial gap in test scores means something is wrong with the Black test takers—and not the tests." After all, testing rose to prominence *because* scores depict White superiority. Otherwise, the results would not have justified eugenic policy and practice. Indeed, well into the twenty-first century, the model is performing as it was designed, ensuring its results repeat across time and circumstance. From this perspective, testing can only be perceived as a tool of oppression.[27]

Some, it seems, cannot yet see the racist ideology grounded in the assumption that these divisions represent something that is real. They cling to something they have come to value about the process—or its results. Yet those who accept the use of mass testing must accept its two basic premises: test scores indicate true differences in mental abilities, and these differences are important enough to justify organizing a society around them.

Educational testing has become so normalized that few seem to question the integrity of the scores, the model that produces them, or the meaning assigned to them. Instead, various factions argue about what *causes* the score discrepancies. Their differing answers lead to political disagreement about how scores should be used, but all sidestep critical questions about *why* such high value is placed on the use of test scores. Why do these results continue to draw the nation to this practice? By asking "what" instead of "why," we have avoided the issue's root. Could it be that we fear the answer?

As things now stand, one group argues that the history of racism in the United States has given White test takers greater access to opportunities of all kinds, and that the test score divide reflects the impact of those differences. They refer to the test score gap as an opportunity gap. They accept the use of test scores because they believe tracking those gaps is the first step toward achieving equality. They watch hopefully for signs the gaps are closing, the intent policy makers claim, not realizing that the model is designed to spread student scores and repeat past results. In short, this faction has not yet recognized that current test-based policy creates *further* opportunity gaps among demographic groups. Because their argument focuses on closing these score gaps, we might presume that if no such gaps existed, they would agree to using large-scale test scores to make high-stakes decisions. From this perspective, it is fine to grant greater opportunity to those considered more deserving as long as merit is fairly defined and everyone has an equal shot at the top. Testing is seen as a means to achieve that end.

Other testing proponents adhere to the original premise that test results truly reveal human mental ability, so test-based education policy allows a meritocracy to function as it should. From this perspective, what causes gaps in mental abilities is not as important as the fact that the tests show they exist.

Some continue to cite genetic evidence. Yet geneticist James F. Crow confirms that human DNA is largely similar. He explained, "Most of our DNA determines that we are human, rather than determining how we are different from any other person. So it is not so surprising that the DNA of any two humans is 99.9% identical."[28]

There are, however, still obvious differences among individuals and between groups, and it's complicated to explain their cause. Genes are long stretches of DNA, and the proteins they produce play a role in genetic variation. "Some of the genetic changes that seem so significant to us," like skin color or hair texture, Crow explained, "depended on a very tiny fraction of our DNA." He adds that that these differences may be "small—but they are real."[29]

Crow then makes an important point. He contends that there is no reason for society to shy away from noting genetic differences, even among groups. Human variation is, after all, devoid of meaning. *Society* has created false correlations, and therein lies the problem. It is obvious that dividing people by skin color and manufacturing a tiered correspondence with mental functioning is a racist act. This illusory connection with racist ideas causes some to shy away from evidence suggesting differences among racial groups. Yet the mere suggestion of difference is not racist—racism comes from how society perceives and treats those differences.[30]

Even so, Vivian Chou explained that "science has yet to find evidence that there are genetic differences in intelligence between populations." Despite this lack of evidence, however, we continue to organize society according to demographically divided test scores that make such differences appear to be real. *This* is the racist act.[31]

So we return to the question of what test scores actually mean and how they are contemporarily applied. Kendi noted that "few testing critics are bursting its biggest bubble: the existence of the achievement gap itself." In 1995, for example, just as America was poised to reform its system of education, the American Psychological Association (APA) conducted a study to try to find the source of test score gaps. The conclusion? After examining and rejecting every existing hypothesis, they revealed that they have no idea why demographic score gaps exist.[32]

When it comes to the use of test scores, it turns out that society has been flying blind, acting on assumptions and beliefs rather than evidence. We have accepted a narrative that outlines false dichotomies about normalcy and difference, all in the name of producing a hierarchy that has kept White people and wealthy people in the seats of power.

It doesn't have to be this way. It is not a given that society should be organized around the imagined trait of intelligence. Nothing suggests we should assign it importance, attempt to measure it, and rank people accordingly. These ideas were all birthed in the human imagination. Yet American institutions are built upon these illusions.

Crow concluded, "A test of our democratic institutions will be the degree to which people can accept all our differences and find ways to fit them into a smooth-working, humanitarian society. . . . To achieve political and social equality, it is not necessary to maintain a fiction that important human differences do not exist."[33]

We are free to pursue an egalitarian society no matter what geneticists discover. Racism and anti-racism are determined by how we handle information. *We* collect and manipulate data; *we* assign them meaning. And absent the false notion of human hierarchy, there is no need to argue about where there may be genetic differences among us. Outside the medical field , it wouldn't, and shouldn't, matter. Caste is not a natural order; illusions created around what is considered superior or inferior can be shattered. We do not have to continue to allow test scores to determine our children's futures—and the future of our nation.

11

Inferences and Assumptions
Testing's Conceptual Framework

> When people have lived with assumptions long enough, passed down through the generations as incontrovertible fact, they are accepted as the truths of physics, no longer needing even to be spoken. They are as true and as unremarkable as water flowing through rivers or the air that we breathe.
>
> —Isabel Wilkerson, *Caste*

We are left with this: with no acknowledgment that large-scale tests have always resulted in demographic divides, no fundamental change in the testing model, and no apparent evidence, policy makers began talking about the need to close achievement gaps. We are acting on assumptions. Based on common core standards created by business and government leaders, testing organizations were asked to test this broad concept called academic achievement and to guide states in specifying the score parameters that would categorize contemporary American students. Anyone who cared to study the data trends could have easily predicted the social implications of such policy.

By now we can see that educational testing is essentially a story about what political leaders *would like to be able to do* and the methods psychometricians developed to deliver a result as close to that as possible. Unfortunately, this tends to create the illusion that the impossible is possible. Psychometricians are not pretending, of course. They are manipulating statistics so testing companies can fulfill political requests. To this end, psychometrics has become a unique culture, operating according to its own norms and standards. Testing procedures and the interpretation of results can only be understood within the context of that culture.

Inside the world of psychometrics, everyone understands that the testing model can never achieve a pure result because many factors interfere with a score's meaning. For those forced to live with the results, the gap we really need to understand is the one that exists between what is imagined and what is real.

The pretending comes on the part of policy makers, politicians, and administrators who admonish us to treat test scores as if they represent reality.

Or maybe they are not pretending. Perhaps their faith is blind because they, too, know little about how scores are produced. Or perhaps, like story of the emperor, they hope and believe their edicts will persuade us see clothing that is not actually there.

As we explore psychometric culture, we quickly find ourselves mired in a world where magical thinking reigns, at least from my vantage point. For those steeped in the norms of the testing model, its basic tenets create an alternate reality based on theories developed over the course of a century. While testing's eugenic origins are rarely discussed, remnants of the past are embedded in the model. Its most basic concepts are purely conceptual, yet they alone explain the model's operation and what meaning is assigned to scores. From the perspective on the other side of this cultural divide, it looks like pure illusion.

So at the very least, we need to understand what is real and what exists only in theory. To that end, I'll name the illusions and try to simplify the psychometric perspective. That may allow us to consider how these concepts connect and collectively contribute to a system that rests on faith rather than science. Code-switching between worldviews is taxing, to be sure, but if it helps us see that testing is one of caste's primary supports, the effort is worth the struggle.[1]

The G-Factor

The g-factor forms the core of psychometric theory. Chapter 8 introduced the g-factor as a concept no one quite knows how to describe—or whether it even exists. Because psychometric culture is built around its mirage, we have a hard time knowing what large-scale tests actually measure. Illusion lies at the center of a psychometric culture constructed to justify and maintain the US educational, social, and economic hierarchy. Faith placed in this theory leads us to believe test-based decisions are based on a type of merit worthy of organizing our society around.

Educational psychologist Linda Gottfredson is a believer. She teaches that the g-factor "describes mental aptitude," demonstrated as "the ability to deal with cognitive complexity." Her read of the data leads her to believe that the g-factor regulates learning and that test results are reasonable predictors of potential success. She asks readers and students to accept her view of a reality where "people are in fact unequal in intellectual potential—and they are born that way." She explained that differences in *g* are therefore "likely to result in social inequality" that we should all learn to accept. Galton preceded Gottfredson by more than a century, yet they seem to view the word through a similar lens.[2]

The only evidence to back this view is produced by large-scale tests. Believers assume the g-factor exists because people's results are consistent across different types of tests. Gottfredson explained, "People who do well on one kind of test tend to do well on the others, and people who do poorly generally do so across the board. This overlap, or intercorrelation, suggests that all such tests measure some global element of intellectual ability as well as specific cognitive skills." Psychometrician Arthur Jensen concurred. He described the g-factor as "the most important factor in the cognitive domain," and "the chief 'active ingredient' . . . in virtually all tests of concern."[3]

Neither Gottfredson nor Jensen, however, bothers to mention what we now know: the model that produces each of these tests intentionally establishes this consistency. Instead, their conviction that tests reveal truth leads them to interpret consistent results as proof that each test has successfully tapped the mysterious milieu presumed to guide our mental functioning. This conclusion supports their assumptions and also the efficacy of large-scale tests.

The g-factor is another example of a conceptual choice used to explain the model's procedures and to justify how meaning is interpreted from test scores. Psychometrician Michael Kane explained, however, that at least in some stages of the testing model's development there may be nothing in the data to suggest one way of interpreting meaning is truer than another. In such cases, strategic choices are made. As the model expanded, each procedure became normalized. Gottfredson explained that one result is that "most intelligence experts now use g as the working definition of intelligence."[4]

Our entire educational system, and therefore our society, is now organized around an idea that exists only as it relates to the network of ideas, beliefs, and assumptions that comprise psychometric theory. This web of ideas is testing's conceptual framework.

It's interesting, then, that when Charles Spearman first conceptualized the g-factor, the idea met strong opposition from leaders in the field, including Edward Thorndike and Karl Pearson. Spearman's papers were housed in an archive in danger of closing, which attracted the attention of Julie Perk, who wanted to investigate his raw data while she still had the chance. She described his bizarre experiments. In 1904, for example, Spearman published a paper claiming he had isolated g by correlating the results of three tests of sensory discrimination with those of three tests of intellectual ability. The sensory tests included the degree to which a person could discern musical pitch; tests of light that evaluated sight, depth, and tone; and measures of how precisely a person could differentiate among objects of different weights. Spearman correlated these results with those of separate tests that had evaluated "cleverness in school and . . . two assessments of common sense." Perk explained, "He then amalgamated the three 'gradings' of discrimination, and the three 'intel-lective gradings,' and recorded the correlation between these two new catego-ries: 'general discrimination' and 'general intelligence.'" Spearman was so pleased with the results that he claimed his procedures should replace those of previous intelligence tests.[5]

Spearman's work was not well received, however, so when his most famous book, *The Abilities of Man*, was published in 1927, statistician E. B. Wilson said it took the tone of someone who was "under considerable criticism." Yet some-how the idea of the g-factor caught on anyway, perhaps because its theory allows the testing model to be broadly applied.[6]

With the g-factor at the heart of the testing model, there was no need to create new models for tests used for different purposes. Gottfredson explained, "The general factor explains most differences among individuals in perfor-mance on diverse mental tests. This is true regardless of what specific ability a test is meant to assess, regardless of the test's manifest content (whether words, numbers or figures) and regardless of the way the test is administered (in written or oral form, to an individual or to a group)." Psychometric theory conceives that no matter what a test claims to measure, from intelligence to academic achievement to classroom-readiness, all are influenced by the g-factor and are therefore reflected in the results. Whatever a test claims to measure is therefore theoretically contained within the score. The advantage to the testing industry eventually led to the theory's wide acceptance, and Spearman rose to fame.[7]

The g-factor encompasses intelligence, and Spearman's theories assume Galton's claims that mental ability is stable over a person's lifetime, and that measurements across the population would naturally produce a bell curve. As a result, psychometric theory presumes that test scores align test takers according to the degree of their mental capacity, as if the g-factor can be measured like sand in a bucket.

If we accept the assumption that the g-factor is stable, it means we should not expect it to change—not through education or experience. This certainly raises questions about why educators are held accountable for closing so-called achievement gaps. It's as if twenty-first-century education policy was built around an instrument policy makers knew nothing about—or, worse yet, they could foresee its impact and implemented it anyway.

Jensen, who passed away in 2012, and Gottfredson are contemporary advo-cates of large-scale testing. They would, however, be under no illusion that score gaps will close. In 2002, Jensen wrote, "In the 96 years since Spearman's discov-ery, *g* has been found to be absolutely ubiquitous, to some degree, in every kind of mental task. . . . This is not a theory but an empirical fact." The evidence

Jensen cites is, of course, test scores. Based on the results of improved testing between Galton's time and now, he concluded that most of Galton's hypotheses were correct. This includes the size of the gap between people considered Black or Brown and those designated as White. Jensen matter-of-factly described the size of this gap as 1.31 standard deviations—which represents twenty IQ points.[8]

Based on the evidence of test scores, Jensen and Gottfredson believed these differences are real, and they therefore would agree with those who conclude that the laws of nature guide people into their social positions. Because they believed the g-factor is fixed, they concluded that social rankings are as solid as the test scores used to explain them, and any effort to disrupt this order is a waste of time and resources. This argument, too, has remained stable over time.[9]

Conceptualizing Error: Positive and Negative Space

When I read about the g-factor, the rationale for the testing model's procedures finally clicked into place. It is the only context in which I found it possible to make any sense of what to me seemed nonsensical. Understanding this basic assumption positions us, finally, to see *why* score stability might be considered the mark of a successful test.

Psychometricians reason that if *g* does not change over time or across contexts, then neither should the scores presumed to quantify it. This led psychometricians to conclude that when the scores of people or groups continually appear in the same order on the bell curve, it means the test has located at least a portion of the g-factor and has ranked them accordingly. An accurate test should therefore produce the same results every time, and this result should be consistent across all high-quality tests.

This presented a problem early on, however, because as psychometricians gave more tests, the results were *not* as stable as expected. The gap between theory and practice must have left psychometricians with two choices. They could admit they were mistaken about the theory and the model: perhaps tests did not measure the g-factor; maybe there is no way to accurately measure mental functioning; and what if the demographic differences they expected to show didn't actually exist after all? The other option was to come up with a way to explain why scores were not consistent. Psychometricians chose the latter, and as a result expanded their framework to include what they call the theory of error.[10] When we hear the word *error,* we tend to get nervous, especially when we're talking about evidence used to make important decisions. Because we equate error with mistakes, the very mention of the word threatens to disrupt our notion of test scores as accurate, objective representations of human capacity.

The truth is that test scores are *full* of error. So in a conceptual feat, psychometricians found a way to explain that the erroneous information contained in every score is irrelevant and does not impact the part of the score they believe is based in truth.

It's hard to imagine how this is possible, but in fact theory is built around the error known to result from the testing process. If error was somehow removed, the entire picture would fall apart. You see, psychometricians use error in much the way artists perceive negative space—as a way to define an object's parameters. Psychometricians, however, are trying to outline something that has no shape or form. Because the g-factor has no volume or definition, psychometricians use error, which does exist, to conceptualize *g*. To further complicate things, while every score contains error, only a small fraction of it can even be estimated. Yet in the culture of testing, the shadow of error is presumed to shine light on some nebulous milieu presumed to be the g-factor.[11]

This, of course, stretches the limits of our imaginations, as psychometrician Michael Kane explained in the introduction of his speech published by ETS. "Paradoxically, errors of measurement don't exist, and yet they are essential." Even within a framework built of illusions, Kane suggested, measurement error is particularly hard to conceptualize. If the testing procedures described in previous chapters seemed haphazard, as they did to me, it's because we haven't yet grasped the theory built to support them. Once we do, we can decide whether or not we are convinced of its truth. Gaining that vantage point, as Kane's statement suggests, will require some mental calisthenics.[12]

The Role of Theory

In most cases, solid corroborating evidence is required for a theory to become widely accepted. Yet the evidence provided to back testing theory comes only from the results the tests themselves produce. And in fact the tests are constructed to generate those results.

As we learn the extent to which psychometric theory is based on conjecture, we may find our minds resisting. These ideas cause upset on many levels. They counter our socialized belief that large-scale testing is based in science. And when we understand that the impact of test-based practice further harms those marginalized by other American policies, we may begin to feel complicit in supporting a system we believed might lead to greater equity. We've somehow been blinded to the fact that the outcomes of contemporary education policy are the opposite of its stated goals. Yet we only need to look at the data to see that a system reliant on test scores continues to create the same social hierarchy it always has, allowing the legacy of eugenics to continue.

People react differently once we understand the level of absurdity involved and the extent of the damage that results. We might become defensive and try to deny the possibility that rhetoric has convinced us to accept practices we would never choose to support. Or we might feel greater responsibility to work to change the system that causes such harm. However you're feeling, know that if we can keep our minds and hearts open, cognitive or emotional dissonance often signals the potential for transformation. Discomfort often results in change, and change is learning's primary outcome.

Problems and Solutions: The Theory of Error

As we return to the world of psychometrics, let's compare theory with reality. Theoretically, a test that accurately quantifies the g-factor would produce the same score for the same group of people every time they take a test. The definition of perfection is complete score stability. Of course, in reality, there is no such thing as a perfect test. Psychometricians recognize that many outside variables influence a score and, counter to the requirements of the scientific method, most of these cannot be controlled in the testing experiment. Even more challenging is the fact that the g-factor, the presumed "object" to be measured, is a not an object at all. It, too, exists only in theory. For the purpose of differentiating scores, however, the g-factor is perceived as a quantity.[13]

It appears that nearly every part of the attempt to represent differences in mental capacity is hypothetical. When psychometricians found that tests did not produce stable scores, for example, they created the theory of measurement error and simply went on with their work. Kane cautioned, however, that "this kind of generalization greatly simplifies our conceptual frameworks, but it involves inferential risk." In short, the meaning of scores had been sacrificed to psychometric convenience. As we add yet another assumption to a pile that has grown into a mountain, we have to wonder how far reality can be bent until it is no longer reality at all.[14]

Like magic, this psychometric schema not only explains score inconsistencies, it also declares them to be insignificant. A double win. Kane explained, "We are ignoring some of the variability in our data and effectively relegating this variability to the dustbin that we call *errors of measurement.*" What once was a problem was simply swept away in a decision about how psychometricians would conceptualize a test score.[15]

Imagine a score as having two separate sections, like an apple's core and its fruit. The core represents the part of the score that has defined the stable g-factor. The apple's fruit, then, is perceived as if it is comprised purely of error resulting from all the uncontrolled, interfering variables. As such, the part of a score represented by the fruit is never stable. Theory explains that this section of the apple is the reason scores fluctuate, even while the g-factor remains steady.

By imagining the two parts as disconnected, the theory of error safeguards scores from claims of inaccuracy. Psychometricians rest in the belief that while error causes part of a score to be inaccurate, it *also* contains a solid, accurate representation of the g-factor. It seems ironic that recognizing inherent error provided psychometricians a way out of their dilemma, avoiding what could have been the death knell for large-scale testing. At the same time, it conserved the idea that general intelligence is stable, despite any evidence to the contrary. It's all a matter of perspective.

Faith in the hypothesis of a fixed g-factor is so strong in testing culture that score consistency is cited as evidence of success. This assumption is what led psychometricians to design tests so they produce consistent scores. Tests are, then, created to produce results *that align with psychometricians' theories,* rather than the other way around. There is nothing scientific about that.

Yet score consistency is testing's standard of quality, rooted in a theoretical belief that an element of that truth is buried somewhere within a score. Conveniently, this means a test score's accuracy cannot be disproven. Neither, though, has it been proven. This returns us to Jensen's confident assertion that empirical evidence undoubtedly proves the existence of the g-factor and therefore also the racial hierarchy test scores demonstrate. In the statement following that claim, Jensen wrote, "Those who, for whatever reason, do not like this fact, have never been able to disprove it." And that is true enough, for how would one ever disprove something that is purely imaginary? In fact, why should we have to, given the lack of evidence demonstrating that testing accomplishes much more than supporting and reinforcing hierarchy?[16]

Defining Error

But wait; there's more. The Praxis manual defined error as "the difference between the observed and true scores." The trouble is, true scores don't exist. And while we would expect this to cause quite a lot of worry, somehow it does not.

It's easy to find the observed score: it is reported after a person takes a test. We might think of it as the whole apple, which theoretically includes both the g-factor and error. Defining the true score, on the other hand, stretches the imagination. According to theory, if every bit of the apple's fruit, a score's error, could be carved away (which it can't), only the true score would remain. It would then reveal the pure truth about a person's mental functioning. Psychometricians seem to imagine true scores the way Michelangelo could see figures hidden inside the unsculpted marble waiting to be revealed.[17]

In reality, of course, a test score does not have two discernable parts. So while some believe scores contain an element of truth, there is no doubt they also include error. It's just that no one knows how *much* error and there is no way to differentiate between error and truth. Doesn't it strike you as odd that we are expected to simply ignore these facts? That we are prompted to treat test scores as pure truth, even as the Praxis manual states that "true scores can never be known"? Ultimately, psychometricians seem to be telling us there is no way to know if a score contains any "truth" at all.[18]

We can see that in psychometric culture error and truth are redefined to the extent that they are mirages created for the model's convenience. Kane explained that true scores and error are "both constructs in the sense that we create them to serve our purposes." And as we've witnessed, the model continues to fulfill its original purpose quite well, as scores are repeatedly used to reinforce and justify the nation's social hierarchy, as Jensen's claims make clear.[19]

Setting ethical questions aside for the moment, these theoretical assumptions raise practical issues. How can you define error as the difference between two things if one of them doesn't exist? And how can you possibly discern the meaning of a score that may or may not contain the information you seek?

Theory envisions that a true score would be represented as a stable, clearly defined point on a bell curve. While the apple's fruit may be soft, theoretically the apple's core is rock solid, meaning this number, and its position on the bell curve, would never change. In the world where scores are used, however, we are only presented with a whole apple, and we are told—and we seem to believe—that it reveals truth about ourselves and those around us.

Estimating Error

Don't get me wrong. Psychometricians don't ignore error completely. They do try to limit its influence, using statistical tools to carve as close to the apple's core as possible. In reality, though, the best they can do is slice a few chunks away and live with the knowledge that they will never be able to even identify, let alone eliminate, many of the factors that interfere with a score's meaning.[20]

The theory claims, remember, that error shows up as inconsistencies in test results. Psychometricians have identified three factors that cause scores to fluctuate. They can estimate and report the influence of two of those sources, but not the third. Even then, many people don't know to look for an estimate of error in a score report, and those who find it may not understand its implications. Therefore, most people take a score at face value, believing they are looking at a true score—or at least something very close.[21]

One source of identified error estimates the impact of using multiple forms of the same test. ETS reports the score inconsistencies caused by this variation as standard error of measurement (SEM). SEM is an estimate of the degree to which the use of multiple test forms likely interferes with the accuracy of a score's presumed meaning.

Another source of error is caused by variations in the context in which a test is given. While attempts are made to control the testing environment, complete standardization is impossible. Sometimes a testing room is too hot—or cold. Problems arise with the computers. Test takers themselves vary from day to day. Some days our brains click along nicely, other days not as well. We may not have slept well. As every teacher knows, personal motivation (or lack thereof) is also an important factor. Test anxiety, too, enters the picture. So while these factors are impossible to control and difficult to measure, we know that both the testing environment and the test taker's personal context certainly impact a test score. However, psychometricians can't begin to predict the influence of these intervening factors, so they don't even attempt to estimate how they might affect the result.[22]

Psychometricians can, however, estimate the influence of one other source of score inconsistency. Some sections of some tests are scored by people rather than computers. Despite efforts to standardize rubrics and regulate the responses of scorers, variation among human scorers is inevitable. ETS reports their estimate of the resulting inconsistencies as standard error of scoring (SES). In the United States, however, large-scale tests rely heavily on the use of multiple-choice items, eliminating the need to estimate SES. While written responses convey nuances of skill or understanding that can't be discerned by a computer, test design often prioritizes efficiency over meaning. Nuance is, in fact, not required for the purposes of norm-referencing. As we've seen, though, if scores are used to guide teaching, the information gained should contain as much detail as possible.[23]

The Impact of Error

While score reports might estimate two types of error, this is merely the tip of an iceberg. We'll never know its size because there is no way to tell how much error is mixed into the reported results. SEM or SES estimates give us some idea of the degree to which error undermines a score's accuracy, which in turn gives us a sense of how additional error, from sources known and unknown, might influence a score.

If you're feeling frustrated at how far a score is removed from any semblance of its presumed meaning, it's no surprise. And the situation is even more fraught because policy, too, ignores the impact of error. Say your reported cumulative score on a version of the Praxis Middle School English Language Arts (MSELA) test is 163. This test's scale is 100–200, and its norm is 162.4, so your score is just above the norming group's average.[24]

The SEM for this test is reported as 6.1 points. This is the estimate of how much your score might vary because there are multiple forms of the same test. This means that if you happened to take a different form of the MSELA test, you might just as easily have received a score 6.1 points above or below the reported score. You can use the estimate of 6.1 to draw a score band ranging from 157.1 to 169.1. This is where a true measure of your performance might lie, given the influence of this single source of error. (Remember, many other sources of error are not accounted for). This means that the reported score of 163 is actually a proxy for any score between 157.1 to 169.1. This, however, is certainly not made clear in the arena where scores are used.[25]

While SEM is often the only type of error reported, even it is missing from some Praxis reports. The document *Understanding Your Praxis Scores* explained, "On some tests, the standard error of measurement could not be estimated because there was no edition of the test that had been taken by a sufficient number of examinees. On other tests, the standard error of measure could not be adequately estimated because the test consists of a very small number of questions or tasks, each measuring a different type of knowledge or skill." In those cases, ETS shares none of the impact of measurement error beyond what the testing manual explains.[26]

SES is reported less frequently and only for tests that include human scoring. Even then, ETS explained that this estimate, too, is sometimes absent from score reports for much the same reason. SES does, however, appear, on the report for the Middle School Language Arts test that serves as our example. For this test, SES estimates the score variation caused by human scorers at 2.4 points. When these two sources of error are combined, then, it broadens the range of expected score variation due to error to include scores from 155.5 and 171.5, almost a fifth of the test's scale! Again, this means that because of measurement error, psychometricians estimate that you were as likely to receive a score anywhere in that large range as you were to receive the reported score of 163, accounting for the influence of just these two variables.[27]

Look, this is not a secret. Testing manuals include this information. Yet we've learned that grasping its meaning requires understanding psychometric theory. Given that this requires us to transfer new meanings to common words, it's hard to imagine how a model could be more opaque.

Yet there's still more fog between a test score and truth. Because even if we know our score lies somewhere within a range, that still doesn't locate our true score. That point, remember, is impossible to know. So while psychometricians' conceptual framework allows them to believe a true score may be somewhere within that range, they also know it might not. So, as in any game of chance, they calculate the odds. In this case, psychometricians estimate the probability as two out of three. In other words, there is a one in three chance that your true score for this test would lie outside even the estimated score range.[28]

Take a moment to let that sink in . . . and then we'll contemplate the implications. Confirming testing's long odds, Daniel Koretz explained, "An examinee with any given true score, taking a test once, has a probability of about two-thirds of getting a score within the range from one SEM below that score to one SEM above, and a probability of one in three of obtaining a score more than one SEM away from the true score."[29]

These are the scores used to determine the course of our educational opportunities and therefore our lives. Most of us have no idea policy makers have placed this bet on our behalf. If decisions are not based on data we can trust, the outcomes of those decisions are certainly not trustworthy, either.

So why would ETS create unnecessary confusion by reporting single scores rather than a range for its Praxis series, the SAT, and many other tests? The implications reach far beyond muddying the waters of our understanding. The Commonwealth of Kentucky, for example, takes the single scores reported on a Praxis II report at face value. With ETS guidance, Kentucky set a cut score of 164 for the Praxis test used in our example, and that is just above the test's median. If you are the test taker with a reported score of 163, you would have failed the Praxis exam and would not receive certification.[30]

As it turns out, this determination ignores the real data: the fact that you might just as easily have gotten a passing score. Yet as Roxanne, Ronald, and Jocelyn learned, once you have failed to meet the cut score, no other evidence is even considered. You are, however, cordially invited to take the test as many times as you like, which translates to as many times as you can afford.

So even if someone knows to look for and use SEM in interpreting a test score's meaning, it doesn't really matter. In the twenty-first century, test-based policies ignore the impact of error even when it is known, along with the fact that true scores are a mirage. With no acknowledgment that chance is involved, test takers, educators, schools, and communities are left to take the hit. And when demographically divided scores are measured against cut scores, some people are certainly hit harder than others, test after test. We are left to assume that this is the level of collateral damage deemed acceptable, and we have to wonder why.

Accountability

When it comes to producing test scores, it seems psychometricians' confidence rests more on faith than on science. The abstract of Kane's speech plainly states: "Errors of measurement arise because our observations are affected by many sources of variability, but our conceptual frameworks necessarily ignore much of this variability. Sources of variability that are not included in our models and descriptions of phenomena are treated as error or noise." In other words, the framework is designed to allow psychometricians to disregard data that interfere with the results they expect.[31]

The theory of error ostensibly releases psychometricians from the impossible task of isolating and eliminating error that impacts test scores. They believe that as long as they select items that produce stable results over time and across contexts, it means the scores have revealed the g-factor. Selecting items on the basis of score stability, however, is exactly the *opposite* of what is needed for the criterion-referencing of scores, where educators hope and expect scores will show improvement over time. Now we can see that the model itself distorts even this outcome.

The tests in the Praxis series are described as minimum competency assessments. This implies criterion-referencing. Even so, the manual makes it clear that the tests are built on the standard model despite the fact that procedures aligned with norm-referenced theory *counter* the philosophy and goals of criterion-referencing. The two simply don't mix.

If our purpose really was to measure student progress toward criteria, testing theory and practice could be so much simpler. Score inconsistencies, for example, don't matter at all on tests not standardized for large-scale production. When scores are accepted as snapshots of learning at a point in time and in a particular context, we expect them to fluctuate. In fact, we expect they will continually rise to indicate a greater mastery of test content. There is no need for a complex statistical model if the meaning of a test score is taken at face value because it relates directly to the test's content. Those are, after all, the only results that are helpful to teachers. Most classroom assessments, for example, directly measure the content or skills that were taught, and results are interpreted only in reference to those items. No indirect measurement is involved because there is no need to extrapolate results to imply a greater meaning. For the purposes of teaching and learning, designing tests to ensure score stability is simply absurd. That is what had me so confused. And if psychometricians don't expect scores to be stable, there would be no need to invent a theory to explain why they are not.[32]

The interplay between theory and the interpretation of results reveals a common refrain in testing's story. We sometimes forget that large-scale testing is, in fact, experimental. Scores are not revealed; they are *produced* according to very specific parameters. We've seen how these specifications limit every aspect of test design, from conception to construction. The theory of error is evidence of how an unexpected outcome was remedied not by interrogating the model's methods or procedures but by manipulating the theory.

Clearly, there are questions to raise. Scientific theories are supposed to emerge from trends in the data, not the other way around. Yet Kane explained that testing theories like "errors of measurement play a vital role in quantitative analysis, by making it possible to model data without immediately running into inconsistencies." In other words, theoretical justifications have allowed the model to continue to be used, unhindered by the possible distraction of its methods being called into question.[33]

But what if these theories are dead wrong? What if, in fact, a score contains *no* evidence of general intelligence? Indeed, what if there is no g-factor? How would we ever know if any of these illusions are true? In this era of educational accountability, who, exactly, is accountable for the impact of mandates requiring educators to use test scores as if they are truth—when they so clearly are not?

12

Translation for Liberation

A world without caste would set everyone free.

—Isabel Wilkerson, *Caste*

As we near the end of our overview of large-scale testing, we now know that we cannot place our trust in test scores, as we have been told we must. In testing manuals and speeches, psychometricians tell us they are testing for a generalized intelligence that may or may not exist, that a true score is not true, and that decisions based on test scores are, essentially, left to chance. Yet for over a century, this practice has continued and now, in the twenty-first century, most high-stakes educational decisions are based on test scores.

In light of these observations, the embers of a question still smolder. How have so many been convinced for so long that large-scale testing is a valuable and necessary tool, worthy of determining our children's futures?

We are raised to believe that some are more deserving than others, so we accept that people can be arranged according to their merit. When score-based decisions reproduce a divided social order, we accept it as evidence of hierarchy's truth. Those found to be most worthy are granted the nation's best resources, and the rest of us go along, believing the test anoints the most deserving. Someday, we hope, we might find our own children in that category. These ideas have been normalized for so long that many perceive this system as equitable.

Our faith, it turns out, is blind. The mirage of hierarchy is supported by our trust in scores produced within a theoretical framework we do not understand. This is not entirely our fault. If leaders wanted to be straight with us, we, and especially educators, would learn the history of testing and how scores are produced. We would be taught the inferences and assumptions behind the testing model, and scores would be reported within a range of possibility that fully acknowledges the role of error.

The story of testing is a cautionary tale. We live in a world that increasingly relies on the results of data emanating from statistical models that surpass Adolphe Quetelet's wildest dreams. Learning to communicate across these new languages sheds light into some very dark corners. Algorithms produce data that influence many areas of our lives. Testing is an early example, and by exploring its story, we've caught glimpses of how the larger system operates to preclude challenges, despite racialized and elitist outcomes. Justifications have been carefully crafted. The implications of this example are far-reaching.

Research in the era of Big Data is used to convince us of all kinds of things. The testing model was an instrument designed by eugenic researchers to produce lots of data they then used to "prove" that a particular "breed" of human is further evolved than others. Because testing culture relies on the language of research, it is critical that we understand how terms are operationalized, which models earn the label "research-based," who defines those parameters, and what practices are included or excluded as a result.

With that in mind, let's consider two terms presented in introductory research courses: *reliability* and *validity*. It may seem odd to approach them as we near the book's end, but we now have the background to understand how the terms are applied. When students dutifully record general definitions of these terms, they begin to learn that the world of research is culturally different from the world they have known. We will consider the way these key terms are defined in the world of testing to reveal yet another source of deep misunderstanding between psychometricians and the public. Anyone who uses test scores should speak the language of testing culture. Yet, like me, few even seem aware of the need for translation or that, in fact, psychometricians operate within a separate cultural framework of their own design.

One reason we are convinced to accept the use of high-stakes testing is based on confusion about what psychometricians mean when they use the terms *valid* and *reliable*. These words have specific meanings in common usage but a different meaning within the testing industry. These misunderstandings are rarely corrected, and we are disoriented as a result. This leaves power in the hands of those who create social policy.

Reliability

It would be reasonable to assume that the evaluation of a test's quality should align with its goals. And it does. But we've seen that while the public assumes one set of goals, psychometricians have another.

When testing company representatives present their wares to a state agency or school system, they often use a test's reliability rating as a selling point. Most who hear such presentations naturally assume that a test rated as highly reliable means they can trust the accuracy of its scores enough to use them to make high-stakes decisions. That assumption, however, is mistaken. Tests receive high reliability ratings when their scores consistently align test takers in the same order. That goal actually serves to *maintain* test score gaps.

There is little attempt to clear up confusion around use of the term *reliability*. I have attended presentations by testing representatives in two contexts: in a middle school faculty meeting and a meeting in which a state agency was charged with selecting a test for statewide use. In each case, the room filled with the language of psychometric culture, and no translation was offered. The rare question was answered according to the assumptions of psychometric culture. These responses were obscured by the layers of theory needed to understand them, so consumers simply abandoned any hope of comprehending. Not surprisingly, misunderstandings arise when we don't know psychometricians have assigned common words new meaning.

The resulting confusion allows testing companies to avoid critique that might otherwise emerge. While many educators and parents might sense something is wrong, we often can't quite put our finger on what it is. This book demonstrates the effort it takes to break down what we can view as cultural barriers that conceal some of the illogic around the high-stakes use of test scores. Had we understood, we might have demanded an end to large-scale testing long ago. Instead, even as the social damage intensifies, the model's opacity continues to obscure our view.

The word *reliability* has served as a hook for consumers. When a company provides a test's reliability rating, few are aware this is a statistical estimate that, like all aspects of the testing model, has meaning only in the context of its theoretical framework. While industry representatives carefully explain that reliability ratings indicate a test's quality, they don't clarify how "quality" is defined in psychometric culture. And it wouldn't do much good even if they did. Koretz explained that while reliability ratings are important to statisticians, they have little practical meaning in the world where tests are used.[1]

In an ETS research memorandum, psychometrician Samuel Livingston shared an example that indicates the depth and breadth of this misunderstanding. He cited a chapter of the 2014 *Standards for Educational and Psychological Testing* that repeatedly associated the word *reliability* with precision. Livingston explained that this is "a really bad idea . . . because it is misleading and confusing. Reliability is consistency. Precision is exactness. These two concepts are not the same." This document, remember, provides the only testing guidelines created by practitioners rather than industry insiders. We would hope that, of all people, *its* authors and editors would have a solid grasp of the model and its theoretical basis. Yet Livingston's observation leaves us wondering how few people understand the theory behind the testing model.[2]

To learn how reliability is operationalized in the world of psychometrics, we must return to the illusion of a true score. This unknowable entity provides the theoretical basis for estimating a test's reliability. At this point, you get the picture. Because reliability ratings rely on a mirage, "the reliability of a set of scores cannot be assessed directly, but only estimated." This estimate is then presented to the public as a measure of a test's quality, and consumers mistakenly believe a high rating means they are getting tests that produce outcomes they can trust.[3]

Clearly, the testing industry has constructed its own reality. Viewed from the outside, it seems one absurdity is layered upon another. These cultural differences lead to some strange situations. Livingston, for example, suggested his colleagues should avoid using the words *true* and *measurement error* when speaking in public. Psychometric truth, after all, exists only in some other dimension, a world psychometricians have themselves created. In this world, Livingston explained, psychometricians calculate a true score by averaging "the scores the test taker *would have had* under many circumstances that mostly did not happen." Believe it or not, these imaginary averages are "the basis for the reliability statistics that we report," the data that lead people to believe test scores are trustworthy.[4]

Numbers are solid, even when their meaning is not. Psychometricians can calculate almost anything as long as they continue to operate in the realm of statistics. Without a hint of trouble, Livingston wrote, "We can report reliability statistics based on 'true scores' by using the data from many test takers and *making some reasonable assumptions about the data we do not have.*"[5]

Again, they *can* because they say they can. Yet we, on the outside, run into trouble when we try to bring these numbers into the light of day, assuming they represent meaningful information. Imagine a testing representative explaining to testing consumers that in fact the reliability rating, this measure of a test's quality, is produced using proxies for scores that *don't exist,* from which psychometricians *extrapolate information* about *what might happen if* they had data they *cannot get.*

That, my friends, is truth. It seems each time psychometricians ran into trouble while creating the testing model, they found a way to simply work around it and continue creating procedures, even as a score's meaning vanished ever further from view.

So it seems we've been fooled by psychometric smoke screens and false stories about hierarchy and merit. As a result, despite Young's warnings in *The Rise of Meritocracy,* we now find ourselves in an untenable situation in which scores are assigned meaning and used to organize American society.

Rationalization and Justification

Once we learn that even the meaning of truth has been sacrificed to the parameters of the testing model, there is surely nothing left to debate. Kendi advised that wherever we see policy outcomes divided by race or class, we should follow the tangle of ideas used to justify those results until we reach their source. As we near the end of one such journey, we find that large-scale test scores are illusions we are asked to pretend are true. Whether we choose to comply, of course, is up to us.

In an age-old story, it is clear who benefits and who loses in this system. Certainly the testing industry, and therefore the US economy, benefits from an education policy that has exponentially increased the use of tests. Policy makers used the consistent demographic score divides to justify the need for school reform and claimed their goal was to close achievement gaps. They then proceeded to create a system that increasingly disenfranchises poor communities and people of color because those scores are used to justify closing or privatizing neighborhood schools. All the while policy makers claim that equality is just around the corner. Once those stubborn achievement gaps close, they say, all will be well.

This is a new twist on racism's historic patterns. This time, rather than blaming only those disenfranchised by policy, responsibility for low test scores spreads to include the nation's entire educational system. Policy makers are presented as champions for equity even as their policies further solidify the social hierarchy. Worst of all, this result was highly predictable, supported by an instrument created to ensure test scores' consistency.

Surely there are people positioned to notice the disconnect between the messaging and the outcomes of education policy. Some of these folks look away, while others try to resist. Parents opt their children out of testing; teachers speak out, retire, or simply quit. Yet until resistance reaches a tipping point, the system, and its damage, continues.

And what of the psychometricians?

Kane concluded simply, "We decide how we describe reality." Some who live in the world of testing may believe the apple has a core and their tests have defined it. What of those who recognize there is no core, or at least not one that can be differentiated, and those who recognize the negative social consequences of score-based policy? They might feel they are not responsible for how scores are used, because those decisions are the responsibility of politicians and policy makers.[6]

As a result, it appears that no one at any point in the chain feels accountable for testing's racialized and elitist impact. Nor are they held accountable. And American law and precedent are constructed to defend those outcomes.

Knowing Right from Wrong

The veil of opacity seems to obscure even our view of right and wrong, both literally and figuratively. Because reliability refers only to consistency, a "high-quality" test can produce *any* outcome at all, as long as it occurs consistently.

Given this definition, a test that produces scores that are consistently *wrong* is every bit as reliable as one that would produce scores that are consistently *right*. Yet it seems to me that if a true score doesn't exist, there is no definitive way to separate right from wrong. In the world of theory, scores that are *wrong* have absolutely no correlation with true scores, while scores considered *right* adhere to psychometricians' best estimates of what true scores might be. That is the best they can do.[7]

So when a score is misrepresented as a single point on a bell curve and then compared to a cut score, it's easy to see how test takers might be misclassified—purely as a result of error. And that misclassification should concern us. Our evaluations should be guided by the questions about whether a particular use of test scores leads to the "right" decisions. We're about to see, however, that even this presents a conundrum.[8]

Validity and Systematic Error

There is no doubt in my mind that Ronald, Jocelyn, and Roxanne were misclassified by a Praxis score interpreted to mean that they were not classroom-ready. Every other piece of evidence collected over four and a half years verified that they certainly were. Policy makers have decreed, however, that test score evidence is the data that "counts" most, and teacher education programs are required to follow their mandates or lose their accreditation. Once again, the knowledge and experience of educators are forced to bow to the power granted to policy makers.

Clearly, there are societal consequences to any use of large-scale test results. History makes that painfully clear. When scores are used to make important decisions, it is all the more critical to have evidence verifying that scores are accurate and their use appropriate so we can trust the conclusions drawn from them. For this reason, Koretz described validity as "the single most important criterion for evaluating achievement testing."[9]

Unlike reliability, validity can only be evaluated in the world where tests are used. Samuel Livingston explained that while "reliability tells us how consistently the test scores measure *something* . . . validity tells whether the test scores are measuring *the right things* for a particular use of the test."[10]

Establishing valid use of scores should begin with evidence that demonstrates the accuracy of the decisions made on the basis of the scores. For this reason, Koretz explained that a *test* should never be described as valid or invalid. Instead, validity is established by determining whether or not test scores are *used* appropriately. Koretz wrote, "The question to ask is *how well supported the conclusion is.*" In other words, how solid is the evidence that a test score effectively serves its intended purpose? Data are only useful, after all, if they help us make better decisions.[11]

To understand how psychometricians evaluate validity, Koretz suggests we visualize valid use as a continuum. On one end, the use of test scores is justified by evidence that indisputably proves we can trust them to support the conclusion that is drawn. The other end of the continuum would include scores that are, Koretz explained, "anchored by inferences that simply are not justified."[12]

Accurately interpreting a score's meaning, then, is critical to establishing valid use. The question then becomes: who is doing the interpreting and to what end? So much inference is required to produce large-scale test scores that the interpretation of meaning is open to question, supported only by theoretical assumptions. Assigning meaning to test scores is therefore as subjective as any other human endeavor. History demonstrates that meaning has often been assigned according to political agendas. Because scores are reliably consistent, political leaders could predict the outcomes of score-based decisions right from the start. This made large-scale testing the ideal instrument to meet the social engineering goals of its developers.

As we've seen, there is no way to prove or disprove the veracity of a score presumed to represent an elusive human quality. In turn, it is difficult to verify whether a person has or has not been correctly categorized as a result of a test score. In addition, when NCLB testing mandates were introduced, policy makers dismissed the use of qualitative data, calling it too subjective. This restricted researchers to using test scores as the accepted source of evidence. Essentially, policy created a monopoly that made it nearly impossible to corroborate or deny the accuracy of score-based verdicts.

Clearly, what is difficult to prove is also difficult to disprove. This secured the legal ground for the expansion of test-based policy, no matter what its outcomes. Courts have established precedent that requires proof of discriminatory intent, so anyone who dares to question the racialized or elitist outcomes of test-based policy is asked to prove what can't be proven.

The historic use of test scores puts the onus on test takers to *dis*prove results produced by an incredibly convoluted model. Yet that becomes nearly impossible when regulatory agencies are also allowed to determine what evidence is valid and what is not. The demand to quantify everything, as if "true" data consist of numbers alone, clears the way for the testing industry to be the sole producer of educational data that "count." This is the reason that direct evidence of the quality of Jocelyn's, Roxanne's, and Ronald's teaching skills accrued over a period of four and a half years was dismissed in favor of a single test score. Research courses warn us against trusting decisions based on a single data point, yet education policy prevents us from triangulating the data, as scientific studies require.

The decision to dismiss the use of qualitative data in educational decision making does nothing to protect students and their families. If anything, its effects are harmful. Consider the rich, complex, direct evidence that is lost when qualitative research is declared useless. Removing humans from decision making removes the possibility of reaching humane conclusions. What we call cold, hard evidence is indeed both cold and hard. Policy makers claim that this more "objective" decision making serves an anti-racist purpose because it supposedly removes human bias. Yet the story of test development and application shows this is not the case, and demographic data show the consequences are anything but equitable. In a bait and switch, rhetoric raised fears about the *possibility* that decisions made by educators might be influenced by racist ideas and replaced it with a system that we now know was *certain* to produce racist and elitist results.

The fear of teachers' racism is not a reason to leave critical decisions to test scores. A straightforward way to reduce racial bias is to infuse teacher education and professional development with anti-racist theory and practice. Yet, particularly in the wake of the Trump administration, some politicians are doing everything in their power to prevent that from happening. They claim teaching anti-racism is teaching anti-Whiteness. This argument serves only to tighten the mental links between White identity and racism, the very link these politicians say they want to sever.

The goal of effective anti-racist education is to affirm our connections to one another across artificial lines of divisions. This requires identifying and denouncing practices that, like testing, lead to demographically divided outcomes—and the ideology used to justify them. As things now stand, anti-racist efforts are thwarted by the outcomes of test-based policy. Throughout the history of large-scale testing, whenever critical educational decisions have been based on test scores, a demographically divided hierarchy is the result.

With this understanding, we return to the question of validity. If establishing validity relies on evidence that conclusions are well supported, it seems valid use of test scores should rely on two factors: evidence that backs our trust in a score's meaning and corroborating evidence that the use of these scores results in accurate decisions. Absent solid evidence in either area, how can we even know where a test falls on the validity continuum? After explaining issues that undermine validity, Koretz concludes that "most inferences based on test scores cannot be perfectly valid, but often they are valid enough to be very useful." Clearly, those uses would need to be carefully determined. That determination is difficult, however. Koretz explained, "Some inferences are better supported than others, but because the evidence bearing on this point is usually limited, we have to hedge our bets."[13]

By now, when it comes to psychometric theory, we have grown used to phrases like "we have to hedge our bets." After studying the deeply layered assumptions behind testing procedures and the distance between a score and its meaning, for me, the possibility of valid use of test scores seems dubious at best. Yet testing advocates continue to rebuke critics with phrases like "Don't let the perfect stand in the way of the good." If the closest we can come to "good" is to assign scores a meaning based on ideology, inference, or political will, why would anyone decide to use test scores to make high-stakes decisions? Knowing that these policies produce outcomes divided by race and class, we are left to draw our own conclusions.

To put this in the context of a real-world example, let's see how ETS discusses valid use of its Praxis exams. The glossary of *Understanding Your Praxis Scores, 2014–15* defines validity as "the extent to which test scores actually reflect what they are intended to measure." It adds, "The Praxis Series tests are intended to measure the knowledge, skills, or abilities that groups of experts determine to be important for a beginning teacher." The *Praxis Technical Manual* claims, "The Praxis tests provide states with the appropriate tools to make decisions about applicants for a teaching license."[14]

The ETS *Praxis Study Companion* presents a paradox, however. It says: "The tests do not measure an individual's disposition toward teaching or potential for success, nor do they measure your actual teaching ability. The assessments are designed to be comprehensive and inclusive but are limited to what can be covered in a finite number of questions and question types. Teaching requires many complex skills that are typically measured in other ways, including classroom observation, video recordings, and portfolios." Given this caveat, why, then, would these tests be the appropriate tools for making certification decisions?[15]

Clearly, there are mixed messages here. Yet policy makers can read the statement recommending the tests' use for licensure decisions and feel they have indeed found just what they need: a seemingly simple solution to what even ETS acknowledges is a vastly complex issue. The appropriate-use statement apparently helps them feel justified in creating policy in which a Praxis score is *the* determining factor in awarding or denying teaching certification, such that its scores alone are used to eliminate candidates from the pool.

Once we know the degree of inference and estimates of probability involved in producing a test score, however, we recognize that such lofty claims are illusory. But for some reason, neither testing companies nor policy makers have been required to bear the burden of proof that the decisions based on test scores are "right." Instead, as Stephen Downing wrote in the *Handbook of Test*

Development, psychometric claims of validity rest "primarily and solidly on the adequacy and defensibility of the methods used to define the content domain operationally, delineate clearly the construct to be measured, and successfully implement procedures to systematically and adequately sample the content domain." A page later, Downing added, "The definition of test content is ultimately a matter of human judgment." So, obviously, are the standards of adequacy and defensibility.[16]

In my mind, the preceding chapters of this book demonstrate how *in*adequate and scientifically *in*defensible those methods are to match the purposes twenty-first-century policy makers claim. Although Koretz believes that the available evidence used to back validity might be sufficient when stakes are low, he concludes that even if the many types of evidence are considered together, they are "insufficient when high-stakes are attached to test scores." In addition, the evidence of the policy's inequitable impact is visible to all who have eyes to see. Kendi confirmed that "all forms of racism are overt if our antiracist eyes are open to seeing racist policy in racial inequity."[17]

The public has the right to demand evidence that test-based policy leads educators and the state to make the right decisions about students and teacher education candidates. The demographically divided impact of test-based decisions should indeed raise that question. Yet in a nation where racism and elitism have been normalized to the extent that they are part of the current that carries our culture along, this outcome has simply been taken for granted. We have to pull into the still waters of an eddy to even be able to see how nonsensical it all is.

Do we really believe that higher percentages of White students and wealthier students are more academically able (whatever that means) from the beginning to the end of their schooling? Are people in those two groups consistently more "ready" to become teachers than all other candidates, even after learning together in the same program? Because anytime a large-scale test is given, this is what the test evidence shows.

Of course White people and wealthy people have never been more capable or more "worthy" than anybody else. What should astonish us, then, is that those who have questioned this result for more than a century are continually stymied by research practices, rules, and regulations set up to defend the system that upholds it. We have, in fact, allowed psychometrics to define reality.

Given the lack of evidence to back the theory and procedures of the testing model and to confirm "correct" categorizations based on tests scores, it seems to me the only outcome we can truly count on may be the one large-scale testing was designed for: to validate and maintain a social hierarchy divided by race and class. It continues to serve that purpose very well.

The structures built to justify this system have been carefully constructed. Once a person has been denied opportunity because of a test score, it is very difficult to overturn that decision. As john a. powell, Michelle Alexander, and Isabel Wilkerson have explained, this is how racist systems are locked in place. In the twenty-first century, test-based education policy has created a closed system that cycles from kindergarten through teacher certification. We now have over a quarter century of data across every national metric that makes the impact of test-based policy clear. And still the defense of large-scale testing continues.

Researchers Heather Hill et al. found that few studies have even attempted to compare results of standardized assessments like the Praxis exams to instructional quality in classroom practice. In a 2003 report for the National Board on Educational Testing and Public Policy titled "Errors in Standardized Tests: A Systemic Problem," researchers Rhoades and Madaus describe the testing industry as a "closed system . . . exempt from independent examinations."[18] Similarly, Daniel Koretz observes, "So many people consider test-based accountability systems to be self-evaluating—they assume that if test scores are increasing, we can trust that students are learning more." Self-evaluating? Why, yes, I guess they are . . . because policy allows it. This assumption might be okay, Koretz said, "if we knew students were, in fact, learning more and if the distortions [in scores] were small enough that they did not seriously mislead people and cause them to make incorrect decisions." We can't, however, rely on either of these outcomes because "there is a disturbing lack of good evaluations of these systems, even after more than three decades of high-stakes testing."[19]

Therefore, while the system demands research-based accountability, policy makers and politicians have scant evidence to justify decisions they have made. Again and again, we return to the advice Koretz stated unequivocally: "One of the best ways to avoid misusing test data: don't treat any single test as providing the 'right,' authoritative answer. Ever." Clearly, twenty-first-century leaders ignored even the advice of the psychometricians their policies have positioned as experts.[20]

As I faced these facts near the end of this long learning journey, I recognized the need to put the pieces of this story together in a new way. While my external world looked much the same, I had changed. I now see the world differently. This transformation led me to conclusions I could not have drawn before. Perhaps the same is true for you.

This new learning impacts how I will move forward. But I am not at an end point. As long as I stay open to new perspectives, I will continue to grow. While I have no definitive answers, I do have ideas to offer, and I hope you will find ways to offer your own solutions as well. It will take all of us, working together, to find a better way.

Drawing Conclusions

Testing advocates are a tenacious lot. So, clearly, are those who set policy and continue practices that maintain the social status quo. While their explanations are carefully crafted to persuade the public, some things just don't mix. Just as oil separates from water, hierarchy will never blend with equity or equality.

When the world called the Nazi Party to accountability at the Nuremberg trials, the norms and assumptions of eugenics theory were also called into question. Outwardly, it appeared that as the Nazis' caste system was disassembled, eugenics ideology was banished from the Earth. The United States, however, had taken a more subtle approach, and the systems created to uphold the illusion of White supremacist ideology maintained a firm hold.

Winfield explained, "Using heredity in combination with older hierarchical versions of race theory eugenicists successfully convinced the public that race, ability, and essential human worth were correlated." The journey we have taken was prompted by the need to disentangle these ideas and identify their source. It turns out that by using test scores as verifying evidence, these ideas became deeply embedded in our national psyche.[21]

So much so, in fact, that the practice of large-scale testing has continued unabated, and now, during the twenty-first century, testing is the primary gatekeeper controlling access to power in American society. We all play a role in this system. We are not powerless. As long as we tolerate the high-stakes use of test scores, accepting and acting on their verdicts, we allow eugenic ideas to spread.

Now that we have uncovered and examined testing's roots and exposed the simple fact that test scores are *not* truth, we must question the purpose of mandates requiring mountains of testing data. The change in ideology from eugenics to meritocracy allowed the testing industry to thrive. The balance on the scale that had once leaned more heavily toward "nature" shifted, instead, toward "nurture." Many claimed that environmental factors, rather than biological differences, caused disparities in people's abilities that are reflected in demographic score divides.

While any move away from biological racism may seem like progress, this position continues to assume that the hierarchy depicted by test scores is real. By accepting the verdict of scores, we allow them to continue to create the impression that those with low scores are somehow "less than." It makes no difference if that is interpreted as lower achieving or less intelligent or less able. Neither the "nature" or "nurture" argument digs deeply enough to hit the root of the problem: the fact that test scores are often the sole evidence used to support these claims. No matter the cause, each stance assumes that the hierarchy of test scores reveals some hidden truth about individuals that highlights racial and class differences, and this belief has served as society's undercurrent for many generations.

The crux of the issue, then, is our willingness to accept this verdict. Have we been fooled so well for so long by this carefully constructed illusion of hierarchy that we really believe some are less worthy of society's best offerings? My conversations with testing advocates lead me to believe the answer is yes, although they rarely say it that way. While some continue to argue there is no better way to evaluate student learning, our close look at the testing model provides clear evidence to the contrary. Others fear that removing the filter of test scores might allow "unqualified" people to hold positions of power. They have learned to trust the verdict of test scores so much that they fear what might happen if we *don't* have this way of demarcating who deserves the opportunity to hold the nation's highest positions. It's as if they cannot even imagine other ways to guide people toward careers that best suit their unique skills, talents, and interests—which, ideally, could be carefully nurtured throughout their schooling. Perhaps, then, lack of imagination has allowed testing to guard the gates to positions of power. Or maybe we should name what we are most reluctant to admit: perhaps our judgment is affected by the ongoing influence of racist ideas.

It is sometimes impossible to see hard truths unless or until we shift our vantage point. In *Gods of the Upper Air,* Charles King explained, "The most enduring prejudices are the comfortable ones, those hidden up close; seeing the world as it is requires some distance, a view from the upper air." Clearly, as a nation, we have some shifting—and some soul searching—to do. This narrative invites us to consider familiar systems in a new light. I hope it brings an end to questions about how to replace large-scale testing and leads us, instead, to questions that acknowledge the critical role of education in shaping our nation.[22]

Educators are encouraged to engage in backward planning—to begin with the end in mind. We can be guided by questions I asked my seventh graders: What kind of people do we want to be? What kind of society do we want to live in? If we can envision the desired outcomes, we can outline steps to get there. Constant critical evaluation should allow us to see when policies and practices veer us away from that track. The set of education policies enacted in 2015 is named the Every Student Succeeds Act. Yet the evaluation of success is based solely on a large-scale testing model that, by design, will never allow that goal to be achieved.

If justice is any part of our societal goals, we must reconfigure the educational system that serves as the backbone of our nation. Isabel Wilkerson places this work squarely in our hands, reiterating that we must check our beliefs as well as our practice. She explained, "A caste system persists in part because we, each and every one of us, allow it to exist. . . . If enough people buy into the lie of natural hierarchy, then it becomes the truth or is assumed to be." So each time we accept the use of large-scale test scores as if they are truth, we reinforce one of caste's primary pillars.[23]

Wilkerson explained, "Caste is a disease, and none of us is immune. . . .No one escapes exposure to its message that one set of people is presumed to be inherently smarter, more capable, and more deserving than other groups deemed lower. This program has been installed into the subconscious of every one of us. And, high or low, without intervention or reprogramming, we act out the script we were handed." Large-scale testing plays a critical role in our indoctrination, as test scores are treated as verification that the script they assign is for the only role we deserve.[24]

We are all damaged by the disease of caste, albeit in very different ways. In a 2019 interview, theologian Serene Jones named the ideology of hierarchy as a cause of collective societal trauma. "At the heart of our nation's turmoil is the fact that people honestly do not believe that we are all equal and loved equally and equally valued. They just don't believe that." Maintaining caste requires ongoing inhumanity, which tears at our psyches and our social fabric. Just as surely, the practices enacted to maintain the illusion of hierarchy erode the potential of our nation.[25]

Wilkerson takes this a step farther, and her conclusions show that eugenics practices have achieved the opposite of what its advocates intended. Rather than evolving into superior people, she wrote, "the species has suffered incomprehensible loss over the false divisions of caste. . . . Where would we be as a species had the millions of targets of these caste systems been permitted to live out their dreams or live at all? Where would the planet be had the putative beneficiaries been freed of the illusions that imprisoned them, too, had they directed their energies toward solutions for all of humanity . . . rather than division?" Blinded by their own ideologies, scientists who believed they were aiding human evolution instead compounded the spread of a disease for which we have yet to find a cure.[26]

The guilt and shame brought on by such questions drive some right back into denial. Yet if we allow ourselves to become frozen in the face of our grave mistakes, the status quo continues, recultivating the cycle of shame. Wilkerson concluded, "It is a danger to the species and to the planet to have this depth of unexamined grievance and discontent in the most powerful nation in the world." The only solution is to deal "with the structure that created the imbalance to begin with."[27]

Jones explained that the way to health is blocked only by our fear. The United States, she said, has been paralyzed by its unwillingness to face the truth about racist ideologies and practices built into the nation's systems. She described it as a "strange fear that somehow, if we come to grips with these horrors, we're somehow gonna die from them. And that's simply not true. You're set free, actually, by the telling of truth. . . . And you can [then] move into a place where . . . it actually propels you into the future, through love."[28]

Many contemporary writers and thinkers agree that love is the path we must seek. As I entered the hall at Berea College to attend a memorial for bell hooks, her words loomed large on a screen: "There can be no love without justice . . . without justice there can be no love."

Imagine the actions of our country driven by the forces of love instead of constant attempts to defend its racist past. Imagine an educational system that treats each precious child as our own. A system based on love would change everything. No matter what the rationale, such a system would clearly *not* grant a high-quality education for some while denying it to others. There would be no hierarchy of worth or messages of deficit declaring that some children are not "ready" for the best our nation has to offer.

Test results were the last century's primary justification for such discrimination. The damage is clear, so that past is painful to consider. But we simply cannot deny the past while the impact of contemporary test-based policy continues to stare us in the eye. Large-scale testing was driven by the desire to achieve the very social stratification twenty-first-century education policy reinforces. This ongoing result should not surprise us; as we've seen, the policy is centered around a large-scale testing model that is performing exactly as designed.[29]

Disrupting the educational hierarchy will inevitably impact other related systems that support injustice. Like dominoes in a carefully balanced line, once the first is tipped, the rest are likely to fall. As these pillars of caste begin to topple, we are set free to begin anew.

In Susan Neiman's book *Learning from the Germans: Race and the Memory of Evil,* she explains how, with great effort, Germany managed to rid itself of the structures created to uphold caste during the Nazi reign. This example returns us to Hartheim, where this book began. Through the support of some and the inaction of others, Hitler gained the power to create a caste system that led to mass murders in Nazi Germany. Now German schools teach about Nazi atrocities. They face their past *because they have chosen a different future.*

In the light of these choices, Wilkerson draws a parallel. "It is the actions, or more commonly inactions, of ordinary people that keep the mechanism of caste running, the people who shrug their shoulders at the latest police killing, the people who laugh off the coded put-downs of marginalized people shared at the dinner table and say nothing for fear of alienating an otherwise beloved uncle. The people who are willing to pay higher property taxes for their own children's schools but who balk at taxes to educate the children society devalues." And at this point, it seems appropriate to add *the people who welcome opportunities awarded by their own or their children's high test scores, with the understanding that low-scoring children are denied those opportunities.* Wilkerson concluded her list of examples with "the people who sit in silence as a marginalized person, whether of color or a woman, is interrupted in a meeting, her ideas dismissed (though perhaps later adopted), for fear of losing caste, each of these keeping intact the whole system that holds everyone in its grip."[30]

For fear of losing caste. As hard as some might try to deny it, at some level we recognize caste's rule over our lives. So if we are honest, perhaps maintaining caste has been the point all along. Wilkerson explained, "You cannot solve anything that you do not admit exists, which could be why some people may not want to talk about it: it might get solved." So the real question is the question Germans faced after World War II: do we *want* to create a just society?[31]

While we cannot go back and change the beginning of America's story, our choices certainly influence how it will progress. With racial unrest and class division at the forefront, the United States finds itself standing at a crossroads that will determine our next chapter. The caste system's skeleton has been laid bare. Wilkerson wrote: "Once awakened, we then have a choice. We can be born to the dominant caste but choose not to dominate. We can be born to a subordinated caste but resist the box others force upon us. And all of us can sharpen our powers of discernment. . . . We need not bristle when those deemed subordinate break free, but rejoice that here may be one more human being who can add their true strengths to humanity."[32]

Now *there* is a goal worthy of our nation's claims: to support people in ways that allow them to recognize and enhance their unique gifts. To that end, educator Bettina Love suggests that rather than constantly trying to reform an educational system constructed upon hierarchy, we should simply begin again, guided by a focus on equity and a commitment to the promise and potential of all of our children.[33]

Allow your body to viscerally experience the relief in that thought.

Just as racist systems were created, they can be dismantled. Yes, it is complicated; yes, it will be hard. But what better work could there be than to create a system that nurtures each of our children in ways that allow them to thrive? Guides like Dr. Love are forging that path right now, pointing the way to freedom. Whether we will summon the courage to follow their lead is up to us.

Epilogue
Hope

Hope is our superpower. . . . Hope is the thing that gets you to stand up when others say, Sit down. It's the thing that gets you to speak when others say, Be quiet.

—Bryan Stevenson, "Love Is the Motive"

The narrative you just read does not have to be *the* story of US education, just as racism does not have to define the entire history of the United States. Pages are yet to be written, and what those pages will contain is up to us. There is no denying the damage caused by the false illusions of hierarchy, but let this be a turning point. If our next steps are taken with care, we can influence the present in ways that will change the trajectory of the future. This is where hope lies. The possibility of enacting the vision of the world we want for our grandchildren carries people into the streets, to the voting booth, and into law offices, schools, and boardrooms. It summoned me to my writing desk. Bryan Stevenson describes hope as our superpower, and it is strongest when we act in concert, each playing a different yet harmonizing role. After all, the arc of history will only bend toward justice once we collectively push it past its tipping point.

In working to transform our nation, we may find that we, too, are transformed. In researching and writing this book, my growth has been enhanced by a remarkable group of writers publishing books that influenced me right when I needed them. The history of racist ideas shows that ideologies spread through narrative. So while I was learning about the history of testing, racist ideas, and statistical modeling from authors like Lemann, Au, Koretz, Kendi, Winfield, O'Neil, and Wilkerson, I also discovered the work of educators who give me hope as they envision a new way forward. In this epilogue you'll see how their work weaves together in my mind.

I am heartened to know that these remarkable people are out there, striving to create something that has not yet existed in this country: an educational system designed to serve all of our children. In short, their ideas bolster my belief in the possibilities of public education, as we begin anew. The starting point on any path toward liberation relies on carefully redesigning the goals, policies, and practices that guide the education of our precious children. This system will be designed by and for the range of people it is supposed to serve, rather than representatives of corporate and elite interests, so that justice is finally practiced and emerges as an outcome. The stones that mark this path are already being laid, and all are welcome to join the effort. Now is the time to make the turn, with faith, hope, and resolve, toward a just future.

This work, of course, will not be easy. There are systems and rhetoric in place to prevent resistance to the status quo, to conjure up our fear. We are too often told that we are helpless, that the system is too complex, that we have no power. We are treated like our voices don't matter. As Ibram X. Kendi explained, "Racist ideas are constantly produced to cage the power of people to resist." They are created to silence us. In turn, our silence effectively supports a social framework engineered to create caste divisions predicated on Whiteness.[1]

This is the mindset that leads people to ask how testing will be replaced. After studying testing's origins, procedures, and implications, it seems they might as well ask: how else will we preserve caste in the United States? Because clearly, this large-scale testing model is not the best way to evaluate teaching or learning.

Growing social divides fracture our nation and threaten our democracy. Our very survival, then, depends on creating communities of belonging, enacting the truth that we *are* each other's keepers, and what is best for my child is also best for yours. For those raised in an individualistic, competitive society, this mindset may feel strange, but it is ancient wisdom.

Once we escape from the grips of false barriers, a whole new world of possibility opens. Once we perceive the world anew, we can dream new kinds of dreams and design, as Bettina Love described, an educational system driven by the forces of "justice, love and equity."[2]

Nurturing Educational Ecosystems

Join me in imagining schools designed as ecosystems of mutual flourishing. Pause for a moment and let the spark of possibility entice you.

Healthy ecosystems require a delicate balance of atmosphere and soil. Together, they sustain life. A forest's health might be evaluated by tracking the diversity of its plants and animals, the growth of its multitude of plants, the cycles needed to maintain rich soil, the quality of the water and air, and the flow of biochemicals that circulate throughout the system. All beings share energy from a single source: our sun. Plants convert that energy into a form they can use, and it is shared throughout the system.[3]

An equally delicate balance is needed to create and sustain the health of human systems, which rely on each person to play a different yet vital role.

Bettina Love suggests that the health of a school should be evaluated by indicators that each student is thriving in every aspect of their being. The health of individuals both relies on and supports community health. Energy circulates freely in systems where people draw what they need and return what they can contribute. Ecosystems themselves operate like a series of overlapping circles. Smaller communities adjoin, intersect, and operate within ever larger environments to create a vast network of connection. From the micro to the macro level, then, maintaining the health of individuals requires nurturing the strength of the whole.[4]

Healthy human ecosystems are spaces of belonging. After all, when our humanity and our dignity are promoted, we thrive. Such environments not only help us recognize our power but support us in becoming more powerful.

We can refuse the image of hierarchy, instead envisioning societies as interconnected ecosystems in which all parts are carefully balanced to ensure the mutual growth of all. This can be the model that guides us in re-creating our schools. And like a pebble tossed into a pond, its effects will ripple outward. Students educated in this system will graduate as leaders, transform the overlapping communities in which they operate, and gradually impact society as a whole. This may, in fact, be our last, best hope for survival.

The work of envisioning and creating healthy communities will strengthen and embolden us. Love explained, "We cannot pursue educational freedom or any type of justice without a model of democracy which empowers all." Working together across perceived differences helps us realize our connections as humans. That alone will help us heal. Any movement toward justice, john a. powell suggests, must honor our interconnections with one another and with the Earth. Botanist Robin Kimmerer of the Citizen Potawatomi Nation describes the rich spaces where seemingly disparate worldviews meet. When ideas emanating from different locations are encouraged to intertwine, they give birth to something new—or remind us of that which is essential as the fragments separated by humans once again join.[5]

An ecosystem out of balance will never thrive. Generations of hierarchy have promoted the health of a few to the detriment of many. Those who colonized much of the world called these systems "civilized." In talking with Isabel Wilkerson about caste in America, Gary Michael Tartakov, an American scholar of caste, diagnosed the underlying problem. "This is a civilization searching for its humanity. . . . It dehumanized others to build its civilization. Now it needs to find its own."[6]

Schools are the place to begin. Our children know a better way. As my middle school students learned about the Nazi Holocaust, they asked questions that prompted us to turn toward the policies of our own country. A theme began to emerge, and from that moment on, it guided the course of my teaching. "Finding Our Humanity" became a touchstone to guide my planning as my students and I practiced being in community with one another. Through literature, history, and the arts, we studied the human capacity for great love and the tragic results of learned hatred. We eventually came to recognize that we were actually studying ourselves, that in every moment we have choices about how we treat the people around us. This both empowered my students and moved them to action, as they thought about ways to spread this message throughout the school.

Therefore, there is no doubt in my mind that it is possible to teach for humanity, and there is every reason to design schools focused on this goal. With love as the driving force, democracy as the organizing principle, and mutual thriving as the educational standard, we have a starting point for creating healthy educational ecosystems. Each policy will be evaluated to ensure its outcomes support communities of mutual growth, exhibited by abilities to make connections, synthesize, consider ideas from different perspectives, and to closely listen to, evaluate, and communicate unique ideas.

Do you feel that small leap in your heart? That, my friends, is the hope that will power the promise of such a future. Across the country and around the world, educators are exploring the elements needed to create healthy atmospheres and produce soils rich enough for each child not only to grow but to thrive.

The strength of these voices is evidenced by a strong and familiar backlash from those who advocate for hierarchy. Former president Trump, for example, demands that his followers declare loyalty to what they call patriotic education, even as it bypasses truth. Such strong resistance to any move to disrupt hierarchy is part of a very old pattern. Yet if we ever truly hope to create a society where Every Student Succeeds, if that goal was not merely tossed out as a distraction, then it is vital that, together, we envision education anew. A community of learning designed on principles of liberty and justice will then serve as a model as we reimagine a nation that might finally begin living up to its promise.

The Path to Freedom

Designing schools as ecosystems of mutual thriving will put us into relationship with each other and with the Earth. As in any ecosystem, it will be important to maintain a careful balance of a healthy atmosphere and a rich substrate of curriculum, policy, and practice. Its health will be measured by its ability to support the diversity and continual growth of students, educators, administrators, and support staff. Human ecosystems, too, must have a source of energy that, like the sun's rays, can be converted into a useful form and shared throughout the system.

We'll consider the source of that energy, but first, let's focus on the fuel it creates: hope. Civil rights lawyer Bryan Stevenson contends that, as difficult as it may be, maintaining hope is our primary task because "injustice prevails where hopelessness persists." In education, the truth in that statement has played out before our eyes in the last quarter century. The injustice rendered by test scores' verdicts has left many educators, parents, and students feeling powerless to resist. Hopelessness often prevails in such situations, which frees harmful systems to expand. Instead, we must stay in touch with the central source of power that can continually fuel hope as it cycles through the system.[7]

What power is strong enough to maintain hope? The answer is recognized by every major religion and practiced by those with no religion. It is as simple as it is complex: love. Ecosystems of belonging are fueled by hope, which is powered by love. Love will forge this path to freedom. If we will trust in the power of love, it will sustain us.

The fact that I have to muster my courage to publicly make such a statement is a sign of how far off course the society of my upbringing has strayed. Some will consider it trite. But Black, Brown, and Indigenous authors have been writing about the importance of love for decades, and the power of their conviction finally helped me find my way to a place where I unabashedly share this conclusion. Their influence has allowed me to see that to deny the critical role of love lends another support for caste's illusions. Exploitation requires the ability to dehumanize those who are oppressed. Love, on the other hand, reveals the humanity and dignity of all.

This makes love a form of resistance. Because love is one of the few forces that can overcome fear; its very mention might feel dangerous to those who maintain power by stoking fear's flames. The times I have freely shared my long-standing belief that my most important job as an educator is to love my students, the response has often been a condescending smile, as if love is not enough. *As if love is not enough.*

Fortunately, some continue to speak and write about the liberatory power of love. Bettina Love, Gholdy Muhammad, bell hooks, angel Kyodo williams, Isabel Wilkerson, Bryan Stevenson, john a. powell, Carla España, Luz Yadira Herrera—each of these thinkers and scholars explain that love is the answer to reclaiming our humanity, individually and collectively. Hearing this view articulated is particularly important for we who have been taught to value objectivity above all else. There is, after all, nothing objective about love. There is also nothing to fear in its lack of objectivity. After all, when we love someone, we strive to serve their best interests and simultaneously open ourselves so we can learn from them. We are often changed by their influence. Our love for others brings meaning and joy to our lives.

These authors allow me to define where foolishness truly lies. Those who downplay the power and importance of love are misguided—or they are trying to misguide me. By freeing myself from rhetoric intended to distract me from the work of justice, by no longer allowing that truth to be denied, I have begun to break the constraints of a system built to encapsulate an illusion of White body supremacy.[8]

In *Caste*'s epilogue, Isabel Wilkerson concluded that we are morally obligated to break the boundaries of hierarchy. The only way we will ever break caste's back, Wilkerson explained, is for each of us to "truly see and connect with the humanity of the person in front of us." We who are favored by the nation's laws and policies must recognize that our only true place is alongside our fellow humans. Embodying that reality requires developing what Wilkerson calls radical empathy "for those who must endure the indignities [we] have been spared." Wilkerson explained that radical empathy "means putting in the work to educate oneself and to listen with a humble heart to understand another's experience from their perspective, not as we imagine we would feel. Radical empathy is not about you and what you think you would do in a situation you have never been in and perhaps never will. It is the kindred connection from a place of deep knowing that opens your spirit to the pain of another as they perceive it." Put simply, radical empathy leads us to care about each other. From this place of caring, we can enact the reality that every person is *worthy* of love. My love. Our love.[9]

Love is the sun that fuels our hope. When we act from a place of love, honoring humanity "in all its manifestations," hope spreads across human communities just as the sun's energy powers a forest ecosystem. Wilkerson offers a compelling image to illustrate its impact. "Multiplied by millions in a given day, it becomes the flap of a butterfly wing that shifts the air and builds to a hurricane across an ocean." This is how the world changes.[10]

A Healthy Educational Ecosystem

This short epilogue cannot contain the depth and detail this educational evolution will require and, of course, the potential solutions will be many. Communities of belonging can only be co-created. My purpose here, then, is to briefly highlight meaningful work already underway and begin to imagine how these projects might intertwine to create new opportunities. Combining these findings with a range of historic and contemporary experience, we might encounter crossroads of possibilities not yet envisioned.

The authors whose work I highlight are helping to define what classrooms and schools can look like when love is the driving force. The Reverend angel Kyodo williams describes the act of love as creating the space inside ourselves to allow others to be who they are, without rank or judgment, remembering that they, like we, are constantly transforming. This leads us to teach in ways that value the differences among individuals. Enacting our love means meeting each student's needs by approaching topics from multiple entry points, using a variety of materials and approaches, and gathering a multitude of tangible evidence to indicate student learning and growth, all while nurturing the health of the community as a whole. Teaching from a place of love means nothing is standard; instead, it is complex and ambiguous, intellectually rigorous, and requires teachers to draw on their experience and rely on their creativity. Teaching with love is a challenge and a joy. It is what keeps teachers in classrooms and students in school.[11]

We'll approach how to create schools as ecosystems of learning and belonging from two different angles. We'll discover, however, that they are inseparable. They work in tandem, each supporting the other. We will focus first on creating and maintaining a healthy, balanced atmosphere and then on producing the rich substrate needed to promote the healthy growth of all.

The Atmosphere

From the moment you enter a school or a classroom, you can sense whether its atmosphere is in or out of balance because it influences how you feel when you are there. Some schools prioritize making students and families feel welcome by ensuring we see both ourselves and others in the range of people, values, and experiences represented in classrooms and hallways. We notice the languages spoken and taught, and the words that are chosen. We take in how school employees and students interact with us, with each other, and with the range of people both in and outside the community. The evidence of these effects is largely intangible but includes a sense of ease and comfort, smiles and laughter, and people communicating with care based on genuine interest. These factors indicate that people are treated with dignity, so their sense of belonging is continually reinforced. When we enter such spaces, we relax, expecting that we, too, will be welcomed as contributing members of this community.

Before the nation's schools were transformed by testing culture, a number of books illustrated the importance of building such communities of learning. From the time I began teaching in the mid-1980s, I was drawn to this literature. I knew from experience that by fostering relationships with and among students, we could carefully cultivate an environment of mutual growth and shared learning. For more than a quarter century, I practiced creating these conditions, and that is the topic I dreamed I'd write about one day. Had I ever predicted the need for the book you hold in your hands, I would likely have chosen a different profession.

Now, after two decades of testing culture, the need for schools to become places of belonging for students, families, and staff, all valued as members of a community, is more important than ever. It is never too late to dream our way to freedom.

So even as we resist harmful policy, it is also important to look ahead with hope and plan with joyful anticipation what we will create together. Director of the Othering and Belonging Institute john a. powell dreams, in fact, that as we embody our inextricable connections to each other and to the Earth, the need to care for the system as a whole will be obvious. In our web of interconnections, a disruption in one segment reverberates and soon impacts us all.[12]

Around the turn of the twenty-first century, the truth of these interconnections prompted a long-term research project in New Zealand called Te Kotahitanga. Its findings provide insight into how schools can purposefully nourish the atmosphere to become spaces of belonging. Insight from this overview will lead us to also contemplate how language affects a school's climate. We'll then consider the ground beneath our feet, exploring elements that will produce a substrate rich enough to promote the growth of students in all their diversity. By weaving connections among these ideas, we may find new ways to restore health to an ecosystem in which many now struggle to survive.

Belonging/En Comunidad/Te Kotahitanga

Peter Block, author of *Community: A Structure of Belonging,* offered two ways to think about belonging. First, he wrote, "to belong is to be related to and a part of something. It is membership, the experience of being at home in the broadest sense of the phrase." At its best, home is a place we can relax, trusting we are loved. Where hierarchy has done its damage, spaces of belonging support healing by carefully reinforcing our humanity.[13]

In New Zealand, many Maori students, like Indigenous students around the globe, struggled in a system constructed by and for the country's European colonizers. The goal of Te Kotahitanga was to first discover and then create conditions in which Maori students, too, would thrive. Researchers began by inviting Maori students to share stories of their school experiences. When school systems are aligned with the cultural norms and values of people of European ancestry, from a young age, children from other cultural groups have to learn to code-switch. While they are in school spaces, they learn to follow those cultural norms. This adds layers of complication to their learning.[14]

It makes sense, then, that the results of these student interviews showed that the learning of Maori students would be enhanced by incorporating elements of Maori cultural values, Kaupapa Maori, into classrooms and schools. The study's findings indicate these would be spaces "where power is shared between self-determining individuals within non-dominating relations of interdependence; where culture counts; where learning is interactive, dialogic and spirals; [and] where participants are connected to one another through the establishment of a common vision for what constitutes excellence in educational outcomes." The researchers explained, "We termed this pedagogy a Culturally Responsive Pedagogy of Relations."[15]

These elements were broken down into specific actions described in the "Effective Teaching Profile" (ETP), a document designed to guide professional development experiences for educators. The ETP emphasized the importance of encouraging, for example, "student voice and participation, the sharing of power with students and their families to develop school reform, the rejection of deficit explanations of Maori student performance, a cross-curricular focus on caring and learning relationships, [and] a shift from traditional transmission modes of pedagogy to more dialogic, interactive modes." These strategies align with the work of Paulo Freire, author of *Pedagogy of the Oppressed,* and also, as we'll see, of educators advocating for schools designed to meet the needs of students of color.[16]

While Te Kotahitanga's outcomes exemplify Block's first definition of belonging, they also demonstrate the second: "To belong to a community," Block wrote, "is to act as a creator and co-owner of that community. . . . It means fostering among all of a community's citizens a sense of ownership and accountability." In the United States, communities once influenced the development of one-room or small local schools. When schools were consolidated into a national system, however, they aligned with state and national policy designed by government officials.[17]

The underlying question that currently confronts our nation is rarely stated: should public schools exclude or include? *We* are the people schools are supposed to serve. All of us. If, together, we clear the air of political wrangling and thoughtfully tend an atmosphere in which every child and family belongs, all will grow and thrive. That outcome is clearly missing from a test-driven system. Yet this should be our bottom line.[18]

Language Shapes Culture

As we witnessed in our study of large-scale testing, language shapes culture in powerful ways. Language defines concepts that influence the way we think about the world. To emphasize this point, Peter Block summarized Werner

Erhard's belief that because "all transformation is linguistic . . . a shift in speaking and listening is the essence of transformation." Our imaginations are limited or freed by the stories we hear and the stories we tell. So, Block continued, "If we have any desire to create an alternative future, it is only going to happen through a shift in our language." Our vocabulary should lend itself to a conversation "that has the power to create something new in the world."[19]

Words and concepts can be used to empower—or restrain—us as effectively as a weapon. Nearly a century ago, Carter G. Woodson wrote, "When you control a man's thinking you do not have to worry about his actions. . . . He will find his 'proper place' and will stay in it."[20]

We have seen that much of the language of testing culture conveys deficit thinking, focused especially on what some children lack. In previous chapters, we witnessed children labeled as morons, idiots, and imbeciles. In the foreword to Gholdy Muhammad's book *Cultivating Genius,* Bettina Love puts this practice into a contemporary context. "In education, we have allowed terms like 'at risk,' 'disadvantaged,' and 'struggling reader' to define our children, never considering that those terms have a history, too. As Gholdy points out, this deficit language that frames Black and Brown children's educational experience is rooted in and guided by Whiteness. It is precisely for that reason that strategies like 'racing to the top' and 'leaving no child behind' always fail because we are not teaching to repair and make our children feel whole and loved through their own identities, skills, intellect, and criticality."[21]

It doesn't have to be this way. While we may not have the power to single-handedly change the system, we each control the language we choose. We take control of our minds by carefully considering which words we will use and which we reject. Refusing the language of deficit changes how we think about our students. Choosing, instead, to focus on what children are capable of also reframes the narrative for those around us. When we find ourselves in conversation with people who use the term *achievement gap,* for instance, we might respond by naming it a *test score gap.* That is, after all, all we know to be true. Now that we understand how scores are derived, we know the probability that they indicate much about a person's intelligence, ability, or achievement is far too low to allow them to influence the trajectory of people's lives. Choosing our language can change the way we think about test scores and also the conclusions drawn from them. If our word choices remind us of the damage wrought when testing is allowed to create and maintain an educational hierarchy, we will less likely be swayed by the rhetoric of testing culture.

In *En Comunidad,* authors Carla España and Luz Yadira Herrera describe language as a critical tool for transforming schools into spaces where all belong. These authors, in fact, introduce a pedagogical approach called *translanguaging* that identifies the cyclical relationship between a school's atmospheric conditions and the curriculum that serves as its soil. In her study of Te Kotahitanga, Professor Emerita Christine Sleeter raised a question about this very relationship. While confirming the positive impact of Te Kotahitanga on Maori students, she speculated about the effect of simultaneously enriching the curriculum.[22]

It only makes sense that the places of belonging España and Herrera, Love, and Muhammad imagine should include a curriculum enriched by a careful balance of nutrients designed to support the healthy growth of all students. The atmosphere and soil are in a reciprocal relationship, so both need careful tending to ensure that energy and nutrients cycle and recycle throughout the system.

Curriculum: Enriching the Soil

The high-stakes use of large-scale testing is an example of a social structure that transforms the illusion of human hierarchy into a lived reality. The outcomes of such systems influence our personal mindsets and prevent us from even imagining that a fully functioning human ecosystem is possible. While we often view the institutional and the personal as separate entities, john a. powell describes their relationship as parts of a whole. Ann Winfield Gibson concurred. "If we fail to recognize racism as it exists in our social institutions, then there can be no hope of recognizing it within ourselves. Conversely, we must recognize racism within ourselves before we can begin the process of extricating it from our institutions." In other words, this relationship, too, is reciprocal. So while systemic reform is certainly needed to bring about justice, it alone is not enough. After generations of socialization, our minds have incorporated the ideas used to justify the inequitable outcomes of these structures, which influences our own ideas and practices. There is no need, then, to argue about which to address first, personal or structural frameworks. Because each influences the other, breaking down hierarchy requires us to attend to both.[23]

A curriculum designed to support a diverse population invites learners to examine the nation's structures, policies, and practices through a lens of justice and evaluate their impact on the trajectories of people's lives. Through introspection, we can sense the array of connections on which our lives depend. As we bring these ideas together, listening to others' stories and processing them individually and collectively, we create a cycle that leads to transformative learning. Synthesizing this information allows us to weigh the outcomes of present practices against our dreams for the future.[24]

While an ecosystem's health is defined by the breadth of its diversity, schools are currently designed to support a monoculture. Therefore, every aspect of the educational system requires our careful attention. España and Herrera conclude, "It is imperative that schooling experiences are liberating and transformative across contexts." Transformative learning relies on trusting relationships guided by hope and the kind of love that patiently nurtures the best in us and will settle for nothing less. Liberation comes with the understanding that children will bloom differently, in their own time, and evidence of growth will therefore be exhibited in many different ways.[25]

We can see now that all parts of an ecosystem are inextricably linked. Any attempt to differentiate the impact of atmosphere and soil is complicated by the fact that these divisions exist only in our minds. The Earth itself operates in concert. It would therefore be wise for us to think about educational conditions in the same light. The curriculum influences the balance in the atmosphere where relationships might be built, and these relationships influence how the curriculum is processed. Here, too, the system is cyclical.

To minds trained to categorize, this integrative thinking can sometimes be frustrating. To gain the full benefit of the studies and recommendations of the authors and research highlighted here, however, it is best to synthesize. Weaving these ideas together could easily take a book in itself—or several books. Because the purpose of this epilogue is to spark hope and give our dreams shape and direction, we'll briefly touch on a few critical points of connection.

Identities, Perspectives, and Studies of Power

While the findings of Te Kotahitanga focused primarily on classroom climate, the state of Montana has forged a path that provides a model for expanding curricular content. In 2005, Montana's Supreme Court upheld a district ruling that a quality education must preserve American Indian cultural identity. Because belonging requires representation, Montana's legislature funded an educational mandate called Indian Education for All (IEFA). Its three primary objectives call for "every Montanan, whether Indian or non-Indian . . . to learn about the distinct and unique heritage of American Indians in a culturally responsive manner"; for all school personnel to develop "an understanding and awareness of Indian tribes to help them relate effectively to Indian students and parents"; and for schools to work "cooperatively with Montana tribes when providing instruction and implementing any educational goals."[26]

Based on seven "Essential Understandings" created by representatives from each Indigenous nation within Montana's borders, educators across the curriculum expanded the scope of their teaching to include Indigenous perspectives. This meant that many non-Native teachers, like me, had much to learn. I've also had much to *unlearn,* as I realized much of what I thought I knew was, simply, wrong.

In an article about IEFA, educator Bobby Ann Starnes explained that the perspectives missing from Eurocentric curricula create a gap in our knowledge, and "the missing content that creates this gap is both significant and telling."[27]

Over the course of a century, the educational curriculum has scaffolded a narrative that sustains and seemingly justifies hierarchy. We study the lives and perspectives of people at the top, implying that these are positions we should envy, occupied by people whose values and practices we should emulate. The many other models of ways we might live upon this Earth are simply left behind. This is why I knew so little, even when I lived just west of the Blackfeet Nation and just north of Salish, Kootenai, and Pend d'Oreilles lands. Centuries of oppressive federal policy decisions had, for the most part, effectively hidden Indigenous cultures from my view, so I was never introduced to that vast diversity of languages, values, perspectives, and lifeways. The choice to omit this information from school curricula was made by someone far removed from my world, yet its absence limited my options as I considered how to live my life.

Some factions of society apparently do not consider these knowledge gaps a deficit, and they continue to advocate strongly for a Eurocentric curriculum. The *patriotic education* former President Trump called for would frame the US government as the hero of every story and omit any example of the negative impact of colonization. Some continue to argue that, like the Indian boarding schools that operated from the mid-1800s through the 1970s, schools should be the flame under a melting pot designed to assimilate everyone to a single set of norms, values, and practices—which also happens to support the long-standing social hierarchy. Trump's supporters have taken up that call and some states have already passed legislation intended to bring about that result.[28]

This fits a historic pattern. Each time there is a strong movement toward justice, a backlash occurs. The eugenics movement in the United States, for example, was a reaction to the success of Black communities as a result of Reconstruction. The public goes along because the knowledge gaps created by a one-sided story impact our ability to critically interpret social power dynamics. Those who argue for the continuation of the master narrative ignore the fact that while curriculum documents declare it is important for students to develop critical thinking skills, this can only happen if students are introduced to a rich array of perspectives. Otherwise, there is little for them to think critically *about.*

For advocates of this view, maybe that is the point. Most of us were educated in a system that glorified the story of the colonizers and omitted studies of power dynamics, leading some to perceive that single perspective as the only *real* history. Many policy makers have benefited from the resulting system. Those who oppose multidimensional studies of history may fear that if enough of us understand how power has been gained and maintained in our country, we will refuse to go along. Controlling the narrative is one way those at the top have defended against the possibility that the caste system itself might one day be destroyed.

The strongest resistance, then, comes from those who know exactly how the social hierarchy is supported because it balances on their shoulders. In her book *Cultivating Genius: An Equity Framework for Culturally and Historically Responsive Literacy,* Gholdy Muhammad demonstrates how nurturing students' abilities to read and interpret the dynamics of power is one of four factors, identity, skill development, intellectualism, and criticality, needed to create schools as spaces that support the learning of all. Muhammad explained, "If students know themselves, they are engaged with the confidence to learn the skills. If they have the skills, they can learn new knowledge and critique that knowledge." In other words, together these four factors nourish the curricular soil in ways essential for the growth of individuals and communities.[29]

España and Herrera support this view. "If we want to provide learning experiences that will help our bilingual Latinx children to thrive, we must construct an educational narrative that places the lives and experiences of these children at the forefront of curriculum design and implementation." In other words, our studies must expand to include everyone involved in our collective story. This view is shared by the many educators who advocate integrating the many perspectives long excluded from Euro-focused curricula. These are not calls to erase the stories of people of European ancestry but to expand and complicate the narrative so it resembles the multiple dimensions of reality. Such enrichment enhances everyone's learning. After all, White students and wealthy students are also hurt by false dichotomies and incomplete narratives. We, too, react with frustration and disappointment when we realize that our education has focused on a small, specific slice of a much larger truth. For schools to become places of belonging, the curricular narrative must be the story of us, represented by a vast array of identities, experiences, and perspectives.[30]

The components of what Muhammad calls criticality harmonize with both Christine Sleeter's synthesis of a 2014 literature review and the *Guide for Racial Justice and Abolitionist Social and Emotional Learning* published by the Abolitionist Teaching Network (ATN). Muhammad defines criticality as "the capacity to read, write, and think in the context of understanding power, privilege, and oppression." The consensus of these authors and researchers is that the curriculum should include both system-wide and local analyses of inequities and their impact on students and families. All stress the importance of developing reciprocal relationships and implementing curricula that encompasses the richness of a wide array of languages, experiences, cultures, and identities. In addition, all call for a curriculum that "explicitly addresses issues of inequity and power," as Sleeter put it. In other words, as Paulo Freire and Donaldo Macedo said, liberatory education requires that people learn to read both the word and the world. When we expand our practice to add identity and criticality to the teaching of knowledge and skills, learning becomes culturally responsive and intellectually invigorating.[31]

Indian Education for All is an example of an effort to narrow knowledge gaps by expanding curricular perspectives. Considered together, the reform efforts of Te Kotahitanga and IEFA encompass the range of elements España and Herrera, Love, Muhammad, and Sleeter call for. Discerning, distilling, and connecting the most effective parts of these endeavors might balance the system's ecological conditions in ways that will light the unique spark of brilliance that exists in every child.

Perhaps these recommendations sync so well because, as Muhammad reminded us, they are not new. "Black people throughout history have laid the groundwork for education for all," recognizing this as the path to justice. All along, the primary challenge has been that such suggestions have been immediately dismissed. The resistance might be based on blindness or fostered by a culture built around the competitiveness of every man for himself. Not yet able to imagine what a model of equity might look like, some may fear overthrow because they fear the possibility that those who have been oppressed will want revenge. If a people's vision is limited to a hierarchical model, they may only imagine that roles would reverse and they would become the oppressed, a fear that has resonated since the time of enslavement.[32]

Those who have not yet released the notion of hierarchy cannot heed the calls of educational leaders like España and Herrera, Love, and Muhammad, who are showing the way toward a system where each child can gain equal footing before stepping into a society redesigned around principles of reciprocity. No one, in fact, has to be at the bottom. If and when we are able to listen, we will hear the voices of leaders around the world forwarding a vision of a society built to create justice for all. Just imagine.

Yes, it is difficult and complicated to undo a caste system and all its trappings. Yet as España and Herrera stated simply and beautifully, "This work is life work." And for those whose hope guides their efforts toward justice, it is life-sustaining work.[33]

The Road Ahead

The future is determined by a nation's system of public education. Imagine policies, practices, and school funding formulas designed to produce equitable outcomes. Imagine schools fueled by hope drawn from the power of love for every child and family.

Creating a new system is, of course, complex and unwieldy. Yet the United States considers itself a land of innovation. Those who try to dissuade us are desperate to preserve a status quo as unsustainable as it is damaging. Indigenous peoples the world over remind us that the Earth is our guide to creating dynamic, interconnected, reciprocal ecosystems.

The opening chapters of this book shared my experience at a school that came as close to this vision as any I have seen. Class sizes were small so relationships could be built, and love was the guiding force. There is more to that story, but within its framework, the rest is detail. Oxford School for Young Children was, in fact, a community of belonging.

By modeling human communities after healthy ecosystems, we will finally recognize that diversity, in all its manifestations, is our greatest defense against destruction. And the United States is one of the most diverse nations on Earth. When we draw upon this collective power, we will grow stronger. At the moment, this potential lies dormant, waiting for us to emerge from the influence of ideas created to separate us. Our children, says author Jason Reynolds, have much to teach us. They name the solution quite plainly: let's just stop being racist. When that domino tumbles, the rest will fall, and we can begin anew.[34]

Love can be our guiding star. Where love exists, everyone belongs. Once my child is your child and your child becomes my child, we will design schools where equity reigns.

Such is the power of love. The solution is as simple—and as complicated—as that. Now let us begin.

Acknowledgments

Although I had dreamed of one day writing a book about teaching—it has been the focus of most of my waking hours for much of my life—this is not the book I had anticipated. While I have long been critical of the restrictions imposed by education policy, I never would have predicted the current scenario. Throughout my career, testing has slowly wrapped itself like a rope around my ankle. The frenzied policy changes that accompanied the passage of NCLB suddenly jerked on that rope and knocked me off my feet. I had no choice but to pay attention, and it changed the course of my research. Please believe that I would rather not have spent the first few hours of every morning for the last five years studying the details of how large-scale tests are constructed or diving ever deeper into the depth of the evil that is eugenics. But the more I learned, the more my sense of responsibility grew. The result, many years later, is the book you now hold.

As it happens, this book emerges in the midst of yet another wave of resistance to a perceived threat to hierarchy, this time aimed directly at our nation's schools. The double-speak around these issues is nothing short of astonishing. These are dangerous times, especially for teachers, and this reality breaks my heart. Yet for the sake of our children and grandchildren, I and many others will continue to work to dream a beloved community into being.

The journey toward this book began with the writing practice and confidence I gained as part of the National Writing Project and specifically the Montana Writing Project. I am grateful for the direction charted by Heather Bruce, who invited me to co-direct a three-week summer institute for teachers in Browning, Montana, on lands of the Blackfeet Nation. Over three years, I had the honor of learning with and from Woody Kipp, Kathy Kipp, Joe Kipp, and Brenda Johnston, who helped me confront the impact of policy created to privilege people like me and to oppress people like them. Their patience with my ignorance and their generous and gentle council set me on a learning journey that will last a lifetime.

During this time, Indian Education for All became law in Montana. Unbeknownst to me, Bobby Ann Starnes, my earliest teaching mentor as the director of Oxford School for Young Children, had been teaching on the Rocky Boy's

Reservation, home to Chippewa Cree peoples. When we reconnected, our conversations about the hope of IEFA and the challenges of implementing it led us to create a nonprofit, Full Circle Curriculum and Materials. Our goal was to work with committees formed by Montana's tribal nations to develop a series of teaching materials for use by teachers across the state. In this process, I met Full Circle advisory council member and Billings school counselor Marcia Beaumont, whose wisdom and experience continue to influence my thinking.

This story circles back to the National Writing Project as through that network, I learned of a Holocaust and human rights organization now named the Olga Lengyel Institute for Holocaust Studies and Human Rights, or TOLI. Brenda Johnston, then my co-director in Browning, and I attended a two-week TOLI summer institute in New York City. There, she and I found connections between the policy that led to the horrors of Nazi Germany and the US policy regarding Indigenous peoples. This led us to design a TOLI seminar for educators that Brenda aptly named Worlds Apart but Not Strangers: Holocaust Education and Indian Education for All. Marcia Beaumont later joined our leadership team, and over the course of nine summers, I had the honor of working with and learning from them and the many colleagues who joined us as seminar participants. From the bottom of my heart, I thank Brenda, Marcia, and Lacy Watson, who joined the team as I prepared to step back. They are not only remarkable, strong leaders, they are friends for a lifetime. And I am deeply grateful for the inspiring work of Sondra Perl and Jennifer Lemberg, TOLI's director and associate director, whose vision dreamed TOLI into being and with whom I still have the honor of working in my role as coordinator of TOLI's regional seminars across the United States. As I continue to learn from them, I am grateful for their faith in my ability to contribute. My thanks also go to TOLI's new executive director, Deborah Lauter, for her willingness to serve as guide as we shape the direction of TOLI's future. It is my privilege to work with the remarkable educators who lead these TOLI seminars, whose deep integrity and devotion to teaching about society's most difficult topics make them the kind of teacher-leaders our children deserve. TOLI's pedagogical approach is relational, and these relationships have supported me through some of life's biggest challenges. I rely on the joy that emanates when we are together.

As No Child Left Behind began to put its stranglehold on education, I accepted a position to teach in the Teacher Education Program at Berea College in Berea, Kentucky and simultaneously began a doctoral program at Morehead State University. There I met the people who most directly influenced this book. I am thankful that David Barnett, chair of my doctoral committee, supported a change in tack and encouraged me to follow my frustrations with large-scale testing to their source. And this is yet another time when Bobby Starnes's leadership impacted my life, as she was then chair of Education Studies at Berea. After my husband's sudden death, Bobby became this book's biggest supporter. She was the first reader of every draft as each chapter took shape, and our long conversations helped hone my thinking. Bobby's support extends far beyond the book, as I continue to learn from her. It is difficult to express all the ways our long friendship has influenced my life. I am forever grateful. I also thank my dear friend and Berea colleague Kathryn Akural for her close reading and invaluable feedback over the course of my writing and Jill Bouma for posing questions that aided my thinking as the writing neared its end. During times I was tempted to quit this project, Bobby and Kathryn encouraged me to continue thinking and writing. If not for their faith in me, this manuscript would likely be languishing in a box somewhere.

Thanks are also due to the editors of the University Press of Kentucky, who bolstered my confidence by accepting my book proposal. Most recently, Director Ashley Runyon patiently stood by as I revised long past our initial deadline.

During the time I've been writing, I have communed with the authors of the many books and podcasts that seemed to arrive just as I needed them. The thinking of these writers has supported and enhanced my work. Most are mentioned in the text and references, but I want to thank them for their influence on my thinking. To name a few: Bryan Stevenson, bell hooks, john a. powell, Michelle Alexander, Ibram X. Kendi, Isabel Wilkerson, Jason Reynolds, Cathy O'Neil, Charles King, Daniel Markovits, Ann Gibson Winfield, Wayne Au, Daniel Koretz, Nicholas Lemann, James Whitman, Susan Neiman, Bettina Love, Gholdy Muhammad, Carla España, Luz Yadira Herrera, Thomas Peacock, Robin Kimmerer, and Suzanne Simard.

Because I end this book with the conclusion that love is the answer to our most vital questions, I will follow that path as I thank my parents, my dear mother Nayda Colomb, whose love continues to light my way, and her husband Henry Colomb, whom we recently lost and whose last conversation with me was about this book. My own father's memory accompanies me daily, and I continue to benefit from his love and guidance. My parents were my first teachers in matters of justice as they kept me, as a young child, acutely aware of all that was happening during the social movements of the 1960s. I also thank my brother Jim Zagray, sister-in-law Cindy, and their much-loved and multitalented daughter Kayla for their ongoing love and support.

My deepest gratitude goes to my husband Bob Warren, whose memory truly is a blessing. I am eternally grateful for the strength I continue to draw from his love and support gained during our marriage of thirty-one years. Bob was my primary thinking partner, and his generosity and encouragement provided space for me to write the proposal for this book. Our many conversations during the course of my learning deepened my understanding of some of its intricacies. The proposal was accepted by the University Press of Kentucky just a few months after he passed, and he would be pleased and proud to see it make its way into the world. While I've missed his feedback and support during this long period of writing and revising, at times I've been able to imagine his input, especially when the subject matter drew close to molecular biology, the subject of his close study. I am forever grateful for the cadre of dear friends who continue to help me through the impossible grief of his passing. In this, my thoughts and thanks turn to Van, whose loving care has returned life's music to my world.

I will end by thanking you, the reader, for accompanying me on this journey. You have been with me during each early morning as I struggled to predict how each word might be read and perceived. I look forward to the conversations sure to arise as we share perspectives in our pursuit of creating a country that is worthy of our children.

Notes

Introduction

Epigraph: Excerpt from CASTE (OPRAH'S BOOK CLUB): THE ORIGINS OF OUR DIS-CONTENTS by Isabel Wilkerson, copyright © 2020 by Isabel Wilkerson. Used by permission of Random House, an imprint and division of Penguin Random House LLC. All rights reserved.

1. Cold Spring Harbor Laboratory, "Carnegie Institution of Washington."
2. Schloss Hartheim, "Euthanasia Centre: 1940–1944."
3. Kendi, *Stamped from the Beginning*; Wilkerson, *Caste*.
4. Muhammad, *Cultivating Genius,* 120; Wilkerson, *Caste,* 70.
5. Wilkerson, *Caste,* 84–87.
6. Kendi, *Stamped from the Beginning,* 9.
7. Love, *We Want to Do More Than Survive,* 65–68.

1. A Façade of Assumptions

Epigraph: Excerpt from *The New Jim Crow: Mass Incarceration in the Age of Colorblindness* - Copyright © 2010, 2012, & 2020 by Michelle Alexander. Reprinted by permission of The New Press. www.thenewpress.com

1. Koretz, *Measuring Up,* 34.
2. See introduction for information about Hartheim
3. Kendi, *How to Be an Antiracist,* 19.
4. Gould, *The Mismeasure of Man,* 20.
5. Gould, *The Mismeasure of Man,* 54.
6. Gould, *The Mismeasure of Man,* 38–39; more on this history in chapters 5 and 6.
7. Gould, *The Mismeasure of Man,* 55.
8. Gould, *The Mismeasure of Man,* 55, 368.
9. Gould, *The Mismeasure of Man,* 57.
10. Gould, *The Mismeasure of Man,* 52, 55.
11. Garcia and Weiss, *The Teacher Shortage Is Real.*
12. O'Neil, *Weapons of Math Destruction,* 134–37.
13. Section 2 explains this in detail.
14. The impetus behind the rise of large-scale testing is described in detail in chapters 4 and 5.
15. Au, "Hiding behind High-Stakes Testing."
16. Kendi, *How to Be an Antiracist,* 122.
17. Starnes and Phi Delta Kappan, "Change, Sputnik, and Fast Food."

2. A Nation at Risk

Epigraph: Excerpt from WEAPONS OF MATH DESTRUCTION: HOW BIG DATA INCREASES INEQUALITY AND THREATENS DEMOCRACY by Cathy O'Neil, copyright © 2016 by Cathy O'Neil. Used by permission of Crown Books, an imprint of Random House, a division of Penguin Random House LLC. All rights reserved.

1. Read the "Great Commitments" of Berea College here: https://www.berea.edu/wp-content/uploads/2016/06/2017-Great-Commitments-Re-articulated.pdf.

2. Kentucky Legislative Research Commission, "Standards for Admission to Educator Preparation"; PraxisExam.org, "The Difference between Praxis I and Praxis II."

3. Burnside, "Day Law."

4. Bennett, McWhorter, and Kuykendall, "Will I Ever Teach?"

5. DuFour, *In Praise of American Educators,* 9–12.

6. Schanzenbach and Larson, "Is Your Child Ready for Kindergarten?"

7. Stearns et al., "Staying Back and Dropping Out."

8. See Friere and Macedo, *Literacy.*

9. Educational Testing Service, *Praxis Technical Manual,* 4; see also Warren, "Justice for All?" 97.

10. You can learn more about KIPP at their website: https://www.kipp.org/.

11. Koretz, *Measuring Up,* 99; emphasis added.

12. Koretz, *Measuring Up,* 98–99.

13. Nettles et al., *Performance and Passing Rate Differences,* 9; see also Warren, "Justice for All?" 123.

14. Kentucky policy later changed to also accept scores from other tests to determine educator preparation entry. See Educational Testing Service, "Kentucky Test Requirements."

15. Nettles et al., *Performance and Passing Rate Differences,* 35; see also Warren, "Justice for All?" 124; Koretz, *Measuring Up,* 98.

16. Ravitch, *The Death and Life of the Great American School System,* 286; Koretz, *Measuring Up,* 127.

17. Koretz, *Measuring Up,* 115; Berliner quoted in Au, "Hiding behind High-Stakes Testing," 13; see also Warren, "Justice for All?" 126.

18. Koretz, *Measuring Up,* 320; Educational Testing Service, *Praxis Technical Manual* 23, 25, 46; see also Warren, "Justice for All?" 115–16.

19. Ibram X. Kendi, "Why the Academic Achievement Gap is a Racist Idea."

20. Koretz, *Measuring Up,* 99.

21. O'Neil, *Weapons of Math Destruction,* 33.

22. O'Neil, *Weapons of Math Destruction,* 2–3.

23. O'Neil, *Weapons of Math Destruction,* 3.

24. O'Neil, *Weapons of Math Destruction,* 33, 2.

25. O'Neil, *Weapons of Math Destruction,* 47.

26. Lamb, "Review: *Weapons of Math Destruction.*"

27. O'Neil, *Weapons of Math Destruction,* 3.

28. O'Neil, *Weapons of Math Destruction,* 208.

29. O'Neil, *Weapons of Math Destruction,* 21, 208.

30. O'Neil, *Weapons of Math Destruction,* 3.

31. O'Neil, *Weapons of Math Destruction*, 31, 227.

32. O'Neil, *Weapons of Math Destruction*, 12.

33. O'Neil, *Weapons of Math Destruction*, 29.

34. Lemann, *The Big Test*, 96–108.

35. Rosner, "The SAT," 108, 116–17; Rhoades and Madaus, *Errors in Standardized Tests*, 8, 10, 30; see also Warren, "Justice for All?" 117.

36. Hibpshman, *Considerations Related to Setting Cut Scores*, 3–4; powell, *Racing to Justice*, 5; see also Warren, "Justice for All?" 156–59.

37. O'Neil, *Weapons of Math Destruction*, 12.

38. O'Neil, *Weapons of Math Destruction*, 27.

39. O'Neil, *Weapons of Math Destruction*, 48.

40. Ravitch, *The Death and Life of the Great American School System*, 246.

41. O'Neil, *Weapons of Math Destruction*, 48.

42. Saad, *Me and White Supremacy*, 3.

3. Constructing an Illusion

Epigraph: Excerpt from Jessica Singer Early, *Stirring Up Justice: Writing and Reading to Change the World* (Portsmouth: Heinemann, 2006). Used by permission of Jessica Singer Early.

1. "Berea College Early History"; Carl Day in Burnside, "Day Law."

2. Jordan, "Middletown School Alumni Gather at Historic Berea School Site."

3. Isabel Wilkerson, *Caste*; Loewen, *Lies My Teacher Told Me*.

4. This understanding came over time as a result of reading the many sources listed in the bibliography, including Ibram X. Kendi's comprehensive *Stamped from the Beginning*, as well as many personal conversations.

5. Kendi, *Stamped from the Beginning*, 6–11; Library of Congress, "The Founders and the Vote."

6. Rosamond, "Hegemony."

7. Kendi, *How to Be an Antiracist*, 20.

8. Montana Office of Public Instruction, *Essential Understandings regarding Montana Indians*.

9. Kendi, *How to Be an Antiracist*, 18, 20. See also Kendi, "Why the Academic Achievement Gap Is a Racist Idea."

10. Kendi, *Stamped from the Beginning*, 52; Carter and Snyder, "What Does It Mean to Be Antiracist?"

11. Wilkerson, "America's Caste System"; Wilkerson, *Caste*, 70.

12. Wilkerson, *Caste*, 84–85, 70.

13. Wilkerson, *Caste*, 66.

14. Wilkerson, *Caste*, 74–75.

15. Palmer, "Hegemony."

16. Palmer, "Hegemony."

17. Whitman, *Hitler's American Model*, 113–31.

18. Kendi, *How to Be an Antiracist*, 18–23; Wilkerson, *Caste*, 384–85.

19. Bell, *Storytelling for Social Justice*, 23.

20. Bell, *Storytelling for Social Justice*, 23.

21. powell, *Racing to Justice,* 84.

22. Bell, *Storytelling for Social Justice,* 23.

23. Strauss, "Trump's 'Patriotic Education' Report"; Flaherty, "Diversity Work, Interrupted."

24. Kendi, *Stamped from the Beginning,* 52; Wilkerson, *Caste,* 54.

25. Karen Fields in Gomer and Petrella, "White Fragility, Anti-Racist Pedagogy, and the Weight of History."

26. Daley, "Genetic Study Shows Skin Color Is Only Skin Deep"; Wilkerson, *Caste,* 66–67.

27. Menakem, *My Grandmother's Hands,* 4–12; Wilkerson, *Caste,* 17.

28. Kendi, *Stamped from the Beginning,* 23–24; quote Francis Gardiner Davenport (1917) in Newcomb, "Five Hundred Years of Injustice."

29. Kendi, *Stamped from the Beginning,* 9–10.

30. Newcomb, "Five Hundred Years of Injustice," section 1.

31. Newcomb, "Five Hundred Years of Injustice," section 1.

32. United Nations Office of Genocide, "Genocide."

33. Kendi, *Stamped from the Beginning,* 36, 31.

34. Kendi, *Stamped from the Beginning,* 38.

35. Battalora, *Birth of a White Nation,* 1–8; Tochluk, *Witnessing Whiteness,* 57–61.

36. Battalora, *Birth of a White Nation,* 17–20; Tochluk, *Witnessing Whiteness,* 58–59; McCulley, "Bacon's Rebellion."

37. Tochluk, *Witnessing Whiteness,* 58.

38. Information for this section is based on Battalora, *Birth of a White Nation,* 20–27; Kendi, *Stamped from the Beginning,* 53–57; Tochluk, *Witnessing Whiteness,* 59–66.

39. Battalora, *Birth of a White Nation,* 21–22.

40. Kendi, *Stamped from the Beginning,* 38.

41. Kendi, *Stamped from the Beginning,* 33, 47–49.

42. George Best in Kendi, *Stamped from the Beginning,* 32.

43. Kendi, *Stamped from the Beginning,* 50–51.

44. Aristotle in Kendi, *Stamped from the Beginning,* 17. For the scientific revolution, see Kendi, *Stamped from the Beginning,* 55–56; for Harvard, see Kendi and Reynolds, *Stamped,* 15–17.

45. Kendi, *Stamped from the Beginning,* 75.

46. Kendi, *Stamped from the Beginning,* 55; Gould, *Mismeasure of Man,* 106.

47. Kendi, *Stamped from the Beginning,* 45.

48. Kendi, *Stamped from the Beginning,* 55.

49. Kendi, *Stamped from the Beginning,* 56.

50. Kendi, *Stamped from the Beginning,* 56.

51. Kendi, *Stamped from the Beginning,* 75.

52. Powell, *Racing to Justice,* xviii, xxiv.

53. Tochluk, *Witnessing Whiteness,* 60–61, 64.

54. Newcomb, "Five Hundred Years of Injustice," sections 2 and 3.

55. Newcomb, "Five Hundred Years of Injustice," section 3; Montana Office of Public Instruction, *Essential Understandings regarding Montana Indians,* "Essential Understanding 5"; Whitman, *Hitler's American Model,* 9–10.

56. Kendi, *How to Be an Antiracist,* 18; Wilkerson, *Caste,* 17–20.

4. Measuring Human Worth

Epigraph: Excerpt from GODS OF THE UPPER AIR: HOW A CIRCLE OF RENEGADE ANTHROPOLOGISTS REINVENTED RACE, SEX, AND GENDER IN THE TWENTI-ETH CENTURY by Charles King, copyright © 2020 by Charles King. Used by permission of Doubleday, an imprint of the Knopf Doubleday Publishing Group, a division of Penguin Random House LLC. All rights reserved.

1. Au, "Meritocracy 2.0," 43–46; Wilkerson, "Isabel Wilkerson on America's Caste System."
2. Cowan, "Francis Galton's Statistical Ideas," 512; Donnelly, *Adolphe Quetelet,* 1, 4, 113–15.
3. Donnelly, *Adolphe Quetelet,* 5–6.
4. Donnelly, *Adolphe Quetelet,* 111–17; Fendler and Muzaffar, "The History of the Bell Curve," 71–74; Pentland, "Social Physics Can Change Your Company (and the World)."
5. Donnelly, *Adolphe Quetelet,* 114.
6. Hacking, *The Taming of Chance,* 107; Sartori, "The Bell Curve in Psychological Research and Practice," 410–13.
7. Hacking, *The Taming of Chance,* 107; Donnelly, *Adolphe Quetelet,* 111–17.
8. Hacking, *The Taming of Chance,* 107; Donnelly, *Adolphe Quetelet,* 119.
9. Donnelly, *Adolphe Quetelet,* 120, 130–34.
10. Donnelly, *Adolphe Quetelet,* 153.
11. Donnelly, *Adolphe Quetelet,* 130–33.
12. Hacking, *The Taming of Chance,* 107; Donnelly, *Adolphe Quetelet,* 115, 127, 121–23, 130–33.
13. Donnelly, *Adolphe Quetelet,* 123, 125.
14. Donnelly, *Adolphe Quetelet,* 1–2; Caponi, "Quetelet, the Average Man, and Medical Knowledge."
15. Goertzel, "The Myth of the Bell Curve" Donnelly, *Adolphe Quetelet,* 3, 127–30; Mordkoff, "Assumption(s) of Normality"; Caponi, "Quetelet, the Average Man, and Medical Knowledge"
16. Donnelly, *Adolphe Quetelet,* 6; Frank Manuel in Donnelly, *Adolphe Quetelet,* 6.
17. Fendler and Muzaffar, "The History of the Bell Curve," 80–82.
18. Peter Buck in Donnelly, *Adolphe Quetelet,* 5; Donnelly, *Adolphe Quetelet,* 5–6, 135–58.
19. Donnelly, *Adolphe Quetelet,* 6.
20. Fendler and Muzaffar, "The History of the Bell Curve," 74; Goertzel, "The Myth of the Bell Curve."
21. Kendi, *Stamped from the Beginning,* 209–11; Winfield, *Eugenics and Education in America,* 50–57.
22. Winfield, *Eugenics and Education in America,* 5–6, 52–57, 153; Kendi, *Stamped from the Beginning,* 210–11; King, *Gods of the Upper Air,* 205.
23. King, *Gods of the Upper Air,* 45.
24. Winfield, *Eugenics and Education in America,* 54, 57.
25. Wilkerson, *Caste,* 78–88; Hutson, "Social Darwinism Isn't Dead"; Fair, "Eugenics and the Modern Conservative Movement."
26. King, *Gods of the Upper Air,* 64.

27. Sartori, "The Bell Curve in Psychological Research and Practice," 411; King, "What Is Inferential Statistics?" For details about how tests produce scores, see chapters 8–12.

28. Fancher, "Francis Galton's African Ethnography"; King, *Gods of the Upper Air,* 65; Gould, *Mismeasure of Man,* 36–44.

29. King, *Gods of the Upper Air,* 64; Sartori, "The Bell Curve In Psychological Research and Practice, 411–14; Fendler and Muzaffar, *The History of the Bell Curve,* 73–75; King, "What Is Inferential Statistics?"

30. Galton Institute, "Sir Francis Galton." *Note:* The Galton Institute website no longer exists. In 2021 the institute was renamed the Adelphi Genetics Forum.

31. Winfield, *Eugenics and Education in America,* 5–7.

32. Sir Francis Galton quoted in Galton Institute, "Later Life."

33. Uenuma, "Better Baby Contests."

34. Weikart, "The Role of Darwinism in Nazi Racial Thought," 537–38.

35. Dana White quoted in Winfield, *Eugenics and Education in America,* 57; Winfield, *Eugenics and Education in America,* 85–88; Fox, "Nearly 2,000 Black Americans Were Lynched during Reconstruction"); Bruinius, *Better for All the World,* 35.

36. Winfield, *Eugenics and Education in America,* 57–59, 151–53.

37. O'Neil, *Weapons of Math Destruction,* 208; Winfield, *Eugenics and Education in America,* 99, 151–53, 163–64. For details about *Weapons of Math Destruction,* see chapter 2.

38. Winfield, *Eugenics and Education in America,* 108, 114; Pilgrim, "What Was Jim Crow?"

39. Galton quoted in Eugenics Archive, "Eugenics"; King, *Gods of the Upper Air,* 89; Galton Institute, "Developing Ideas."

40. Cowan, "Francis Galton's Statistical Ideas," 510; King, *Gods of the Upper Air,* 64.

41. Fancher, "Biographical Origins of Francis Galton's Psychology."

42. Galton in Fancher, "Galton's African Ethnography," 71; Fancher, "Galton's African Ethnography," 78–79.

43. Fancher, "Galton's African Ethnography," 79; Galton Institute, "Developing Ideas."

44. Winfield, *Eugenics and Education in America,* 65; Cowan, "Francis Galton's Statistical Ideas," 511.

45. Cowan, "Francis Galton's Statistical Ideas," 511.

46. Fendler and Muzaffar, "The History of the Bell Curve," 74; Sartori, "The Bell Curve in Psychological Research and Practice," 407; Cowan, "Francis Galton's Statistical Ideas," 514; Stahl, "The Evolution of the Normal Distribution," 111.

47. Cowan, "Francis Galton's Statistical Ideas," 516–28; Fancher, "Biographical Origins of Francis Galton's Psychology," 227–28.

48. King, *Gods of the Upper Air,* 174; Arthur Jensen, "Galton's Legacy to Research on Intelligence," 145–48.

49. Jensen, "Galton's Legacy to Research on Intelligence," 149.

50. Jensen, "Galton's Legacy to Research on Intelligence," 148.

51. Cowan, "Francis Galton's Statistical Ideas," 510, 527.

52. Winfield, *Eugenics and Education in America,* 153.

53. *Merriam-Webster,* "Intelligence." For Enlightenment values, see chapter 3; Benson, "Intelligence across Cultures," 56.

54. Lemann, *The Big Test,* 23.

55. Black, *War against the Weak,* 208, 259; Stoskopf, "Echoes of a Forgotten Past," 131; see also Warren, "Justice for All?" 130–36.

56. United Stated Holocaust Memorial Museum, "Nazi Camps"; Winfield, *Eugenics and Education in America*, 68–69; Wilkerson, *Caste*, 78–88; United States Holocaust Memorial Museum, "Euthanasia Program and Aktion T-4."

57. Gould, *The Mismeasure of Man*, 36.

58. O'Neil, *Weapons of Math Destruction*, 21.

59. O'Neil, *Weapons of Math Destruction*, 21.

5. Evaluating Human Worth

Epigraph: Excerpt from WEAPONS OF MATH DESTRUCTION: HOW BIG DATA INCREASES INEQUALITY AND THREATENS DEMOCRACY by Cathy O'Neil, copyright © 2016 by Cathy O'Neil. Used by permission of Crown Books, an imprint of Random House, a division of Penguin Random House LLC. All rights reserved.

1. Koretz, *Measuring Up*, 1; O'Neil, *Weapons of Math Destruction*, 1–13.

2. O'Neil, *Weapons of Math Destruction*, 136.

3. Sartori, "The Bell Curve in Psychological Research and Practice," 114.

4. Koretz, *Measuring Up*, 327.

5. Winfield, *Eugenics and Education in America*, 99–100.

6. Brutlag, "The Development of Correlation and Association in Statistics"; Karl Pearson in Norton, "Karl Pearson and Statistics," 10; see also Warren, "Justice for All?" 148–49.

7. Karl Pearson in Pearce, "Eugenics: Historic and Contemporary."

8. Delzel and Poliak, "Karl Pearson and Eugenics," 1059.

9. Norton, "Karl Pearson and Statistics," 4; Delzel and Poliak, "Karl Pearson and Eugenics," 1060, Amazon, "Groundwork of Eugenics"; see also Warren, "Justice for All?" 148–49.

10. Delzel and Poliak, "Karl Pearson and Eugenics," 1058; Pearson and Moul in Denzel and Poliak, "Karl Pearson and Eugenics," 1060–61.

11. Delzel and Poliak, "Karl Pearson and Eugenics," 1068, 1069.

12. Pearson in Sartori, "The Bell Curve in Psychological Research and Practice," 414.

13. Pearson in Stahl, "The Evolution of the Normal Distribution," 112; Pearson in Sartori, "The Bell Curve in Psychological Research and Practice," 414.

14. Berlak, "The Need for a New Science of Assessment," 10–11.

15. Sartori, "The Bell Curve in Psychological Research and Practice," 416.

16. Goertzel, "The Myth of the Bell Curve."

17. Stoskopf, "Echoes of a Forgotten Past," 127–28; Au, "Hiding behind High-Stakes Testing," 8; see also Warren, "Justice for All?" 131.

18. Winfield, *Eugenics and Education in America*, 117; Goddard, "Mental Tests and the Immigrant," 243.

19. Goddard, "Mental Tests and the Immigrant," 243.

20. Goddard, "Mental Tests and the Immigrant," 244.

21. Goddard, "Mental Tests and the Immigrant," 243–44.

22. Goddard, "Mental Tests and the Immigrant," 252, 247, 251; Winfield, *Eugenics and Education in America*, 117.

23. Goddard, "Mental Tests and the Immigrant," 252, 243.

24. Goddard, "Mental Tests and the Immigrant," 243.

25. Goddard, "Mental Tests and the Immigrant," 261, 271; for explanations and samples of tests, see 261–71.

26. Winfield, *Eugenics and Education in America*, 85.

27. Winfield, *Eugenics and Education in America*, 92, 8–9, 90–91, 73.

28. Wilkerson, *Caste*, 69–72.

29. Simkin, "Education in Nazi Germany"; Winfield, *Eugenics and Education in America*, 91.

30. "Text of the White House Statements on the Human Genome Project."

31. Wilkerson, *Caste*, 121; Whitman, *Hitler's American Model*, 129–31.

32. Winfield, *Eugenics and Education in America*, 88; Whitman, *Hitler's American Model*, 12.

33. Winfield, *Eugenics and Education in America*, 97.

34. Black, *War against the Weak*, xvi, 3–7; Bruinius, *Better for All the World*, 5–9; Disability Justice, "The Right to Self-Determination"; Harris, "Why *Buck v. Bell* Still Matters."

35. Flaherty, "An Intelligent Argument on Race?"

36. Winfield, *Eugenics and Education in America*, xx.

37. Kendi, "Why the Academic Achievement Gap Is a Racist Idea."

38. Kendi, *How to Be an Antiracist*, 17–18; Kendi, "Why the Academic Achievement Gap Is a Racist Idea."

39. Winfield, *Eugenics and Education in America*, 100.

40. Stoskopf, "Echoes of a Forgotten Past," 128; Bruinius, *Better for All the World*, 204.

41. Plucker, "Lewis Madison Terman"; Leslie, "The Vexing Legacy of Lewis Terman."

42. Terman in Stoskopf, "Echoes of a Forgotten Past," 129.

43. Terman in Stoskopf, "Echoes of a Forgotten Past," 129.

44. Bruinius, *Better for All the World*, 202.

45. Winfield, *Eugenics and Education in America*, 77, Goddard, "Mental Tests and the Immigrant," 268.

46. Goddard, "Mental Tests and the Immigrant," 269; Black, *War against the Weak*, 247, references the "lethal chamber," Wilkerson, *Caste*, 131–40.

47. Au, "Meritocracy 2.0," 39–48; Winfield, *Eugenics and Education in America*, 77.

48. Dewey, *Democracy and Education*, 207; Winfield, *Eugenics and Education in America*, 132–33.

49. Allen, "Intelligence Tests and Immigration to the United States," 2–3; Stoskopf, "Echoes of a Forgotten Past," 129; Becker, *History of the Stanford-Binet Intelligence Scales*, 1–3.

50. Plucker, "Lewis Madison Terman."

51. Stoskopf, "Echoes of a Forgotten Past," 128; Allen, "Intelligence Tests and Immigration," 2; Lemann, *The Big Test*, 30.

52. Allen, "Intelligence Tests and Immigration," 2–3.

53. Lemann, *The Big Test*, 29–30; Allen, "Intelligence Tests and Immigration," 3.

54. Stoskopf, "Echoes of a Forgotten Past," 130.

55. Au, "Hiding behind High-Stakes Testing," 9.

56. Brigham in Graves and Johnson, "The Pseudoscience of Psychometry and the Bell Curve," 277–78.

57. Lemann, *The Big Test*, 29.

58. Allen, "Intelligence Tests and Immigration," 2.

59. Terman in Stoskopf, "Echoes of a Forgotten Past," 129.

6. "Experts," Opposition, and Obfuscation

Epigraph: Excerpt from Walter Lippmann, "The Great Confusion," *New Republic* (January 1923).

1. Stoskopf, "Echoes of a Forgotten Past," 129–30.
2. Winfield, *Eugenics and Education in America*, 90.
3. Stoskopf, "Echoes of a Forgotten Past," 129.
4. Stoskopf, "An Untold Story of Resistance."
5. DuBois in Stoskopf, "An Untold Story of Resistance"; Wilkerson, *Caste*, 178–89.
6. Bond in Winfield, *Eugenics and Education in America*, 130; Norton, "The Horace Mann Bond Papers," 29–31.
7. Winfield, *Eugenics and Education in America*, 130; Bond in Winfield, *Eugenics and Education in America*, 130–31.
8. Stoskopf, "An Untold Story of Resistance."
9. Drakeford, "What's Race Got to Do with It?" 20–21.
10. Stoskopf, "An Untold Story of Resistance."
11. Wilkerson, *Caste*, 226.
12. Houts, "Behind the Call for Test Reform," 669.
13. Houts, "Behind the Call for Test Reform," 670.
14. Lippmann, "Debunking Intelligence Experts."
15. Lippmann, "Debunking Intelligence Experts."
16. Allen, "Intelligence Tests and Immigration to the United States," 2.
17. Lippmann in Houts, "Behind the Calls for Test Reform," 670.
18. Houts, "Behind the Calls for Test Reform," 670.
19. Lemann, *The Big Test*, 33.
20. Brigham in Lemann, *The Big Test*, 33.
21. Brigham in Lemann, *The Big Test*, 34.
22. Brigham in Lemann, *The Big Test*, 34.
23. Brigham in Lemann, *The Big Test*, 34, 40.
24. Lemann, *The Big Test*, 40.
25. Lemann, *The Big Test*, 41, 34.
26. Wilkerson, *Caste*, 224.
27. Wilkerson, *Caste*, 134; Winfield, *Eugenics and Education in America*, 99–100.
28. Wilkerson, *Caste*, 229.
29. Wilkerson, *Caste*, 229.
30. Au, "Hiding behind High-Stakes Testing," 9; Houts, "Behind the Calls for Test Reform," 670.
31. Stoskopf, "Echoes of a Forgotten Past," 128.

7. Shifting Rhetoric

Epigraph: Excerpt from THE MERITOCRACY TRAP: HOW AMERICA'S FOUNDATIONAL MYTH FEEDS INEQUALITY, DISMANTLES THE MIDDLE CLASS, AND DEVOURS THE ELITE by Daniel Markovits, copyright © 2019 by Daniel Markovits. Used by permission of Penguin Press, an imprint of Penguin Publishing Group, a division of Penguin Random House LLC. All rights reserved.

1. Au, "Meritocracy 2.0," 53; Wilkerson, *Caste*, 68.

2. Ansalone, "Keeping on Track," 124–25.

3. Wilkerson, *Caste*, 70.

4. Albert Coates in Winfield, *Eugenics and Education in America*, 141.

5. Winfield, *Eugenics and Education in America*, 141, 139.

6. Lemann, *The Big Test*, 115–19.

7. Young in Lemann, *The Big Test*, 117–19.

8. Fox, "Michael Young."

9. Au, "Meritocracy 2.0," 46–47.

10. Young, "Down with Meritocracy."

11. Young, "Down With Meritocracy"; Lemann, *The Big Test*, 347.

12. Lemann, *The Big Test*, 119.

13. Young, "Down with Meritocracy,"

14. Markovits, *The Meritocracy Trap*, 268, ix.

15. Markovits, *The Meritocracy Trap*, 5.

16. Markovits, *The Meritocracy Trap*, 18; Horowitz, Igielnik, and Kochhar, "Trends in Income and Wealth Inequality."

17. Markovits, *The Meritocracy Trap*, 268.

8. Establishing a Culture

Epigraph: Excerpt from MEASURING UP: WHAT EDUCATIONAL TESTING REALLY TELLS US by Daniel Koretz, Cambridge, Mass.: Harvard University Press, Copyright © 2008 by the President and Fellows of Harvard College. Used by permission. All rights reserved.

1. Koretz, *Measuring Up*, 327–28; Hibpshman, *Considerations Related to Setting Cut Scores*, 8.

2. Koretz, *Measuring Up*, 117.

3. O'Neil, *Weapons of Math Destruction*, 227.

4. Koretz, *Measuring Up*, 19–20.

5. Koretz, *Measuring Up*, 30–34.

6. Koretz, *Measuring Up*, 19; emphasis added.

7. Koretz, *Measuring Up*, 19.

8. Popham, "Criterion-Referenced Measurement," 62.

9. Jensen, "The G-Factor," 37 (abstract).

10. Charles Spearman in Perks, "Spearman and the Importance of Archives," 37; Jensen, "The G-Factor," 37 (abstract).

11. Jensen, "The G-Factor," 37 (abstract).

12. Josue, "Understanding the Normal Curve and its Parameters in Standardized Tests," 62.

13. Popham, "Criterion-Referenced Measurement," 62.

14. Popham, "Criterion-Referenced Measurement," 62–66.

15. Popham, "Criterion-Referenced Measurement," 64.

16. Popham, "Criterion-Referenced Measurement," 63.

17. Koretz, *Measuring Up*, 23.

18. Young and Zucker, *The Standards-Referenced Interpretive Framework*, 2–3.

19. Young and Zucker, *The Standards-Referenced Interpretive Framework*, 4.

20. Young and Zucker, *The Standards-Referenced Interpretive Framework*, 5.

21. Young and Zucker, *The Standards-Referenced Interpretive Framework,* 5–6.
22. Young and Zucker, *The Standards-Referenced Interpretive Framework,* 4, 6.

9. Test Design

Epigraph: Excerpt from WEAPONS OF MATH DESTRUCTION: HOW BIG DATA INCREASES INEQUALITY AND THREATENS DEMOCRACY by Cathy O'Neil, copyright © 2016 by Cathy O'Neil. Used by permission of Crown Books, an imprint of Random House, a division of Penguin Random House LLC. All rights reserved.

1. Educational Testing Service, "How Tests and Test Questions Are Developed."
2. Educational Testing Service, *Technical Manual for the Praxis Series,* 13.
3. Educational Testing Service, *Technical Manual for the Praxis Series,* 19; Knapp and Knapp, "Practice Analysis," *Licensure Testing: Purposes,* 93–94.
4. Educational Testing Service, "Praxis National Advisory Committees (NACs)"; Educational Testing Service, *Technical Manual for the Praxis Series,* 17, 14.
5. Knapp and Knapp, "Practice Analysis," 100.
6. Educational Testing Service, *Technical Manual for the Praxis Series,* 12–15.
7. Educational Testing Service, *Technical Manual for the Praxis Series,* 14.
8. Knapp and Knapp, "Practice Analysis," 94.
9. Educational Testing Service, *Technical Manual for the Praxis Series,* 14–15.
10. Rosenfeld and Kocher, *A Job Analysis of the Content Knowledge and Skill Areas Important for Newly Licensed (Certified) Elementary School Teachers.*
11. Educational Testing Service, *Technical Manual for the Praxis Series,* 17.
12. Educational Testing Service, *Technical Manual for the Praxis Series,* 13.
13. Educational Testing Service, *Technical Manual for the Praxis Series,* 14.
14. Educational Testing Service, "How Tests and Test Questions Are Developed."
15. Educational Testing Service, "Item Development."
16. Berlak, "The Need for a New Science of Assessment," 10.
17. Berlak, "The Need for a New Science of Assessment," 10–11; emphasis added.
18. Popham and Husek, "Implications of Criterion-Referenced Measurement," 2.
19. Livingston, "Item Analysis," 421–22.
20. Livingston, "Item Analysis," 422.
21. Livingston, "Item Analysis," 431; Varma, *Preliminary Item Statistics,* 3, 6.
22. Varma, *Preliminary Item Statistics,* 6.
23. Rosner, "The SAT," 115; Livingston, "Item Analysis," 433; Varma, *Preliminary Item Statistics,* 3.
24. Cole, "History and Development of DIF," 27.
25. Cole, "History and Development of DIF," 27; Hoff, "ETS President Cole Announces Retirement."
26. Varma, *Preliminary Item Statistics,* 6–7.
27. Rosner, "Why the New SAT Isn't as Transparent as the College Board Want You to Believe"; emphasis added.
28. Rosner, "Why the New SAT Isn't as Transparent as the College Board Wants You to Believe"; emphasis added.
29. Warren, "Justice for All?" 143–46.
30. Strauss, "Here's the Very First SAT."

31. Rosner, "Why the New SAT Isn't as Transparent as the College Board Want You to Believe"; Rosner, "The SAT," 105.

32. Kidder and Rosner, "How the SAT Creates Built-in Headwinds."

33. Rosner, "Why the New SAT Isn't as Transparent as the College Board Want You to Believe."

34. Gitomer, "Teacher Quality in a Changing Policy Landscape," 18–27; see also Warren, "Justice for All?" 138.

10. Collateral Damage

Epigraph: Excerpt from Harold Berlak et al., *Toward a New Science of Educational Testing and Assessment* (Albany: SUNY Press, 1992), 12.

1. powell, *Racing to Justice,* 106.

2. Koretz, *Measuring Up,* 324.

3. Koretz, *Measuring Up,* 324.

4. Popham, "Criterion-Referenced Measurement," 65.

5. Andrew Ho in Shafer, "When Proficient Isn't Good."

6. Educational Testing Service, *Praxis Technical Manual,* 26–27.

7. Educational Testing Service, *Praxis Technical Manual,* 27.

8. Educational Testing Service, *Praxis Technical Manual,* 27; emphasis added.

9. Educational Testing Service, *Praxis Technical Manual,* 27.

10. Warren, "Justice for All?" 100–101.

11. Educational Testing Service, *Praxis Technical Manual,* 28.

12. Code of Federal Regulations, title 29, section 1607.4 D in Hibpshman, *Considerations Related to Setting Cut Scores for Teacher Tests,* 5; see also Warren "Justice for All?" 156.

13. Hibpshman, *Considerations Related to Setting Cut Scores for Teacher Tests,* 5; see also Warren, "Justice for All?" 156–57.

14. Bejar, "Standard Setting," 1.

15. Rosner, ""The SAT," 107–8; see also Warren, "Justice for All?" 145.

16. Zieky, "Fairness Reviews in Assessment," 360.

17. Educational Testing Service, *2014 ETS Standards for Quality and Fairness,* 2.

18. Educational Testing Service, *2014 ETS Standards for Quality and Fairness,* 2.

19. Zieky, "Fairness Reviews in Assessment," 361–62; Educational Testing Service, "Fairness Guidelines."

20. Zieky, "Fairness Reviews in Assessment," 363.

21. Educational Testing Service, "Item Development."

22. Zieky, "Fairness Reviews in Assessment," 373–74; Educational Testing Service, *2014 ETS Standards for Quality and Fairness,* 56.

23. Zieky, "Fairness Reviews in Assessment," 373.

24. Zieky, "Fairness Reviews in Assessment," 373–74.

25. Zieky, "Fairness Reviews in Assessment," 362–63; Rosner, "Why the New SAT Isn't as Transparent as the College Board Wants You to Believe."

26. Note also Berea College's motto: "God has made of one blood all peoples of the earth." https://www.berea.edu/about/1855-to-today/.

27. Kendi, "Why the Academic Achievement Gap Is a Racist Idea."

28. Crow, "Unequal by Nature," 82.

29. Crow, "Unequal by Nature," 83–84.

30. Crow, "Unequal by Nature," 85; Jensen, "Psychometric G and Achievement," 120–21.

31. Crow, "Unequal by Nature," 83; Chou, "How Science and Genetics are Reshaping the Race Debate."

32. Kendi, "Why the Academic Achievement Gap Is a Racist Idea"; Plucker, "Unanswered Questions."

33. Crow, "Unequal by Nature," 87.

11. Inferences and Assumptions

Epigraph: Excerpt from CASTE (OPRAH'S BOOK CLUB): THE ORIGINS OF OUR DISCONTENTS by Isabel Wilkerson, copyright © 2020 by Isabel Wilkerson. Used by permission of Random House, an imprint and division of Penguin Random House LLC. All rights reserved.

1. Kane, *Errors of Measurement,* 4–33.

2. Gottfredson, "The General Intelligence Factor."

3. Gottfredson, "The General Intelligence Factor"; Jensen, "Psychometric G and Achievement," 131, 121.

4. Kane, *Errors of Measurement,* 6–7; Gottfredson, "The General Intelligence Factor."

5. Perks, "Spearman and the Importance of Archives," 722.

6. Perks, "Spearman and the Importance of Archives," 724.

7. Gottfredson, "The General Intelligence Factor"; Perks, "Spearman and the Importance of Archives," 724; Kane, *Errors of Measurement,* 7, 9.

8. Jensen, "Galton's Legacy to Research on Intelligence," 151, 164; Gottfredson, "The General Intelligence Factor."

9. Gottfredson, "The General Intelligence Factor"; Jensen, "Galton's Legacy to Research on Intelligence," 154.

10. Kane, *Errors of Measurement,* 7.

11. Kane, *Errors of Measurement,* 4–33.

12. Kane, *Errors of Measurement,* 5.

13. Kane, *Errors of Measurement,* 31–32.

14. Kane, *Errors of Measurement,* 7.

15. Kane, *Errors of Measurement,* 7.

16. Kane, *Errors of Measurement,* 26–28, 31; Jensen, "Galton's Legacy to Research on Intelligence," 151.

17. Educational Testing Service, *Praxis Technical Manual,* 39; Kane, *Errors of Measurement,* 7–9.

18. Educational Testing Service, *Praxis Technical Manual,* 39.

19. Kane, *Errors of Measurement,* 9.

20. Kane, *Errors of Measurement,* 15.

21. Koretz, *Measuring Up,* 145–53.

22. Au, "Hiding behind High-Stakes Testing," 15.

23. Koretz, *Measuring Up,* 145–53.

24. Educational Testing Service, *Technical Manual for the Praxis Series,* 56.

25. Koretz, *Measuring Up,* 153–57.

26. Educational Testing Service, *Understanding Your Praxis Scores.*

27. Educational Testing Service, *Understanding Your Praxis Scores,* 2; Koretz, *Measuring Up,* 153–57.

28. Koretz, *Measuring Up,* 153.

29. Koretz, *Measuring Up,* 155.

30. Educational Testing Service, "Kentucky Test Requirements."

31. Kane, *Errors of Measurement,* 3.

32. Kane, *Errors of Measurement,* 6–7.

33. Kane, *Errors of Measurement,* 7, 5.

12. Translation for Liberation

Epigraph: Excerpt from CASTE (OPRAH'S BOOK CLUB): THE ORIGINS OF OUR DISCONTENTS by Isabel Wilkerson, copyright © 2020 by Isabel Wilkerson. Used by permission of Random House, an imprint and division of Penguin Random House LLC. All rights reserved.

1. Koretz, *Measuring Up,* 157–62.

2. Livingston, "Test Reliability," 18.

3. Educational Testing Service, *Praxis Technical Manual,* 39.

4. Livingston, "Test Reliability," 10.

5. Livingston, "Test Reliability," 10; emphasis added.

6. Kane, *Errors of Measurement,* 32.

7. Koretz, *Measuring Up,* 223–24.

8. Koretz, *Measuring Up,* 159–61, 324–25.

9. Koretz, *Measuring Up,* 31.

10. Livingston, "Test Reliability," 7.

11. Koretz, *Measuring Up,* 31.

12. Koretz, *Measuring Up,* 219.

13. Koretz, *Measuring Up,* 31, 223, 219.

14. Educational Testing Service, *Understanding Your Praxis Scores,* 2; Educational Testing Service, *Praxis Technical Manual,* 11.

15. Educational Testing Service, *Praxis Study Companion,* 46.

16. Downing, "Twelve Steps for Effective Test Development," 7–8.

17. Koretz, *Measuring Up,* 236, 223; Kendi, *How to Be an Antiracist,* 221.

18. Hill et al., "Teacher Quality and Quality Teaching," 490; Rhoades and Madaus, *Errors in Standardized Tests,* 8; see also Warren, "Justice for All?" 117–18.

19. Koretz, *Measuring Up,* 331.

20. Koretz, *Measuring Up,* 320.

21. Winfield, *Eugenics and Education in America,* 97.

22. King, *Gods of the Upper Air,* 345.

23. Wilkerson, *Caste,* 380.

24. Wilkerson, *Caste,* 380, 384.

25. Jones, "Grace in a Fractured World."

26. Wilkerson, *Caste,* 377–78. In the last chapter of *How to Be an Antiracist,* Kendi, too, describes racism as a cancer.

27. Wilkerson, *Caste,* 381.

28. Jones, "Grace in a Fractured World."
29. See description in Love, *We Want to Do More Than Survive,* 16–31.
30. Wilkerson, *Caste,* 383.
31. Wilkerson, *Caste,* 385.
32. Wilkerson, *Caste,* 380.
33. Love, *We Want to Do More than Survive,* 101–3.

Epilogue

Epigraph: Bryan Stevenson, quoted from the *On Being* with Krista Tippett episode "Finding the Courage for What's Redemptive" (December 2020).

1. Kendi, *How to Be an Antiracist,* 124.
2. Love, *We Want to Do More Than Survive,* 102.
3. Schlesinger, "What Makes a Healthy Ecosystem?"
4. Love, *We Want to Do More Than Survive,* 120–23.
5. Love, *We Want to Do More Than Survive,* 68; powell, *Racing to Justice,* 227; Kimmerer, "The Intelligence of Plants."
6. Wilkerson, *Caste,* 357.
7. Stevenson, "Love Is the Motive."
8. Resmaa Menakem uses the term "white body supremacy" in *My Grandmother's Hands,* 6–7.
9. Wilkerson, *Caste,* 386.
10. Wilkerson, *Caste,* 387.
11. williams, "The World Is Our Field of Practice."
12. powell, "Creating the Conditions for Belonging and Breathing in a Toxic Environment."
13. Block, *Community,* xii.
14. Te Kete Ipurangi, "Mihi"; Te Kete Ipurangi, "History of the Project."
15. Rangahau, "Principles of Kaupapa Maori"; Te Kete Ipurangi, "The Development of Te Kotahitanga."
16. Wise Qatar Foundation, "Te Kotahitanga"; Effective Teaching Profile outlined in Sleeter, *Professional Development for Culturally Responsive and Relationship-Based Pedagogy,* 40.
17. Block, *Community,* xii.
18. Love, *We Want to Do More Than Survive,* 63, 65.
19. Block, *Community,* 15.
20. Carter G. Woodson in Kendi, *How to Be an Antiracist,* 142.
21. Love, foreword, 6–7.
22. España and Herrera, *En Comunidad,* 20–22; Sleeter, *Power, Teaching, and Teacher Education,* 229.
23. Winfield, *Eugenics and Education in America,* 165.
24. España and Herrera, *En Comunidad,* 4–16.
25. España and Herrera, *En Comunidad,* 17.
26. Supreme Court of Montana, Columbia Falls Schools et al. v. The State of Montana; Juneau and Broaddus, "And Still the Waters Flow," 194.
27. Starnes, "Montana's Indian Education for All," 185.

28. See, for example, Ragar, "Montana's Schools Superintendent Pushes Back."

29. Muhammad, *Cultivating Genius,* 58–60.

30. España and Herrera, *En Comunidad,* 17.

31. Sleeter, "Deepening Social Justice Teaching," 3; Abolitionist Teaching Network, *Guide for Racial Justice;* Muhammad, *Cultivating Genius,* 12; Friere and Macedo, *Literacy.*

32. Muhammad, *Cultivating Genius,* 43.

33. España and Herrera, *En Comunidad,* 167.

34. Reynolds, "Imagination and Fortitude."

Bibliography

Abolitionist Teaching Network. *Guide for Racial Justice and Abolitionist Social and Emotional Learning,* August 2020. https://abolitionistteachingnetwork.org/guide.

Alexander, Michelle. *The New Jim Crow: Mass Incarceration in the Age of Colorblindness.* New York: New Press, 2010.

Allen, Garland. "Intelligence Tests and Immigration to the United States, 1900–1940." *ResearchGate* (September 2006): 1–5. doi:10.1002/9780470015902.a0005612.

Amazon. "Groundwork of Eugenics." Accessed October 16, 2022. https://www.amazon.com/gp/product/B007I770QA/ref=dbs_a_def_rwt_hsch_vapi_tkin_p1_i1.

Ansalone, George. "Keeping on Track: A Reassessment of Tracking in Schools." *Race, Gender, and Class in Education* (Part 1) 7, no. 3 (2000): 108–32. https://www-jstor-org.berea.idm.oclc.org/stable/41674950?seq=3#metadata_info_tab_contents.

Au, Wayne. "Hiding behind High-Stakes Testing: Meritocracy, Objectivity, and Inequality in U.S. Education." *International Education Journal: Comparative Perspectives* 12, no. 2 (January 2013): 7–19. https://www.researchgate.net/publication/282187943_Hiding_behind_high-stakes_testing_Meritocracy_objectivity_and_inequality_in_US_education.

———. "Meritocracy 2.0: High-Stakes Standardized Testing as a Racial Project of Neoliberal Multiculturalism." *Educational Policy* 30, no. 1 (November 2015): 39–62. doi:10.1177/0895904815614916.

Battalora, Jacqueline. *Birth of a White Nation: The Invention of White People and Its Relevance Today.* Houston: Strategic Book, 2013.

Becker, Kirk. *History of the Stanford-Binet Intelligence Scales: Content and Psychometrics.* Stanford-Binet Intelligence Scales 5th ed., Assessment Service Bulletin no. 1. Itasca, IL: Riverside, 2003. https://www.hmhco.com/~/media/sites/home/hmh-assessments/clinical/stanford-binet/pdf/sb5_asb_1.pdf?la=en.

Bejar, Isaac I. "Standard Setting: What Is It? Why Is It Important?" *ETS R&D Connections* 7 (October 2008). https://www.ets.org/Media/Research/pdf/RD_Connections7.pdf.

Bell, Lee Anne. *Storytelling for Social Justice: Connecting Narrative and the Arts in Antiracist Teaching.* New York: Routledge, 2010.

Bennett, Christine L., Lynne M. McWhorter, and John A. Kuykendall. "Will I Ever Teach?" *American Educational Research Journal* 43, no. 3 (2006): 531–75.

Benson, Etienne. "Intelligence across Cultures: Research across Africa, Asia, and Latin American Is Showing How Culture and Intelligence Interact." *American Psychological Association* 34, no. 2 (2003). https://www.apa.org/monitor/feb03/intelligence.

Berea College. "Berea College Early History," July 9, 2021. https://www.berea.edu/about/history/.

———. "The Great Commitments." Accessed October 8, 2022. https://www.berea.edu/wp-content/uploads/2016/06/2017-Great-Commitments-Re-articulated.pdf.

———. "Our Inclusive History: From 1855 to Today," 2022. https://www.berea.edu/about /1855-to-today/.

Berlak, Harold. "The Need for a New Science of Assessment." In *Toward a New Science of Educational Testing and Assessment*, 1–20. Albany: SUNY Press, 1992.

Black, Edwin. *War against the Weak: Eugenics and America's Campaign to Create a Master Race*. New York: Four Walls Eight Windows, 2003.

Blakemore, Erin. "The Little Known History of the Forced Sterilization of Native American Women." *JSTOR Daily*, August 25, 2016. https://daily.jstor.org/the-little-known-history-of-the-forced-sterilization-of-native-american-women/.

Block, Peter. *Community: A Structure of Belonging*. San Francisco: Berrett-Koehler, 2018.

Bracey, Gerald W. "Thinking about Tests and Testing: A Short Primer in 'Assessment Literacy.'" American Youth Policy Forum, 2000. https://webpages.uncc.edu/~rglamber /Rsch6109%20Materials/article%202.pdf.

Bruinius, Harry. *Better for All the World: The Secret History of Forced Sterilization and America's Quest for Racial Purity*. New York: Knopf, 2006.

Brutlag, Jake. "The Development of Correlation and Association in Statistics," 5th ed. December 2007. http://buttelake.com/corr.htm.

Burnside, Jacqueline. "Day Law." Early History of Black Berea, 2001. //community.berea .edu/earlyblackberea/daylaw.html.

Camera, Wayne. "Standards for Educational and Psychological Testing: Historical Notes." American Educational Research Association, 2014. http://www.aera.net/portals/38 /docs/outreach/standards_hill_briefing_slides_final.pdf?timestamp=1410876719244.

Caponi, Sandra. "Quetelet, the Average Man, and Medial Knowledge." *História ciências saúde-Manguinhos* 20, no. 3 (July–September 2013): 830–47. http://www.scielo.br/scielo .php?pid=S0104-59702013000300830&script=sci_arttext&tlng=en.

Carter, Jordan, and Ian Snyder. "What Does It Mean to Be Antiracist?" National League of Cities, 2021. https://www.nlc.org/article/2020/07/21/what-does-it-mean-to-be-an-anti-racist/.

Chou, Vivian. "How Science and Genetics Are Reshaping the Race Debate of the 21st Century." *Science in the News,* April 17, 2017. Harvard University. https://sitn.hms .harvard.edu/flash/2017/science-genetics-reshaping-race-debate-21st-century/.

Cold Spring Harbor Laboratory. "Carnegie Institution of Washington." Accessed October 3, 2022. https://www.cshl.edu/archives/institutional-collections/carnegie-institution-of-washington/.

Cole, Nancy. "History and Development of DIF." In *Differential Item Functioning*, edited by Paul W. Holland and Howard Wainer, 25–30. New York: Routledge, 2012.

Cowan, Ruth Schwartz. "Francis Galton's Statistical Ideas: The Influence of Eugenics." *The History of Science Society: The University of Chicago Press Journals* 63, no. 4 (1972): 509–28. https://www.jstor.org/stable/229774.ind.

Crow, James F. "Unequal by Nature: A Geneticist's Perspective on Human Differences." *Daedalus* (Winter 2002): 81–88. https://www.jstor.org/stable/20027739.

Daley, Jason. "Genetic Study Shows Skin Color Is Only Skin Deep." *Smithsonian Magazine,* October 17, 2002. https://www.smithsonianmag.com/smart-news/genetic-study-shows-skin-color-just-skin-deep-180965261/.

Delzel, Darcie A. P., and Cathy D. Poliak. "Karl Pearson and Eugenics: Personal Opinions and Scientific Rigor." *Science and Engineering Ethics* 19 (2013): 1057–70. doi:10.1007 /s11948-012-9415-2.

Dewey, John. *Democracy and Education: An Introduction to the Philosophy of Education.* New York: Macmillan, 1922. https://www.google.com/books/edition/Democracy_and _Education/jqROAAAAMAAJ?hl=en&gbpv=0.

Disability Justice. "The Right to Self-Determination: Freedom from Involuntary Sterilization." 2022. https://disabilityjustice.org/right-to-self-determination-freedom-from-involuntary-sterilization/.

Donnelly, Kevin. *Adolphe Quetelet, Social Physics and the Average Men of Science, 1796– 1874.* Pittsburgh: University of Pittsburgh Press, 2016. https://www.jstor.org/stable /j.ctt1dfnth2.5.

Downing, Steven M. "Twelve Steps for Effective Test Development." In *Handbook of Test Development,* edited by Steven M. Downing and Thomas M. Haladyna, 3–25. Mahwah, NJ: Lawrence Erlbaum Associates, 2006.

Drakeford, Lillian Dowdell. "What's Race Got to Do with It? A Historical Inquiry into the Impact of Color-Blind Reform on Racial Inequality in America's Public Schools." Ph.D diss., Antioch University, 2010. https://aura.antioch.edu/etds/647/.

DuFour, Richard. *In Praise of American Educators: And How They Can Become Even Better.* Bloomington, IN: Solution Tree, 2015.

Early, Jessica Singer. *Stirring Up Justice: Writing and Reading to Change the World.* Portsmouth, NH: Heinemann, 2006.

Educational Testing Service. "About ETS," 2020. https://www.ets.org/about/what.

———. "Data Requests," 2020. https://www.ets.org/research/contact/data_requests/.

———. "Fairness Guidelines." About ETS, 2020. https://www.ets.org/about/fairness /guidelines/.

———. "How Tests and Test Questions Are Developed." *How ETS Approaches Testing,* 2020. www.ets.org/understanding_testing/test_development.

———. "Item Development." ETS K-12 Student Assessment Programs, 2020. https://www .ets.org/k12/capabilities/item-development/.

———. "Kentucky Test Requirements." ETS Praxis, 2014. https://www.ets.org/praxis/ky /requirements/.

———. "Praxis National Advisory Committees (NACs)." ETS Praxis, 2021. https://www.ets .org/praxis/states_agencies/about/content_current/nac.

———. *Praxis Study Companion: Elementary Education Three Subject Bundle; Mathematics, Social Studies and Science.* Princeton: Educational Testing Service, 2020. https://www .ets.org/s/praxis/pdf/5901.pdf.

———. *Praxis Technical Manual.* Rev. ed. Princeton: Educational Testing Service, 2010.

———. *2014 ETS Standards for Quality and Fairness.* Princeton: Educational Testing Service, 2014. https://www.ets.org/s/about/pdf/standards.pdf.

———. *Technical Manual for the Praxis Series and Related Assessments.* Princeton: Educational Testing Service, 2015.

———. *Understanding Your Praxis Scores, 2013–14.* Princeton: Educational Testing Service, 2013.

Educational Testing Service Research. "ETS Policy and Research Reports," 2020. https:// www.ets.org/research/policy_research_reports.

España, Carla, and Luz Yadira Herrera. *En Comunidad: Lessons for Centering the Voices and Experiences of Bilingual Latinx Students.* Portsmouth, NH: Heinemann, 2020.

Eugenics Archive. "Eugenics." Accessed February 15, 2020. https://eugenicsarchive.ca /discover/connections.

Fair, Alexandra. "Eugenics and the Modern Conservative Movement." *Black Perspectives: African American Intellectual History Society,* January 19, 2018. https://www.aaihs.org /eugenics-and-the-modern-conservative-movement/.

Fancher, Raymond E. "Biographical Origins of Francis Galton's Psychology." *Isis* 74, no. 2 (June 1983). https://www.jstor.org/stable/233104.

———. "Francis Galton's African Ethnography and Its Role in the Development of His Psychology." *British Journal for the History of Science* 16, no. 1 (March 1983): 67–79. https://www.jstor.org/stable/4026094.

Fendler, Lynn, and Irfan Muzaffar. "The History of the Bell Curve, Sorting and the Idea of Normal." *Educational Theory* 58, no. 1 (2008): 63–82. doi:10.1111/j.1741–5446.2007 .0276.x.

Flaherty, Colleen. "Diversity Work, Interrupted." *Inside Higher Ed,* October 7, 2020. https://www.insidehighered.com/news/2020/10/07/colleges-cancel-diversity-programs-response-trump-order.

———. "An Intelligent Argument on Race?" *Inside Higher Ed,* January 23, 2020. https://www .insidehighered.com/news/2020/01/23/intelligent-argument-race?utm_source= Inside+Higher+Ed&utm_campaign=172c035ca4-DiversityMatters_COPY_01&utm _medium=email&utm_term=0_1fcbc04421–172c035ca4–236288829&mc_cid= 172c035ca4&mc_eid=d9a476ab80.

Fox, Alex. "Nearly 2,000 Black Americans Were Lynched during Reconstruction." *Smithsonian Magazine,* June 18, 2020. https://www.smithsonianmag.com/smart-news/nearly-2000-black-americans-were-lynched-during-reconstruction-180975120/.

Fox, Margalit. "Michael Young, 86, Coined, Mocked 'Meritocracy.'" *New York Times,* January 25, 2002. https://www.nytimes.com/2002/01/25/world/michael-young-86-scholar-coined-mocked-meritocracy.html.

Friere, Paulo, and Donoldo Macedo. *Literacy: Reading the Word and the World.* Westport, CT: Bergin and Garvey, 1987.

Galton Institute. "Developing Ideas: Hereditary Genius." Accessed February 15, 2020. https:// www.galtoninstitute.org.uk/sir-francis-galton/meterology-and-heredity/#genius.

———. "Later Life: The Eugenic Vision." Accessed February 15, 2020. https://www .galtoninstitute.org.uk/sir-francis-galton/eugenics-and-final-years/.

———. "Sir Francis Galton," 2021. https://www.galtoninstitute.org.uk/sir-francis-galton/.

Garcia, Emma, and Elaine Weiss. *The Teacher Shortage Is Real, Large and Growing, and Worse Than We Thought.* Economic Policy Institute, 2019. https://www.epi.org /publication/the-teacher-shortage-is-real-large-and-growing-and-worse-than-we-thought-the-first-report-in-the-perfect-storm-in-the-teacher-labor-market-series/.

Gitomer, Drew H. "Teacher Quality in a Changing Policy Landscape: Improvements in the Teacher Pool." Educational Testing Service, 2007. http://www.ets.org/Media /Education_Topics/pdf/TQ_full_report.pdf.

Glaser, Robert. "Instructional Technology and the Measurement of Learning Outcomes: Some Questions." *American Psychologist* (1963): 519–21. https://doi.org/10.1111 /j.1745–3992.1994.tb00561.x .

Goddard, Henry H. "Mental Tests and the Immigrant." *Journal of Delinquency* 5, no. 2 (September 1917): 243–77. https://www.gwern.net/docs/iq/1917-goddard.pdf.

Goertzel, Ted. "The Myth of the Bell Curve." Ted Goertzel's Home Page, 1981. http://crab .rutgers.edu/~goertzel/normalcurve.htm.

Gomer, Justine, and Christopher Petrella. "White Fragility, Anti-Racist Pedagogy, and the Weight of History." *Black Perspectives: African American Intellectual History Society,*

July 27, 2017. https://www.aaihs.org/white-fragility-anti-racist-pedagogy-and-the-weight-of-history/.

Gottfredson, Linda S. "The General Intelligence Factor." *Scientific American,* November 1998. http://www2.psych.utoronto.ca/users/reingold/courses/intelligence/cache/1198 gottfred.html.

Gould, Stephen J. *The Mismeasure of Man.* New York: Norton, 1996.

Graves, Joseph L., and Amanda Johnson. "The Pseudoscience of Psychometry and the Bell Curve." *Journal of Negro Education* 64, no. 3 (Summer 1995): 277–94. https://www.jstor.org/stable/2967209.

Hacking, Ian. *The Taming of Chance.* Cambridge: Cambridge University Press, 1990.

Harris, Jasmine E. "Why *Buck v. Bell* Still Matters." *Bill of Health: Examining the Intersection of Health Law, Biotechnology, and Bioethics,* October 14, 2020.

Hibpshman, Terry. *Considerations Related to Setting Cut Scores for Teacher Tests.* Frankfort: Kentucky Educational Professional Standards Board, 2004.

———. *Design of an Education Professional Standards Board (EPSB) Preparation and Accountability System for Teacher Training Programs.* Frankfort, Kentucky: Kentucky Education Professional Standards Board, 2013.

Hill, Heather C., Kristin Umland, Erica Litke, and Laura R. Kapitula. "Teacher Quality and Quality Teaching: Examining the Relationship of a Teacher Assessment to Practice." *American Journal of Education* 118, no. 4 (August 2012): 489–519.

Hoff, David. "ETS President Cole Announces Retirement." *Education Week,* January 19, 2000. https://www.edweek.org/teaching-learning/ets-president-cole-announces-retirement /2000/01.

Horowitz, Juliana Menasce, Ruth Igielnik, and Rakesh Kochhar. "Trends in Income and Wealth Inequality." Pew Research Center, January 9, 2020. https://www.pewsocialtrends .org/2020/01/09/trends-in-income-and-wealth-inequality/.

Houts, Paul. "Behind the Call for Test Reform and Abolition of the IQ." *Phi Delta Kappan* 54, no. 10 (June 1976): 669–73. https://www.jstor.org/stable/20298432.

Hutson, Matthew. "Social Darwinism Isn't Dead: Rich People Think They Really Are Different from You and Me." *Slate,* January 3, 2014. https://slate.com/technology/2014/01 /social-darwinism-and-class-essentialism-the-rich-think-they-are-superior.html.

Jensen, Arthur. "Galton's Legacy to Research on Intelligence." *Journal of Biosocial Science* 34, no. 2 (April 2002): 145–72. doi:10.1017/S0021932002001451.

———. "The G-Factor: Psychometrics and Biology." In *The Nature of Intelligence: Novartis Foundation Symposium 233,* edited by Jamie A. Goode, Kate Webb, and Gregory R. Bock, 37–57. Novartis Foundation, 2000. http://arthurjensen.net/wp-content/uploads /2014/06/The-g-Factor-Psychometrics-and-Biology-With-Added-Discussion-2000-by-Arthur-Robert-Jensen.pdf.

———. "Psychometric G and Achievement." In *Policy Perspectives on Educational Testing: Evaluation in Education and Human Services,* edited by B. R. Gifford, 32:117–227. SpringerLink, 1993. https://doi.org/10.1007/978-94-011-2226-9_4.

Jones, Serene. "Grace in a Fractured World." Interview with Krista Tippett. *On Being,* December 5, 2019. https://onbeing.org/programs/serene-jones-grace-in-a-fractured-world/#transcript.

Jordan, Tim. "Historical Marker Unveiled at Middletown School." Berea College, 2016. https://www.berea.edu/tag/middletown-school/.

———. "Middletown School Alumni Gather at Historic Berea School Site." Berea College, July 5, 2016. https://www.berea.edu/tag/middletown-school/.

Josue, Editha E. "Understanding the Normal Curve and Its Parameters in Standardized Tests." Houston Teachers Institute. Accessed October 26, 2022. https://www.uh.edu /honors/Programs-Minors/honors-and-the-schools/houston-teachers-institute /curriculum-units/pdfs/2006/probability/josue-06-math.pdf.

Juneau, Denise, and Mandy Smoker Broaddus. "And Still the Waters Flow: The Legacy of Indian Education for All in Montana." *Phi Delta Kappan* 88, no. 3 (November 2006): 193–97.

Kane, Michael. *Errors of Measurement, Theory, and Public Policy.* William Angoff Memorial Lecture Series. Princeton: Educational Testing Service, 2010.

Kendi, Ibram X. *How to Be an Antiracist.* New York: Penguin Random House, 2019.

———. *Stamped from the Beginning: The Definitive History of Racist Ideas in America.* New York: Nation, 2016.

———. "Why the Academic Achievement Gap Is a Racist Idea." *Black Perspectives: African American Intellectual History Society,* 2016. https://www.aaihs.org/why-the-academic-achievement-gap-is-a-racist-idea/.

Kendi, Ibram X., and Jason Reynolds. *Stamped: Racism, Antiracism, and You.* New York: Little, Brown, 2020.

Kentucky Legislative Research Commission. "Standards for Admission to Educator Preparation, 16 KAR 5:02." Accessed May 19, 2014. http://www.lrc.state.ky.us/kar /016/005/020.htm.

Kidder, William C., and Jay Rosner. "How the SAT Creates Built-in Headwinds: An Educational and Legal Analysis of Disparate Impact." *Santa Clara Law Review* 43, no. 1 (2002): 131–211. https://digitalcommons.law.scu.edu/cgi/viewcontent.cgi?referer= &httpsredir=1&article=1285&context=lawreview.

Kimmerer, Robin Wall. "The Intelligence of Plants." Interview with Krista Tippett. *On Being,* February 26, 2016. https://onbeing.org/programs/robin-wall-kimmerer-the-intelligence-of-plants/.

King, Charles. *Gods of the Upper Air: How a Circle of Renegade Anthropologists Reinvented Race, Sex, and Gender in the Twentieth Century.* New York: Doubleday, 2019.

King, Paul. "What Is Inferential Statistics?" *Magoosh Statistics Blog,* January 2, 2018. https:// magoosh.com/statistics/what-is-inferential-statistics/.

Knapp, Joan E., and Lenora G. Knapp. "Practice Analysis: Building the Foundation for Validity." In *Licensure Testing: Purposes, Procedures, and Practices,* vol. 9, edited by James C. Impara, 93–116. Lincoln, NE: Buros Institute of Mental Measurements, 1995. https://digitalcommons.unl.edu/buroslicensure/9.

Koretz, Daniel. *Measuring Up: What Educational Testing Really Tells Us.* Cambridge, MA: Harvard University Press, 2008.

Lamb, Evelyn. "Review: *Weapons of Math Destruction.*" *Scientific American,* August 31, 2016. https://blogs.scientificamerican.com/roots-of-unity/review-weapons-of-math-destruction/#.

Lemann, Nicholas. *The Big Test: The Secret History of the American Meritocracy.* New York: Farrar, Strauss and Giroux, 1999.

Leslie, Mitchell. "The Vexing Legacy of Lewis Terman." *Stanford Magazine,* July–August 2000. https://stanfordmag.org/contents/the-vexing-legacy-of-lewis-terman.

Library of Congress. "The Founders and the Vote." Accessed February 2, 2018. https://www .loc.gov/classroom-materials/elections/right-to-vote/the-founders-and-the-vote/.

Lippmann, Walter. "Debunking Intelligence Tests: Walter Lippmann Speaks Out." *History Matters,* n.d. Accessed August 30, 2020. http://historymatters.gmu.edu/d/5172/.

———. "The Great Confusion: A Reply to Mr. Terman." *New Republic,* January 3, 1923. https://archive.org/details/sim_new-republic_1923-01-03_33_422/page/144/mode/2up.

Livingston, Samuel A. "Item Analysis." In *Handbook of Test Development,* edited by Steven M. Downing and Thomas M. Haladyna, 421–41. Mahwah, NJ: Lawrence Erlbaum Associates, 2006.

———. "Test Reliability: Basic Concepts." Research Memorandum 18-01, Princeton: Educational Testing Service, 2018.

Loewen, James. *Lies My Teacher Told Me: Everything Your American History Textbook Got Wrong.* New York: New Press, 1995.

Love, Bettina. Foreword to *Cultivating Genius: An Equity Framework for Culturally and Historically Responsive Literacy,* by Gholdy Muhammad. New York: Scholastic, 2020.

———. *We Want to Do More Than Survive: Abolitionist Teaching and the Pursuit of Educational Freedom.* Boston: Beacon, 2019.

Loveless, Tom. *The 2012 Brown Center Report on American Education: How Well Are Americans Learning?* Brown Center on Education Policy. Brookings, February 16, 2012.

Markovits, Daniel. *The Meritocracy Trap: How America's Foundational Myth Feeds Inequality, Dismantles the Middle Class, and Devours the Elite.* London: Allen Lane, 2019.

McCulley, Susan. "Bacon's Rebellion." Historic Jamestowne, National Park Service, 1995. https://www.nps.gov/jame/learn/historyculture/bacons-rebellion.htm.

Menakem, Resmaa. *My Grandmother's Hands: Racialized Trauma and the Pathway to Mending Our Hearts and Bodies.* Las Vegas: Central Recovery, 2017.

Merriam-Webster. "Intelligence." Accessed January 3, 2020. https://www.merriam-webster.com/dictionary/intelligence.

Montana Office of Public Instruction. *Essential Understandings regarding Montana Indians,"* 2007. http://svcalt.mt.gov/education/textbook/EssentialUnderstandings.pdf.

Mordkoff, J. Toby. "Assumption(s) of Normality." J. Toby Mordkoff, 2016. http://www2.psychology.uiowa.edu/faculty/mordkoff/GradStats/part%201/I.07%20normal.pdf.

Muhammad, Gholdy. *Cultivating Genius: An Equity Framework for Culturally and Historically Responsive Literacy.* New York: Scholastic, 2020.

Neiman, Susan. *Learning from the Germans: Race and the Memory of Evil.* New York: Farrar, Straus and Giroux, 2019.

Nettles, Michael T., Linda H. Scatton, Johnathan H. Steinberg, and Linda L. Tyler. *Performance and Passing Rate Differences in African American and White Prospective Teachers on Praxis Examination.* Educational Testing Service, 2011. https://www.ets.org/Media/Research/pdf/RR-11–08.pdf.

Newcomb, Steve. "Five Hundred Years of Injustice: The Legacy of Fifteenth Century Religious Prejudice." *Native Web,* Fall 1992. http://ili.nativeweb.org/sdrm_art.html.

New Zealand Ministry of Education (Te Tahuhu o te Matauranga). "About History of the Project." *Te Kete Ipurangi.* Accessed April 26, 2021. https://tekotahitanga.tki.org.nz/About/The-Development-of-Te-Kotahitanga/History-of-the-Project.

———. "About Mihi." *Te Kete Ipurangi.* Accessed April 26, 2021. https://tekotahitanga.tki.org.nz/About/Mihi.

———. "About Te Kotahitanga." *Te Kete Ipurangi.* . Accessed April 26, 2021. https://tekotahitanga.tki.org.nz/About.

———. "About the Development of Te Kotahitanga." *Te Kete Ipurangi.* Accessed April 26, 2021. https://tekotahitanga.tki.org.nz/About/The-Development-of-Te-Kotahitanga.

Norton, Bernard J. "Karl Pearson and Statistics: The Social Origins of Scientific Innovation." *Social Studies of Science* 8, no. 1 (1978): 3–34. http://www.jstor.org/stable/284855.

Norton, Rita. "The Horace Mann Bond Papers: A Biography of Change." *Journal of Negro Education* 53, no. 1 (Winter 1984): 29–40. http://www.jstor.com/stable/2294982.

O'Neil, Cathy. *Weapons of Math Destruction: How Big Data Increases Inequality and Threatens Democracy.* New York: Broadway Books, 2016.

Palmer, Nathan. "Hegemony: The 'Haves' and the 'Soon to Haves.'" *Sociology in Focus,* February 8, 2012. https://sociologyinfocus.com/hegemony-the-haves-and-soon-to-haves-2/.

Pearce, JMS. "Eugenics: Historic and Contemporary." *Hektoen International: A Journal of Medical Humanities,* Fall 2019. https://hekint.org/2019/12/16/eugenics-historic-and-contemporary/.

Pellegrino, James. *The Evolution of Educational Assessment: Considering the Past and Imagining the Future.* Princeton: Educational Testing Service, 2004. https://www.ets.org/Media/Research/pdf/PICANG6.pdf.

Pentland, Sandy. "Social Physics Can Change Your Company (and the World)." WNYC New York Public Radio, *Harvard Business Review Ideacast,* April 24, 2014. https://www.wnyc.org/story/401-social-physics-can-change-your-company-and-the-world/.

Perks, Julie. "Spearman and the Importance of Archives." *Psychologist* 19, no 12 (December 2006): 722–25. https://thepsychologist.bps.org.uk/volume-19/edition-12/spearman-and-importance-archives.

Pilgrim, David. "What Was Jim Crow?" Ferris State University Jim Crow Museum, 2012. https://www.ferris.edu/jimcrow/what.htm.

Plucker, Jonathan. "Lewis Madison Terman." *Human Intelligence,* April 29, 2018. //www.intelltheory.com/terman.shtml.

———. "Unanswered Questions." In *The APA 1996 Intelligence Task Force Report.* Human Intelligence, Fall 2002. https://www.intelltheory.com/apa96.shtml#questions.

Popham, W. James. "Criterion-Referenced Measurement: Half a Century Wasted?" *Educational Leadership* 71, no. 6 (March 2014): 62–66.

Popham, James W., and T. R. Husek. "Implications of Criterion-Referenced Measurement." *Journal of Educational Measurement* 9, no. 1 (1969): 1–9. https://www.jstor.org/stable/1433917.

powell, john a. "Creating the Conditions for Belonging and Breathing in a Toxic Environment." Bioneers Conference, January 13, 2020. https://www.youtube.com/watch?v=IpxT-8Qodnw.

———. *Racing to Justice: Transforming Our Conceptions of Self and Other to Build an Inclusive Society.* Bloomington: Indiana University Press, 2012.

PraxisExam.org. "The Difference between Praxis I and Praxis 2," 2022. https://praxisexam.org/praxis/difference-between-praxis-i-praxis-ii/.

Ragar, Shaylee. "Montana's Schools Superintendent Pushes Back against Critical Race Theory." Montana Public Radio, May 14, 2021. https://www.mtpr.org/montana-news/2021-05-14/montanas-schools-superintendent-pushes-back-against-critical-race-theory-in-schools.

Rangahau. "Principles of Kaupapa Maori." Accessed May 25, 2021. http://www.rangahau.co.nz/rangahau/27/.

Ravitch, Diane. *The Death and Life of the Great American School System.* New York: Basic Books, 2011.

Reynolds, Jason. "Imagination and Fortitude." Interview with Krista Tippett. *On Being,* June 25, 2020. https://onbeing.org/programs/jason-reynolds-imagination-and-fortitude/.

Rhoades, Kathleen, and George Madaus. *Errors in Standardized Tests: A Systemic Problem.* Boston: National Board on Educational Testing and Public Policy, 2003. https://www.bc.edu/research/nbetpp/statements/M1N4.pdf.

Rosamond, Ben. "Hegemony." *Encyclopedia Britannica.* Accessed November 9, 2020. https://www.britannica.com/topic/hegemony.

Rosenfeld, Michael, and Gregory K. Kocher. A Job Analysis of the Content Knowledge and Skill Areas Important for Newly Licensed (Certified) Elementary School Teachers (K-6). Educational Testing Service, June 1998. https://www.ets.org/Media/Research /pdf/RR-98-26.pdf.

Rosner, Jay. "Lessons Learned on My Journey to the Fisher Sports Brief, and Beyond." *University of San Francisco Law Review* 48, no. 2, article 5 (2014): 315–26. https:// repository.usfca.edu/usflawreview/v0148/iss2/5/.

———. "The SAT: Quantifying the Unfairness behind the Bubbles." In *SAT Wars: The Case for Test-Optional College Admission,* edited by Jay Soares, 104–17. New York: Teachers College Press, 2012.

———. "Why the New SAT Isn't as Transparent as the College Board Wants You to Believe." *Los Angeles Times,* April 29, 2016. https://www.latimes.com/opinion/op-ed/la-oe-0501-rosner-sat-transparency-20160501-story.html.

Saad, Layla. *Me and White Supremacy: Combat Racism, Change the World, and Become a Good Ancestor.* Naperville, IL: Sourcebooks, 2020.

Sartori, Riccardo. "The Bell Curve in Psychological Research and Practice: Myth or Reality?" *Quality and Quantity* 40, no. 3 (2006): 407–18. doi:10.1007/s11135–005–6104–0.

Schanzenbach, Diane Whitmore, and Stephanie Howard Larson. "Is Your Child Ready for Kindergarten? Redshirting May Do More Harm Than Good." *Education Next* 21, no. 3 (2021).https://www.educationnext.org/is-your-child-ready-kindergarten-redshirting-may-do-more-harm-than-good/.

Schlesinger, Bill. "What Makes a Healthy Ecosystem?" *Translational Ecology,* December 5, 2018. Duke Nicholas School of the Environment. https://blogs.nicholas.duke.edu /citizenscientist/what-makes-a-healthy-ecosystem/.

Schloss Hartheim. "Euthanasia Centre, 1940–1944." Schloss Hartheim, 2020. https://www .schloss-hartheim.at/en/memorial-exhibition/historic-site/euthanasia-centre-1940–1944.

Shafer, Leah. "When Proficient Isn't Good." Useable Knowledge: Relevant Research for Today's Educators. Harvard Graduate School of Education, January 24, 2016. https://www.gse.harvard.edu/news/uk/15/12/when-proficient-isnt-good.

Simkin, John. "Education in Nazi Germany." Spartacus Educational Publishers, May 2022. https://spartacus-educational.com/GEReducation.htm.

Simon, Stephanie. "No Profit Left Behind." *Politico,* February 10, 2015. https://www.politico .com/story/2015/02/pearson-education-115026.

Sleeter, Christine. "Deepening Social Justice Teaching." *Journal of Language and Literacy Education@UGA,* February 2014. http://jolle.coe.uga.edu/wp-content/uploads/2014 /01/SSO_Feb2015_Template.pdf.

———. *Power, Teaching, and Teacher Education: Confronting Injustice with Critical Research and Action.* New York: Peter Lang, 2013.

———. *Professional Development for Culturally Responsive and Relationship-Based Pedagogy.* New York: Peter Lang, 2011.

Stahl, Saul. "The Evolution of the Normal Distribution." *Mathematics Magazine* 79 (2006): 96–113. https://www.maa.org/programs/maa-awards/writing-awards/the-evolution-of-the-normal-distribution.

Starnes, Bobby Ann. "Montana's Indian Education for All: Toward an Education Worthy of American Ideals." *Phi Delta Kappan* 88, no. 3 (November 2006): 184–92.

Starnes, Bobby Ann, and *Phi Delta Kappan*. "Change, Sputnik, and Fast Food." *Education Week,* April 1, 2011. https://www.edweek.org/education/opinion-change-sputnik-and-fast-food/2011/04.

Stearns, Elizabeth, Stephanie Moller, Judith Blau, and Stephanie Potochnick. "Staying Back and Dropping Out: The Relationship between Grade Retention and School Dropout." *Sociology of Education* (July 2007). https://www.jstor.org/stable/20452707?seq=1.

Stevenson, Bryan. "Love Is the Motive." Interview with Krista Tippett. *On Being,* December 3, 2020. https://onbeing.org/programs/bryan-stevenson-love-is-the-motive /#transcript.

Stoskopf, Alan. "Echoes of a Forgotten Past: Eugenics, Testing, and Education Reform." *Educational Forum* 66, no. 2 (Winter 2002): 126–33. doi:10.1080/00131720208984814.

———. "An Untold Story of Resistance: African-American Educators and IQ Testing in the 1920's and 30's." *Rethinking Schools* (Fall 1999). https://rethinkingschools.org/articles /an-untold-story-of-resistance/.

Strauss, Valerie. "Here's the Very First SAT, from 1926. Can You Pass It?" *Washington Post,* April 22, 2014. https://www.washingtonpost.com/news/answer-sheet/wp/2014/04/22 /heres-the-very-first-sat-from-1926-can-you-pass-it/.

———. "Trump's 'Patriotic Education' Report Excuses Founding Fathers for Owning Slaves and Likens Progressives to Mussolini." *Washington Post,* January 19, 2021. https://www.washingtonpost.com/education/2021/01/19/trump-patriotic-education-report-slavery-fascists/.

Supreme Court of Montana. Columbia Falls Schools et al. v. The State of Montana, no. 04-390, March 22, 2005. LexisNexis. https://leg.mt.gov/content/Publications/fiscal /Education/CF-Decision-I-Supreme-Court.pdf.

"Text of the White House Statements on the Human Genome Project." *New York Times,* June 27, 2000. https://archive.nytimes.com/www.nytimes.com/library/national/science /062700sci-genome-text.html.

Tochluk, Shelly. *Witnessing Whiteness: The Need to Talk about Race and How to Do It.* Lanham, MD: Rowman and Littlefield Education, 2007.

Uenuma, Francine. "Better Baby Contests Pushed for Much-Needed Infant Health but Also Played into the Eugenics Movement." *Smithsonian Magazine,* January 17, 2019. https://www.smithsonianmag.com/history/better-babies-contests-pushed-infant-health-also-played-eugenics-movement-180971288/.

United Nations Office of Genocide and the Responsibility to Protect. "Genocide." Accessed July 10, 2021. https://www.un.org/en/genocideprevention/genocide.shtml.

United States Holocaust Memorial Museum. "Euthanasia Program and Aktion T-4." Last edited October 7, 2020. https://encyclopedia.ushmm.org/content/en/article/euthanasia-program.

———. "Nazi Camps." *Holocaust Encyclopedia.* Accessed July 18, 2021. https://encyclopedia .ushmm.org/content/en/article/nazi-camps.

Varma, Seema. *Preliminary Item Statistics Using Point Biserial Correlation and P-Values.* Educational Data Systems, Inc. Accessed December 31, 2018. https://jcesom.marshall .edu/media/24104/Item-Stats-Point-Biserial.pdf.

Warren, Wendy Zagray. "Justice for All? Costs and Consequences of Standardized Testing Requirements in Teacher Education Reform Policy." 3700888. Ann Arbor, MI: Pro-quest Dissertations, 2015.

Weikart, Richard. "The Role of Darwinism in Nazi Racial Thought." *German Studies Review* 36 (2013): 537–56. https://www.csustan.edu/sites/default/files/History/Faculty/Weikart/Darwinism-in-Nazi-Racial-Thought.pdf.

Whitman, James Q. *Hitler's American Model: The United States and the Making of Nazi Race Law.* Princeton: Princeton University Press, 2017.

Wilkerson, Isabel. "America's Caste System." Interview with Rund Abdelfatah and Ramtin Arablouei. NPR, *Throughline*, August 6, 2020. https://www.npr.org/2020/08/04/898918916/americas-caste-system.

———. *Caste: The Origins of Our Discontents.* New York: Random House, 2020.

———. "Isabel Wilkerson on America's Caste System." Interview with Terry Gross. NPR, *Fresh Air*, August 4, 2020. https://www.npr.org/2020/08/04/898981897/isabel-wilkerson-on-americas-caste-system.

williams, angel Kyodo. "The World Is Our Field of Practice." Interview with Krista Tippett. *On Being,* April 19, 2018. https://onbeing.org/programs/angel-kyodo-williams-the-world-is-our-field-of-practice/.

Wilson, Robert. "Eugenics." Eugenics Archive, 2013. https://eugenicsarchive.ca/discover/connections.

Winfield, Ann Gibson. *Eugenics and Education in America: Institutionalized Racism and the Implications of History, Ideology, and Memory.* New York: Peter Lang, 2007.

Wise Qatar Foundation. "Te Kotahitanga." Last updated December 22, 2020. https://www.wise-qatar.org/project/te-kotahitanga-new-zealand/.

Young, Michael. "Down with Meritocracy." *Guardian,* June 29, 2001. https://www.theguardian.com/politics/2001/jun/29/comment.

Young, Michael J., and Sasha Zucker. *The Standards-Referenced Interpretive Framework: Using Assessments for Multiple Purposes.* Pearson Assessment Report. San Antonio: Pearson, 2004. http://images.pearsonassessments.com/images/tmrs/tmrs_rg/Interpretive Frameworks.pdf.

Zieky, Michael. "Fairness Reviews in Assessment." In *Handbook of Test Development,* edited by Steven M. Downing and Thomas M. Haladyna, 359–76. Mahwah, NJ: Thomas Erlbaum Associates, 2006.

Zucker, Sasha. *Fundamentals of Standardized Testing.* Pearson Assessment Report. San Antonio: Pearson, 2003.

Index